THE SEARCH FOR PSYCHIC POWER

the reason why people should be skeptical in psychic power

here are some of the reasons why people should be skeptical in psychic powers.

THE SEARCH FOR PSYCHIC POWER

ESP & PARAPSYCHOLOGY REVISITED

C.E.M. HANSEL

PROMETHEUS BOOKS
BUFFALO, NEW YORK

To
Gwenllian

Published 1989 by Prometheus Books
700 East Amherst Street, Buffalo, New York 14215

Copyright © 1989 by C. E. M. Hansel

Library of Congress Cataloging-in-Publication Data

Hansel, C. E. M. (Charles Edward Mark), 1917-
     The search for psychic power : ESP and parapsychology revisited /
by C. E. M. Hansel.
          p.   cm.
     Bibliography: p.
     Includes index.
     ISBN 0-87975-516-4—ISBN 0-87975-533-4 (pbk.)
     1. Psychical research. 2. Extrasensory perception. I. Title.
BF1031.H256   1989
133.8'072—dc19   89-3665
                                                                           CIP

Preface

I would like to acknowledge my indebtedness to all those who collaborated with me in preparing my two earlier books, on which the present edition is based. In particular, thanks are due to Professor Emeritus R. T. Birge and to Mr. Martin Gardner.

Thanks are also due to Mr. Kenneth Heuer, former Science Editor at Charles Scribner's Sons; to Dr. Trevor M. Hall; Dr. Christopher Scott; and to Mr. Alan Wesencraft, who has permitted me to consult references in the Harry Price Library of the University of London.

Finally, I am indebted to Professor Paul Kurtz for making this publication possible; to my editor, Steven L. Mitchell of Prometheus Books; and to my wife, Gwenllian, who has spent much time correcting the manuscript and proofs.

Contents

5

Part One

Early Forms of Investigation

1

The Origins of Psychical Research

INTRODUCTION

Our awareness of objects in the world outside arises through the use of the senses. Scientific knowledge explains how this comes about: we see an object because light is reflected from it into our eyes. It also makes clear the conditions under which seeing cannot take place: light is necessary for vision, therefore, without it we cannot see.

Personal experience also tells us that our thoughts remain private unless expressed by voice or action. Another person's thoughts can be guessed, but few would claim to be able to know them as they would if the person were thinking aloud. There are exceptions. On the stage, men appear to see when blindfolded and to read thoughts; but such performances are classified as magic, and it is known that the magician uses tricks that enable him to appear to do what common sense says is impossible.

During the past one hundred years, however, the public has become aware of reports that abilities such as clairvoyance and telepathy have been demonstrated in the laboratory by means of rigorously controlled experiments. These claims are puzzling to many persons who are interested in natural processes and scientific experimentation, for the investigators claim to have established, by means of experiments, the reality of phenomena that conflict with well-established principles.

Experimental evidence has been claimed for four such processes:

1. *Telepathy,* a person's awareness of another's thoughts in the absence of any communication through sensory channels.

2. *Clairvoyance,* knowledge acquired of an object or event without the use of the senses.

3. *Precognition,* knowledge of another person's future thoughts (precognitive telepathy) or of future events (precognitive clairvoyance).

4. *Psychokinesis,* a person's ability to influence a physical object or an event, such as the toss of a die, by thinking about it.

Since the first three of these processes would involve an act of perception, and also because they are, by definition, independent of activity in the sense organs, each is commonly referred to as a kind of extrasensory perception, or ESP.

It will be seen that the supposed processes are consistent with beliefs that have long been a part of folklore and superstition. Telepathy is a new name for mind reading; clairvoyance for second sight; precognition for divination or premonition; and psychokinesis for the process whereby a man thinks, for example, that he can get good weather for his holiday by praying for it. For this reason, the experiments, if they can be relied on and if their results satisfy normal scientific requirements, would imply that much of what has in the past been regarded as superstition must now be included in the domain of natural science.

THE START OF ORGANIZED RESEARCH

Preoccupation with these beliefs was responsible for the emergence at the end of the nineteenth century of psychical research, in which the study of thought transference and other related phenomena became an organized discipline. At that time there was a great deal of speculation about the possibility of strange new human powers. Stories of extraordinary happenings that seemed to contravene accepted scientific principles were popular, just as they are today. In the later half of the nineteenth and well into the twentieth century, much publicity was given to spiritualist mediums, who supposedly received messages from the dead and whose exploits attracted considerable scientific interest.

But, at that time science displayed a unity in that when a new discipline, such as biology, revealed facts involving new types of processes, they were always consistent with other scientific knowledge. Thus, principles of physics and chemistry operated in the new discoveries of biology. As D'Arcy Thompson (1860–1948), the Scottish biologist, wrote, ". . . no physical law, any more than gravity itself, not even among the puzzles of stereo-chemistry, or of physiological surface-action and osmosis, is known to be transgressed by the bodily mechanism."[1]

In the realm of the senses, the eye was found to employ principles known to optics, and the ear to contain mechanisms that might be expected from the study of sound. Messages were transmitted along nerve fibers from the sensory organs to the brain; the nervous system behaved in a manner consistent with knowledge of other physical systems.

While it was not clear at that time whether psychological events would ever be fully explicable in terms of the natural laws already known to science, nothing in human behavior seemed at variance with known processes. The precise changes arising in the brain that were responsible for, say, memory were not known, but remembering displayed no very strange characteristics; similar processes, such as the camera's recording of a photographic image or the creation of a charge in a condenser, were well understood. However, if a man had shown himself to be capable of knowing about things before they happened, that would have involved a process of quite a different order, as if the photograph could emerge before the film had been exposed in the camera. While telepathy seemed unlikely but not impossible—for it was conceivable that some sixth sense together with some means of transmitting information lay undiscovered—precognition displayed characteristics foreign to science, since, in this case, an effect seemed to precede its cause.

Not all scientists were skeptical about the reports of what appeared to be paranormal happenings. A number of eminent British scientists, including the chemist Sir William Crookes (1832–1919), the physicists Sir William Fletcher Barrett (1844–1925) and Sir Oliver Joseph Lodge (1851–1940), the mathematician Augustus De Morgan (1806–1871), and the biologist Alfred Russel Wallace (1823–1913), thought that there was more in the reports than orthodox science would admit.

THE SOCIETY FOR PSYCHICAL RESEARCH

After some early unsuccessful attempts to bring these matters to the serious attention of the scientific world, a group of scholars at Cambridge University decided that the time had come to set up a learned society to examine those human faculties, real or supposed, that appeared inexplicable to science. As a result, the Society for Psychical Research was founded in 1882, with Henry Sidgwick (1838–1900), professor of moral philosophy at Cambridge, as its first president. An American Society for Psychical Research was established a few years later, with the distinguished astronomer Simon Newcomb (1835–1909) as its president. Today there are similar groups in many countries.

Since those early beginnings, a considerable amount of research has been conducted by the societies, by private individuals, and in universities. Today, psychical research, or *parapsychology* as it is now known, has come to be regarded as an accepted field of scientific study: investigations are in progress in some university departments; several laboratories and associations are committed to full-time research; and higher degrees are awarded in the topic. In 1969, the Parapsychological Association was granted affiliation with the American Association for the Advancement of Science.

ATTITUDES TOWARD ESP

For a student of psychology, the position is puzzling. Most of the leading British psychologists who have had anything to say on the matter of extrasensory perception have left no doubt that they regard its existence as proved. Professor Eysenck, head of the Department of Psychology at the Maudsley Hospital, London, wrote in 1957:

> Unless there is a gigantic conspiracy involving some thirty university departments all over the world and several hundred highly respected scientists in various fields, many of them originally hostile to the claims of the psychical researchers, the only conclusion the unbiased observer can come to must be that there does exist a small number of people who obtain knowledge existing either in other peoples' minds, or in the outer world, by means yet unknown to science.[2]

The student finds that a similar viewpoint has been expressed by other well-known scientists and philosophers. Yet parapsychology is unlikely to appear in his curriculum and little reference is made to it in his textbooks. If he questions his teachers, he is likely to find that they know very little about psychical research, or, if they are critical of it, that they have few facts with which to support their criticisms. Thus, the late Dr. Samuel George Soal, a mathematician at London University, and Britain's best-known parapsychologist, wrote:

> There is, of course, no shortage of people who feel that, because they are qualified in psychiatry or psychology, they are competent to pass judgment on the work of the parapsychologist. The "expert" knowledge of such persons is usually based on some quite elementary books on the subject which omit the essential experimental details without which a proper evaluation of the work is not possible. It would be interesting to meet the psychiatrist or psychologist who has perused every page of the 49 volumes of the *Proceedings* of the Society for Psychical Research, and who remains a skeptic. It is no coincidence that those most skeptical of ESP research are almost invariably those who are least acquainted with the facts.[3]

Even in the beginnings of psychical research, the conflict between skeptic and believer existed. Members of the new Society for Psychical Research thought that a strong *a priori* case for telepathy and kindred phenomena existed in the numerous reports of "inexplicable" experiences. Many scientists, however, adopted the attitude that such phenomena were, *a priori*, so unlikely in view of existing knowledge that there was no point in bothering about them.

Toward the end of the nineteenth century the great German scientist Hermann Ludwig von Helmholtz (1821–1894) expressed this viewpoint when he declared: "Neither the testimony of all the Fellows of the Royal Society, nor even the evidence of my own senses, would lead me to believe in the transmission of thought from one person to another independently of the recognized channels of sense."[4] Helmholtz was speaking with some authority, since he was the greatest living expert on sensory communication. To him, the manner in which information accrued through the activity of the sense organs and the relationship between bodily processes and mental processes made the idea of telepathy as scientifically untenable as that of a flat earth.

In Helmholtz's time, the evidence for telepathy was almost entirely of an anecdotal nature; but during the last century, numerous experiments have been carried out that are claimed to provide evidence for the existence of ESP. It may be that any *a priori* theoretical objections must now be relinquished in the light of empirical evidence; but before such a drastic step is taken, it is necessary to be quite certain that the experimental results obtained by parapsychologists are due to paranormal rather than to normal processes, and that the experiments establish this fact according to the accepted criteria of scientific investigation and proof.

A close inspection of the work of the parapsychologists is, in any case, important for two reasons: if their claims are justified, a complete revision in contemporary scientific thought is required at least comparable to that made necessary in biology by Charles Darwin and in physics by Albert Einstein. On the other hand, if ESP is merely an artifact, it is then necessary to understand how what may appear to be conventional experimental methods can yield results leading to erroneous conclusions.

THE SUBJECT MATTER OF PARAPSYCHOLOGY

Telepathy

For telepathy to exist, the receiver, or percipient, must learn without the use of his sense organs what the sender, or agent, is thinking about. It is also usually implied that there is no special activity on the part of the agent. That is, his thoughts become known to the percipient whether he wishes it or not and without his making any effort at communication. Furthermore, information is said to pass from one person to another without the use of special apparatus. It does not involve the setting up of disturbances, such as those created by voice or movements, and it does not require any activity of the known senses. Telepathy implies the existence of human abilities unknown to psychology or physiology and the presence of properties of matter unknown to physics.

Clairvoyance

Clairvoyance differs from telepathy in that only one person is involved: the percipient is said to become aware of an object or event without the involvement of a second person. If clairvoyance is possible, the agent in a telepathy experiment might appear to play a minor role, since there would be little point in him transmitting a message giving the identity of an object to a percipient, who can identify it without his aid by clairvoyance.

Precognition

In some experiments on either telepathy or clairvoyance the subject's guess is checked against a target that is not decided until after he has made his guess. If scores above the chance level are obtained under this condition, he is said to display telepathic or clairvoyant precognition.

Psychokinesis

Psychokinesis differs from the processes already described in that a person is claimed to influence a physical object by thinking about it. He causes something to happen in the external world, rather then himself being influenced by an external event.

NOTES

1. D'Arcy Thompson, *Growth and Form* (Cambridge, England: Cambridge University Press, 1942), p. 13.
2. H. J. Eysenck, *Sense and Nonsense in Psychology* (London: Penguin Books, Ltd., 1957), p. 13.
3. S. G. Soal and F. Bateman, *Modern Experiments in Telepathy* (London: Faber & Faber, Ltd., 1954), p. 24.
4. Quoted in Rosalind Heywood, *Beyond the Reach of Sense* (New York: E. P. Dutton & Co., Inc., 1961), p. 11.

2

Early Investigations

THE CREERY SISTERS

Soon after the formation of the Society for Psychical Research in 1882, a Committee on Thought Reading was set up, headed by William Barrett, then professor of physics in the Royal College of Science for Ireland, together with Edmund Gurney (1847–1888), who devoted his energies to psychical research, and Frederic Myers (1843–1901), an inspector of schools, both formerly fellows of Trinity College, Cambridge. Later in the year, Frank Podmore (1855–1910), a post office official, joined the committee. Henry Sidgwick, in his presidential address to the society in July 1882, introduced the first report of this committee by saying:

> We must drive the objector into the position of being forced either to admit the phenomena as inexplicable, at least by him, or to accuse the investigators either of lying or cheating or of a blindness or forgetfulness incompatible with any intellectual condition except absolute idiocy.
>
> I am glad to say that this result, in my opinion, has been satisfactorily attained in the investigation of thought reading. Professor Barrett will now bring before you a report which I hope will be only the first of a long series of similar reports which may have reached the same point of conclusiveness.[1]

Sidgwick lived to eat his words, for the investigation described in that report concerned the five young daughters (Mary, Alice, Maud, Kathleen, and Emily) of an English clergyman, the Reverend A. M. Creery. During sitting after sitting, the girls and a young servant, Jane, convinced the investigators of their telepathic abilities. Then, six years later, in 1888, they were caught using a code and admitted to having deceived the researchers.

In the first report of the committee, mention was also made of a G. A. Smith whose telepathic abilities were supposedly developed to the highest degree.

The second and third committee reports contained details of tests carried out on Smith, that for nearly twenty years were accepted as providing evidence for thought transference.

THE SMITH-BLACKBURN EXPERIMENTS

On August 26, 1882, a letter by Douglas Blackburn, editor of *The Brightonian,* appeared in the spiritualist magazine *Light.* This read:

> The way Mr. Smith conducts his experiment is this: He places himself en rapport with myself by taking my hands: and a strong concentration of will and mental vision of my part has enabled him to read my thoughts with an accuracy that approaches the miraculous. Not only can he, with slight hesitation, read numbers, words and even whole sentences which I alone have seen, but the sympathy between us has developed to such a degree that he rarely fails to experience the taste of any liquid or solid I choose to imagine. He has named, described, or discovered small articles he has never seen when they have been concealed by me in the most unusual places, and on two occasions, he has successfully described portions of a scene which I either imagined or actually saw.[2]

This letter came to the attention of Myers and Gurney, who forthwith went to Brighton and carried out tests on Smith and Blackburn. They found that Smith, when blindfolded, could name words that had been shown to Blackburn even when there was no contact between the two men. Smith was also able to reproduce drawings of simple figures shown to Blackburn, provided he touched him. The two subjects then went to London and were investigated in a long series of tests carried out by the Committee on Thought Reading. One of the tests was later vividly described by Blackburn:

> These were the conditions: Smith sat in a chair at the large table. His eyes were padded with wool, and, I think, a pair of folded kid gloves, and bandaged with a thick dark cloth. His ears were filled with one layer of cotton-wool, then pellets of putty. His entire body and the chair on which he sat were enveloped in two very heavy blankets. I remember, when he emerged triumphant, he was wet with perspiration, and the paper on which he had successfully drawn the figure was so moist that it broke during the examination by the delighted observers. Beneath his feet and surrounding his chair were thick, soft rugs, rightly intended to deaden and prevent signals by foot shuffles. Smith being rendered contact proof and perfectly insulated, my part began.
> At the farther side of the room—a very large dining room—Mr. Myers showed me, with every precaution, the drawing that I was to transmit to the brain beneath the blankets. It was a tangle of heavy black lines, interlaced, some curved, some straight, the sort of thing an infant playing with a pen

or pencil might produce, and I am certain absolutely indescribable in words, let alone in a code. I took it, fixed my gaze on it, pacing the room meanwhile and going through the usual process of impressing the figure upon my retina and brain, but always keeping out of touched distance with Smith. These preliminaries occupied perhaps ten or more minutes, for we made a point of never hurrying. I drew and redrew many times openly in the presence of observers, in order, as I explained and they allowed, to fix it on my brain.[3]

Blackburn went on to describe how he then stood in silence behind Smith's chair while Smith produced an almost line-for-line reproduction of Myers's original drawing. As a result of their tests, the investigators concluded that they had eliminated the possibility of information reaching Smith through any of the known senses.

Not everyone accepted the claims of the Committee on Thought Reading. Sir Horatio Donkin (1845–1927), a physician and a prominent critic, stated in the *Westminster Gazette* of November 26, 1907, that he had been told of two occasions when outside observers were invited to see Smith and Blackburn in action. Once, precautions taken to prevent possible auditory communication put a stop to the thought transference. On the other occasion, precautions against visual communication had a similar effect. Donkin pointed out that no mention was made in the published accounts of the presence of these observers or of the tests that were applied and the effects that were observed.

One of the observers, Sir James Crichton–Browne (1886–1940), a neurologist, confirmed these observations in the *Westminster Gazette* of January 29, 1908. He, together with the British scientist, Francis Galton (1822–1911), had been present as an observer at one sitting. After witnessing demonstrations of telepathy by Smith, the two had improved the effectiveness of his blindfold and earplugs. Further tests showed "not the smallest response on the part of Mr. S to Mr. B's volitional endeavors. There was no more flashing of images into his mind. His pencil was idle. Thought transference was somehow interrupted."[4]

Notwithstanding these objections, Smith and Blackburn were accepted as authentic by the Society for Psychical Research. Both became members of the group, and Smith acted as Gurney's secretary, assisting him by producing a number of other Brighton youths who gave convincing demonstrations of telepathy after being hypnotized by Smith. For their services to science the youths received financial benefits. After Gurney's suicide in 1888, the experiments were continued by Mrs. Henry Sidgwick, helped by other members of the society. Successful results were reported until 1892, when Smith left the employment of the society. Telepathic phenomena ceased with his departure, except for one occasion in 1894, when he again helped with an experiment. By 1898, the society had given up all hope of finding subjects who could display telepathy under hypnosis.

Blackburn's Confession

Smith came into the news again on December 5, 1908, when Blackburn revealed in a popular magazine, *John Bull,* that he and Smith had used tricks during the 1882 telepathy investigations. More complete details were given by Blackburn in the *Daily News* of September 1, 1911, from which the following extract is taken.   mind guessing

> For nearly thirty years the telepathic experiments conducted by Mr. G. A. Smith and myself have been accepted and cited as the basic evidence of the truth of Thought Transference.
>
> Your correspondent "Inquirer" is one of the many who have pointed to them as a conclusive reply to modern skeptics. The weight attached to those experiments was given by their publication in the first volume of the proceedings of the Society for Psychical Research, vouched for by Messrs. F. W. H. Myers, Edmund Gurney, Frank Podmore, and later and inferentially by Professor Henry Sidgwick, Professor Romanes, and others of equal intellectual eminence. They were the first scientifically conducted and attested experiments in Thought Transference, and later were imitated and reproduced by "sensitives" all over the world.
>
> I am the sole survivor of that group of experimentalists. As no harm can be done to anyone, but possible good to the cause of truth, I, with mingled feelings of regret and satisfaction now declare that the whole of those alleged experiments were bogus, and originated in the honest desire of two youths to show how easily men of scientific mind and training could be deceived when seeking for evidence in support of a theory they were wishful to establish.[5]

Blackburn went on to describe how mediums abounded at the end of the nineteenth century and how he had started an exposure campaign. He had then met Smith, and together they had perfected a thought-reading act. One of their performances, after being described in *Light,* had brought them to the notice of the Society for Psychical Research. He explained how they were then approached by Gurney and Myers and "saw in them only a superior type of spiritualistic crank" by whom they were pestered daily. Their first private demonstration was accepted so unhesitatingly, and the lack of reasonable precautions on the part of the investigators was so marked, that Smith and he felt it their duty to show how utterly incompetent these investigators were. Blackburn concluded by writing:

> In conclusion, I ask thoughtful persons to consider this proposition; if two youths, with a week's preparation, could deceive trained and careful observers like Messrs. Myers, Gurney, Podmore, Sidgwick, and Romanes under the most stringent conditions their ingenuity could devise, what are the chances of succeeding inquirers being more successful against "sensitives" who have had the advantage of more years experience than Smith and I had weeks?

Further, I would emphasize the fact that records of telepathic rapport in almost every instance depend upon the statement of one person, usually strongly predisposed to belief in the occult.[6]

Smith denied all the charges, but Blackburn then provided so much detail of the techniques employed that there was little doubt that tricks had been used. After describing the test in which Smith had been swathed in blankets, Blackburn continued:

I also drew it, secretly, on a cigarette paper. By this time I was fairly expert at palming, and had no difficulty while pacing the room collecting "rapport," in transferring the cigarette paper to the tube of the brass projector on the pencil I was using. I conveyed to Smith the agreed signal that I was ready by stumbling against the edge of the thick rug near his chair.

Next instant he exclaimed: "I have it." His right hand came from beneath the blanket, and he fumbled about the table, saying, according to arrangement: "Where's my pencil?"

Immediately I placed mine on the table. He took it and a long and anxious pause ensued.

This is what was going on under the blanket. Smith had concealed up in his waistcoat one of those luminous painted slates which in the dense darkness gave sufficient light to show the figure when the almost transparent cigarette paper was laid flat on the slate. He pushed up the bandage from one eye, and copied the figure with extraordinary accuracy.

It occupied over five minutes. During that time I was sitting exhausted with the mental effort quite ten feet away.

Presently Smith threw back the blanket and excitedly pushing back the eye bandage produced the drawing, which was done on a piece of notepaper, and very nearly on the same scale as the original. It was a splendid copy.[7]

If Blackburn had kept his secret, this series of experiments might well have gone down in the history of parapsychology as one of the conclusive investigations providing irrefutable evidence for telepathy, since critics such as Donkin and Crichton-Browne get little publicity and are soon forgotten. As it is, the outcome of the investigations of the Creery sisters (see page 19) and of Smith and Blackburn merely demonstrates the fact, confirmed time after time, that intelligent men can be deceived quite easily when their powers of observation are biased by their underlying beliefs.

TYPES OF INVESTIGATION

The two early investigations carried out by members of the Society for Psychical Research, described above, are examples where individuals claiming to have psychic powers attempt to demonstrate their ability. They do this under their own conditions, much in the manner that a stage magician performs before an audience.

Most later investigations employed some form of experiment in which the investigators decide the method and procedure under which a subject is to be tested. The subject follows instructions given him rather than operating wholly or partly under his own conditions. In the case of the Smith-Blackburn tests an experimental element was introduced when the visiting scientists improved the effectiveness of the blindfold and earplugs. The failure of Smith in subsequent tests was not, however, attributed to this change in the conditions.

Demonstration of a Natural Phenomenon

An important feature of the experimental method is that it is described in a report so that other independent investigators can carry out a similar experiment to see whether they get the same result. If any weakness or source of experimental error is suspected, the original design may be modified to remove it. The original result may then be attributed to the presence of that weakness.

After carrying out an initial experiment, the investigator is likely to conduct further experiments introducing additional controls against possible sources of error or making modifications suggested to him until he is satisfied that he can produce an experimental design that will confirm his original result. He is then in a position to give the method, procedure, and conditions for a demonstration of his findings that would permit all interested parties to test for themselves.

The result of an ESP experiment is usually in the form of a score, or the number of hits made by subjects when attempting to guess target symbols. This is compared with the number of hits that would be expected to arise by chance in the absence of ESP. If such a result would only be expected to arise by chance in 5 percent of cases, it is said to be "significant" at the 5 percent level. An investigator may then consider it worthwhile to continue with his experiments, increasing the number of observations made to confirm his own result. Eventually he may be in a position to present an experimental design that is likely to be repeatable so as to confirm his result when carried out by himself or by any other investigator.

In the words of R. A. Fisher: "In order to assert that a natural phenomenon is experimentally demonstrable we need, not an isolated record, but a reliable method of procedure. In relation to the test of significance we may say that a phenomenon is experimentally demonstrable when we know how to conduct an experiment which will rarely fail to give us a statistically significant result."[8]

To provide such a demonstration requires some knowledge not only of the number of observations necessary but also of the number of subjects to be tested, i.e., of the distribution of the ability in the population. A demonstration that fails more often than "rarely" may require an increase in the number of subjects to be tested and in the number of observations to be made on each subject. It may, however, require a change in the experimental plan to ensure that the method and procedure are properly implemented.

If the ability is found in only a very small number of the population, it may then be necessary to experiment on those individuals by passing them to a series of independent investigators. Claims have been made for remarkable powers of ESP in particular subjects; but these subjects have invariably lost their ability following publication of the experimental report. In no case has a subject been produced whose ability has been confirmed by a series of independent investigators under experimental conditions. If such a subject were to become available there would be little difficulty in providing a repeatable demonstration.

The Effects of Error and Trickery

In the normal course of events the effects of error will be detected and removed by modification of the experimental conditions during the development of a repeatable demonstration. Given what is claimed to be a repeatable experiment in which the methods and procedure are stated in an experimental report, the manner in which a further experiment is conducted, the observance of the experimental conditions, and the accuracy of the report submitted are factors that have to be considered.

In the history of parapsychology there has been a high incidence of trickery on the part of those involved in investigations that produced high scores. The repeatable demonstration provides a safeguard against such activity, the possibility of trickery on the part of subjects being reduced by removing sources of experimental error, and on the part of the investigators by developing a demonstration that is confirmed by independent investigators.

In the absence of such a repeatable demonstration emphasis has been placed in the past on isolating investigations that consisted of a series of experiments conducted by a particular investigator or team of investigators. A small number of such investigations have given results having astronomical antichance odds under conditions that are claimed to exclude the possibility of experimental error. In such cases it is clear that ESP is operating, or that some form of error is at present not envisaged by the investigators, or that the result is due to trickery on the part of one or more of the investigators.

The past record of parapsychology indicates that if there is any possibility of participants doing anything to influence the result—anything that is not noted in the experimental report—this possibility must be fully considered.

EARLY EXPERIMENTS ON TELEPATHY: JOHN E. COOVER

The first major experimental research on telepathy was contained in a monograph entitled *Experiments in Psychical Research,* published in 1917 by John E. Coover,[9] professor of psychology at Stanford University. This extensive volume of more than 600 pages contains details of four experiments on thought transference or telepathy.

In the main experiment 100 pairs of subjects each conducted a series of 100 trials. One of the subjects acted as percipient attempting to identify targets selected by the other subject who acted as experimenter. The targets were taken from a pack of playing cards from which the face cards had been removed leaving cards 1 through 10 in each of the four suits. Assuming the selection of the target cards to be random, the result could then be assessed using simple statistical methods either in terms of the card number 1–10 or in terms of the card (number plus suit) 1–40.

Coover's experiment is of interest owing to the use of a control series to allow for the effects of various forms of experimental error. The control series is of particular importance in an experimental situation that may involve unforeseen sources of error or possible forms of error that are difficult to eliminate. In each experiment two series of observations are made—an experimental series and a control series. Conditions in the two series are as near to being identical as possible, except for one factor that is present only in the experimental series. Any difference in the result obtained in the two series is then attributed to the effect of that one factor since it constitutes the only difference between the two series.

Coover's aim was to investigate thought transference—or telepathy—i.e., where the percipient tries to identify cards seen by the agent. He therefore arranged that on approximately 50 percent of trials in each run of 100 the experimenter would see the target card, making telepathy possible; on the remaining trials the experimenter would not see the card, making telepathy impossible. The 100 attempts made by the percipient could then be divided into an experimental series, in which telepathy was possible, and a control series, in which telepathy was impossible.

The experimenter was in the same room as the percipient, and they were positioned at distances of up to 10 meters apart. The procedure adopted was as follows: The experimenter, with a watch before him, shuffled the deck of forty cards, cut the pack, and held the cards concealed. He then shook a box containing a die to determine whether the trial would be allocated to the experimental or control series. If it was to be experimental, he turned over the pack, exposing to his view the under card, tapped once to signal the percipient that the experiment period had begun, and thought of the card "willing the content to be projected into the mind" of the percipient. After 15 to 20 (or more) seconds, he tapped twice to signal the close of the interval. Then, after noting that the reagent (percipient) had recorded his guess he recorded the color, number, and suit of the card and the number of the die spot, which decided whether the trial was to be allocated to the experimental or control series.

Precisely the same procedure was employed when the die indicated that the trial was to be allocated to the control series except that the experimenter did not turn over the cards so that the target card was not revealed to him until after the percipient had recorded his guess. The whole procedure was repeated until 100 cards had been recorded. Using this procedure 100 percipients were tested by 100 experimenters, who also acted as agents.

In the total of 10,000 guesses 5,135 arose in the experimental series and 4,865 in the control series. The results are summarized in table 2-1, which records the numbers of hits achieved when considering only the card number (1–10) and when considering both number and suit for a total of 40 different targets.

TABLE 2-1

Number of Hits Arising in Experimental and Control Series in Terms of
NUMBER (1–10) and NUMBER Plus SUIT Together
with Mean Scoring Rates per 1000 Trials

Series	Trials	Number 1–10		Cards 1–40	
		Hits	Rate	Hits	Rate
Exp'tal	5135	153	104.8	538	2.98
Control	4865	141	100.3	488	2.90

It will be seen that the scoring rates in the experimental and control series do not differ greatly under the conditions for numbers (1–10) or for cards. If the observed numbers of hits for each condition for the experimental and control series are assessed statistically using a chi-square test, the difference, using the criterion of significance adopted by Coover of antichance odds of 50,000 to 1 is not significant, and in fact not significant even at odds of 20 to 1. In addition, it was found that none of the results for the students, when considered individually, revealed any special ability at guessing cards.

Coover concluded therefore that the findings did not support the idea of telepathy, either as some ability found at a low level in the general population or as an ability present in some individuals. To support the latter finding he carried out tests on ten professional psychics who were found to be less successful than his student percipients in obtaining hits.

It was suggested, however, by F. C. S. Schiller in a review of the experiments that Coover had misrepresented his findings.[10] He isolated the scores of the fourteen highest-scoring subjects and compared the mean of these scores with that expected to arise by chance. The score resulting from deviation from chance was then statistically significant with odds greater than 50,000 to 1 against chance. He obtained a similar finding in the case of the control series for those subjects about which there was evidence in the findings to suggest something akin to clairvoyance. He selected the scores obtained by fourteen of the percipients who had obtained the highest scores and compared their total score with the chance expectation score. He did this separately for the experimental and control series and obtained antichance odds of around 50,000 to 1 in both cases. Schiller suggested: "These figures therefore distinctly point to some source of rightness beyond chance in these cases. As it occurs in the 'pure guesses' as well as in the 'experiments' it cannot be of the nature of conscious thought-transference. but may it not be due to a sort of 'lucidity' or clairvoyance in the 'reagent'?"[11]

Schiller's idea was taken further in 1939 when R. H. Thouless pointed out that if the overall scores for the experimental and control series are combined, the excess above-chance expectation (44 hits in 10,000 trials) obtained by Coover had odds of about 200 to 1 against chance occurrence.[12]

Replying to these criticisms, Coover pointed out that Schiller's form of analysis was incorrect and that by selecting particular cases for analysis it was possible to obtain equally high antichance odds for a variety of effects.[13] In the case of Thouless's criticism, any form of error present in both the experimental and control series would produce the same effect. He suggested that there were two possible forms of error that could have been present to account for the small surplus of overall hits. These were: (1) subliminal normal sensory cues and (2) recording errors on the part of the experimenter. He regarded (1) as less likely owing to the fact that tests had been conducted at six different distances between the subject and the cards, but scores were uniformly distributed at these different distances. He regarded recording errors as being more likely owing to the complex task undertaken by the experimenter.

In 1954, S. G. Soal pointed out that a more likely form of experimental error was present owing to the manner in which Coover selected target cards by shuffling and cutting a pack of playing cards, together with preferences of the subjects for particular cards when recording their guesses. In regard to these forms of error, he wrote: "So far as we are aware, however, no one has produced any evidence from Coover's original lists of cards and guesses that factors of this sort were present. . . ."[14]

Coover's control series, in which telepathy was not possible, allowed for sources of error, including those suggested by Soal, provided the difference in scoring rates between the experimental and control series was observed. By lumping together the two series and comparing the total score with that expected by chance, the effect of these forms of error becomes manifest.

To carry out a test for clairvoyance would require a control series in which clairvoyance is not possible. This could be achieved by comparing the number of hits in an experimental series in which no one sees the target, with the number obtained when guesses are checked against targets in the same series other than those for which they were intended.

In his reply to critics in 1939 when criticizing Schiller's use of a selected group of subjects, Coover pointed out that by taking guesses produced by such a group and matching their targets with their preceding guess in the series, he obtained equally antichance odds to those obtained by Schiller. He wrote: "We seem to have proof of prescience, prediction, or prophecy. The relation is between the guess and the following drawing of a card from a newly shuffled pack."[15]

He also checked targets produced by one experimenter against guesses produced by a percipient for whom they were not intended. Again, he obtained high antichance odds and wrote: "Were this extra-chance result to be warranted, we should have to search for some demon that correlates drawings of cards from immediately shuffled packs manipulated by different persons at different places and times."[16] To this day Coover is credited by parapsychologists with having demonstrated clairvoyance. He might equally well have been credited with the discovery of precognition.

Remarkably, in spite of the claim that Coover had produced evidence for clairvoyance, his experiment was not repeated—and reported—by his critics in order to confirm the claim or to reduce possible sources of error present in both the experimental and control series. This could quite easily have been done by employing a better method for randomizing the targets together with the use of a further control series in which clairvoyance would not be possible for each percipient/experimenter pair.

Coover's monograph describes an experiment in which he tested a subject to see if when guessing numbers the subject would fare better if only those guesses were considered in which the subject had confidence that he had made a correct identification. If a subject could correctly identify symbols by ESP or any other means, it might be expected that he would know when he was right or wrong. A subject could demonstrate his ability best by passing on those trials where he was unable to make an identification. Coover's subjects were unable to display any such ability and it has generally been assumed until very recently that subjects do not know when they are right or wrong.

It might also be supposed that if a subject makes a series of guesses at the same list of symbols his percentage of successes would be improved by taking the most frequently arising guess—or the mode—for each item on the list. Again, this has not been the case. In Coover's experiment above he allowed subjects ample time to make a decision on each card. This again might be expected to facilitate the demonstration of any weak ESP ability present. Coover's subjects had 15 to 20 seconds in which to make up their minds. In later experiments this period was reduced until it was of the order of half a second—i.e., as quickly as the targets could be manipulated.

MASS BROADCASTING EXPERIMENT

In 1927 a mass broadcasting experiment was carried out by members of the Society for Psychical Research. Listeners attempted to identify targets viewed by seven agents assembled in a broadcasting studio at 2 Savoy Hill, London. Listeners to the broadcast were asked to attempt to identify each of five targets. Sir Oliver Lodge announced the time at which each target was to be viewed by the agents. Listeners were then given three minutes in which to get their telepathic impressions of the target followed by an interval of two minutes before the next target was viewed. Two of the objects were playing cards— the first target being a 2 of clubs, the fourth target a 9 of hearts—permitting the results to be assessed statistically.

A total of 24,650 persons sent in their lists of guesses, from which it was clear that the chances of success on any card were not 51 to 1 but depended on preferences for particular cards. The result was determined by considering each of the two cards as falling into an experimental and a control series. Thus the first card used was the 2 of clubs. This arose (correctly) 190 times in the experimental series and 145 times (incorrectly) in the control series. The second card was the 9 of hearts, which arose 150 times in the experimental series and 491 times in the control series. It was concluded that the figures "offer no support to the supposition that telepathy is possible under these conditions."[17]

The experimental report provided interesting data to indicate the manner in which particular cards arise more frequently than others. Thus the ace arose most frequently in the overall 49,300 guesses at a playing card. The actual figures were 1,584 (clubs), 3,891 (spades), 2,520 (diamonds), 2,751 (hearts). The knave came second in popularity: 872 (clubs), 795 (spades), 1,000 (diamonds), 777 (hearts). Among the number cards (2–10) odd numbers arose more frequently than even numbers, with the 5 arising most frequently in each suit.

ESTERBROOKS'S EXPERIMENT

A further experiment using playing cards that was similar in some respects to Coover's was reported in 1927 by G. E. Esterbrooks, a graduate student working under William McDougall in the Department of Psychology at Harvard University.[18] Dr. J. B. Rhine, who was to become the most prominent figure in parapsychology over the next fifty years, was also present in the department and took an interest in the experiments.

Esterbrooks used Harvard students as subjects, selecting those who were "positively interested." Esterbrooks himself acted as sender and experimenter with the guesser in a separate part of the room. Three series of experiments were conducted in which 83 subjects divided into three groups were tested over 2,300 trials.

An electric device was used to generate a click every 220 seconds to signal to the subject that he was to make his guess. At the same time Esterbrooks looked at a playing card, continuing to do so over the period of 20 seconds. In the case where a "red" playing card was present he switched on a red light.

The results were analyzed in terms of color and suit, giving antichance odds of 8 million to 1 for color and 900 to 1 for suit.

A fourth series of tests was carried out using mostly subjects who had taken part in the earlier series, with the guessers situated in a separate building some 60 feet away from the sender. Scores were now at the chance level.

At the suggestion of McDougall a control series was obtained after the original tests were completed by retesting some of the subjects under conditions where telepathy was not possible because the experimenter did not see the card. This gave chance results. A further control series was obtained in order to check that effects due to the method of selecting cards (cutting a shuffled pack with a knife) or card preferences of the subjects had not affected the scores. This was done by checking guesses against targets five trials ahead of those for which they were intended. Again, chance results were obtained.

Esterbrooks stated at the end of his report that further tests were being made by his assistant at Springfield College, Springfield, Massachusetts. According to J. B. Rhine, "Esterbrooks' 'telepathy' experiment succeeded for him but was said to have failed the next year when repeated by an assistant."[19]

EARLY EXPERIMENTS ON CLAIRVOYANCE

Experiments on clairvoyance are relatively simple in that only a single individual—the guesser—is involved, whereas a second person—the sender—is required in telepathy experiments.

Such experiments were first reported by the French physiologist Charles Richet in 1884.[20] He enclosed playing cards in envelopes and asked a subject who had been put under hypnosis to identify them. His subject is said to have been highly successful over a series of 133 trials, but when she performed before a group of scientists in Cambridge her powers deserted her. She is reported to have recovered her ability following her return to Paris.[21] The following year Peirce and Pickering reported an experiment in which they tested 36 subjects over 23,384 trials under clairvoyance conditions. They did not obtain significantly above-chance scores.[22]

Following a gap of many years in which the emphasis was on telepathy, an experiment was reported in 1929 by Ina Jephson, a council member of the Society for Psychical Research.[23] She used 240 members of the society as her subjects. Instructions were sent to them by post, asking subjects to complete in their homes 25 trials guessing the identities of playing cards, but making only 5 attempts on any one day.

Each subject was instructed to take a pack of playing cards, shuffle it, and draw out a card at random, keeping it face downward. He had to guess the card, record his guess, and then write next to it the actual value of the card, followed by the suit. He then replaced the card in the pack and repeated the whole operation until he had recorded 5 trials. In this manner each subject completed 5 attempts on each of five days. The 240 subjects thus completed a total of 1,200 sets of 5 trials, giving 6,000 trials in all. The results were assessed in terms of the chances of the card (1/52), its number (1/13), suit (1/4), and color (1/2) being correct.

The 6,000 guesses produced 245 complete identifications against the chance number of 115, giving enormous antichance odds. High above-chance scores were also obtained for number, suit, and color. It was found that subjects scored highest at the start of their run of five. Their scores then dropped but recovered on the fifth card. This was called a "decline effect."

It was suggested by S. G. Soal, a member of the society, that there were several sources of error present in Jephson's tests and that they should be carried out under better conditions. He thought, for example, that some subjects may have made several attempts to guess five cards on the same day and sent in their best result, or that some subjects may not have recorded their guesses until they could start off with a hit. Further tests were then reported by Jephson, Soal, and Theodore Besterman—the research officer of the Society for Psychical Research—to eliminate such possibilities.[24]

A large number of playing cards with plain backs were placed in blue envelopes that exactly fitted the cards. The envelopes were of such a nature that they could not be rendered transparent by strong light, X rays, or solvents nor could they be opened without leaving traces. They bore the impress of the Society for Psychical Research. The envelopes were sealed and sent to 559 subjects in batches of five in five successive weeks.

The whole operation of preparing targets and checking results was supervised by a fourth experimenter named Colonel Dick. He ensured that the other investigators followed the procedure laid down and that the experiment was conducted exactly as planned.

A total of 9,469 guesses showed no trace of any extrachance factor. The original result obtained by Miss Jephson was not confirmed, even though more than twice the number of subjects was tested—including most of those who had taken part in her earlier experiment.

The experiment indicated how data could be obtained from a large group of subject using simple methods. Second, it tested the hypothesis that the original subjects who also acted as investigators were affecting the scores.

NOTES

1. H. Sidgwick, "Presidential Address," *Proceedings of the Society of Psychical Research* 1, 1 (1882): 12.

2. D. Blackburn, letter in *Light* (August 26, 1882).

3. D. Blackburn, *London Daily News* (September 1, 1911).

4. Sir James Crichton-Browne, letter in *Westminster Gazette* (January 29, 1908).

5. Blackburn, *London Daily News* (September 1, 1911).

6. Blackburn, *London Daily News* (September 1, 1911).

7. Blackburn, *London Daily News* (September 1, 1911).

8. R. A. Fisher, *The Design of Experiments* (Edinburgh: Oliver and Boyd, 1935), p. 16.

9. John E. Coover, "Experiments in Psychical Research" in the *Leland Stanford University's Psychical Research Monograph No. 1* (Stanford: published by the university; republished in 1975, New York: Arno Press).

10. F. C. S. Schiller, "Review: *Experiments in Psychical Research,*" *Proceedings of the Society for Psychical Research* 76, (1920): 261-273.

11. Ibid., p. 264.

12. R. H. Thouless, "Dr. Rhine's Recent Experiments on Telepathy and Clairvoyance and a Reconsideration of J. E. Coover's Experiments on Telepathy," *Proceedings of the Society for Psychical Research* 43 (1935): 24-37.

13. J. E. Coover, "Reply to Criticisms of the Stanford Experiments on Thought Transference," *Journal of Parapsychology* 3 (1937): 17-30.

14. S. G. Soal and F. Bateman, *Modern Experiments in Telepathy* (London: Faber & Faber, 1954), p. 13.

15. J. E. Coover (1937), op. cit., p. 22.

16. Ibid.

17. V. J. Woolley, "The Broadcasting Experiment in Mass-Telepathy," *Proceedings of the Society for Psychical Research* 38 (1928): 1-9.

18. G. H. Esterbrooks, "A Contribution to Experimental Telepathy," *Bulletin 5, Boston Society for Psychical Research* 5 (1927): 1-30.

19. J. B. Rhine in *Handbook of Parapsychology,* edited by B. B. Wolman (New York: Van Nostrand, 1977), p. 31.

20. Charles Richet, "Further Experiments on Hypnotic Lucidity or Clairvoyance," *Proceedings of the Society for Psychical Research* 6 (1988): 66-83.

21. J. B. Rhine in *Handbook of Parapsychology,* edited by B. B. Wolman (New York: Van Nostrand, 1977), p. 26.

22. J. M. Peirce and E. C. Pickering, Appendices B and C of *Proceedings of the Society for Psychical Research* 4 (1888): 66-83.

23. Ina Jephson, "Evidence for Clairvoyance in Card-Guessing," *Proceedings of the Society for Psychical Research* 37, 109 (1929): 233-268.

24. T. Besterman, S. G. Soal, and Ina Jephson, "Report of a Series of Experiments in Clairvoyance Conducted at a Distance Under Approximately Fraud-Proof Conditions," *Proceedings of the Society for Psychical Research* 39, 118 (1931): 374-414.

Part Two

Card-Guessing Experiments

3

Experiments at Duke University

WILLIAM MCDOUGALL

In 1920, William McDougall (1871-1938), the well-known British psychologist, was appointed to the chair of psychology at Harvard University. McDougall at that time was president of the British Society for Psychical Research, having become interested in the subject while a student at Cambridge. He found a history of psychical research at Harvard, for ten years earlier, the German psychologist, Hugo Münsterberg—McDougall's predecessor in the chair at Harvard—had exposed the great Italian medium Eusapia Palladino, and an experiment on telepathy had been carried out there in 1916 by L. T. Troland, a professor of psychology in the department.

Psychical research flourished at Harvard during the 1920s. McDougall found funds for the work lying idle and quickly put them to use. Experiments on telepathy were conducted by the psychologists Gardner Murphy and G. H. Esterbrooks, and before long McDougall, together with most of the staff of his department and several senior members of the university, was involved in the investigation of a local medium by the name of "Margery."

While at Harvard, McDougall was contacted by a young Chicago botanist, Joseph Banks Rhine. Rhine and his wife Louisa, who had become interested in psychical research, partly through hearing a lecture on spiritualism given by the English author and physician Sir Arthur Conan Doyle (1859-1930). Rhine began a correspondence with McDougall, and in 1926 he joined the Harvard psychology department as a research assistant. When McDougall moved to the faculty of Duke University in 1927, Rhine went with him.

FIGURE 3-1
ESP Cards (formerly called Zener Cards)

Rhine's first publication on telepathy appeared in 1929 and concerned a telepathic horse named Lady.[1] In view of the considerable doubts about this experiment and the fact that Rhine admitted that the owner of the horse had later resorted to using signals, there is little point in considering it in detail.

In 1934, he published *Extra-Sensory Perception,*[2] in which he gave details of research at Duke University and claimed to have found overwhelming evidence for the existence of extrasensory perception. Further research followed, and in 1940 the Duke Parapsychology Laboratory was formed with Rhine as its director.

EARLY EXPLORATORY TESTS

The first part of the research described in *Extra-Sensory Perception* consisted of exploratory tests made under comparatively loose conditions in which the aim was to discover subjects who would be used in later research.

Some of the major tests carried out during this exploratory period (1930-32) are detailed below:

1. In the summer of 1930, children at a summer recreational school were asked to guess a number (0-9) seen by the experimenter. Approximately a thousand trials were made in this manner, but not a single child was discovered whose performance warranted any further investigation.

2. In the fall, Rhine in collaboration with a colleague in the psychology department, K. E. Zener, carried out clairvoyance experiments on students in class. Tests were made using three types of material: numbers (0-9), letters of the alphabet, and Zener cards. The latter, so named because they had been chosen by Zener, consisted of five different symbols: a circle, a rectangle, a plus sign, wavy lines, and a star. In a total of 1,600 trials, the scores were close to the chance expectation. After the experiment Zener became too burdened with other work and dropped out of the research.

3. In the winter of 1931–32, Rhine obtained what he called his first really convincing result. A clairvoyance test using Zener cards on twenty-four subjects yielded an overall score of 207 hits in 800 trials. As there were five different symbols, the score expected to arise by chance was 160 hits, and the odds were greater than a million to one against a score of 207. Twelve of the twenty-four subjects obtained an average of 5 hits or more in 25 trials, while the other twelve subjects scored below chance. Of the latter group, Rhine said that none of them "developed," and few were tried again. But as, on the average, fewer than 14 trials were made with each of these low-scoring subjects, it is difficult to see how they were given much chance to develop. A surprising feature of these tests was, in fact, the small number of trials some of the subjects made. During each trial the subject might look at the back of the card and pick it up before making his guess; but this would hardly have taken more than about five seconds for each guess. Even so, several subjects recorded only 50 or fewer trials, and the twelve low-scoring subjects averaged fewer than 14 trials—about one and a half minutes work each.

4. Two further experiments yielding significantly high scores were carried out at this time by Dr. Rhine's assistants, but in neither case were the exact conditions of the experiments stated. Charles E. Stuart tested nine subjects and J. G. Pratt, fifteen. In each case, the overall score for the group had high odds against arising by chance. From the meager details given, it would appear that the experimenter sat at a table with the subject and handed him a pack of Zener cards. The subject took each card in turn, holding it face downward, and made his guess, which was recorded by the experimenter. The guesses were, on some occasions, checked for hits after a run of 5 trials and on the other occasions after a run of 24 trials had been completed.

These "early and minor tests," Rhine stated, were published so that the reader might see the whole of the group's work in its infancy. They included 23,550 trials, and the overall score achieved had odds greater than a billion to one against arising by chance. But, as Rhine commented, "Some of the weaknesses of these beginnings one only has to read here to avoid."

A feature of the early tests was the fact that, among a large number of subjects who were tested at this time, only two—A. J. Linzmayer and Stuart, both undergraduate students—later showed themselves capable of obtaining consistently high scores. The experiments gave results that were statistically significant because the groups of subjects scored slightly above the chance level over a large number of trials.

In 1930 and early 1931, progress was slow, and subjects with ESP seemed hard to find; but later in 1931 there were dramatic changes, and by the end of 1932 almost everyone tested among the graduate psychology students at Duke was found to have some ability. Thus, Rhine stated in *Extra-Sensory Perception* that, of the fourteen graduate students in psychology present in the previous two years, six showed ESP ability that was statistically significant, another had been reported to have done work that was appreciably significant, and the remaining seven students had not to his knowledge been tested.

TESTS ON HIGH-SCORING SUBJECTS

The second part of Rhine's research consisted of investigations carried out on eight high-scoring subjects. Each of them in a relatively short time displayed remarkable powers of ESP, and his final assessment of the combined score of his subjects gave odds greater than 10^{1000} to 1 against chance occurrence.

Various types of tests were used, but they had a common characteristic: the subject guessed one of five different symbols that were either depicted on cards or were thought of by some other person. The cards were in packs of 25, containing 5 of each of the different symbols. When a subject guesses the order of such a pack, provided he is not told whether he is correct or not after each trial, an average score of 5 hits per run of 25 is expected to arise. A subject's score will vary in different runs of 25 trials; thus, in 100 runs, several scores of 9, one or two 10s, and with luck a 12 would probably arise. A score of 13 would not be extraordinary (odds are about 6 to 1 against getting a score of 13 in 100 runs), but a 14 would be unlikely. A score of exactly 5 hits would be expected to arise on about 40 occasions.

Rhine's high-scoring subjects would often average 8 or 9 hits over a large number of runs. Thus, the most outstanding subject, Hubert E. Pearce, a student for the Methodist ministry in the School of Religion at Duke, averaged 8 hits per run over 690 runs, constituting a total of 17,250 trials. This performance would not seem remarkable unless an observer were well acquainted with the probabilities of the different-sized scores arising by chance. But, in fact, if a person could average even 5.3 hits per 25 trials over 690 runs, there would be odds greater than 1 million to 1 against this result arising by chance, although the subject would only be averaging 1 extra hit in each 76 guesses.

The experimental techniques employed by Rhine were:

1. BT *(Basic Technique,* later referred to as the "Before Touching" technique). The pack was shuffled, cut, and placed face downward on the table. The subject attempted to guess the first card, which was then removed and placed in a separate pile. He then attempted to guess the second card, and the process continued until he had guessed at the identity of each of the twenty-five cards in the pack. On some occasions, the subject himself took the card from the pack, held it face downward, attempted to guess it, and then placed it in a second pile.

2. DT *(Down Through).* The pack was shuffled, cut, and placed face downward on the table. The subject attempted to guess the cards one by one, from the top, without disturbing the pack.

3. PT *(Pure Telepathy).* Here no cards or records of the targets were used; the aim was to study telepathy as distinct from clairvoyance. Thus, a second person, the agent, had to think of a symbol; but it was argued that if a pack of cards was used, the subject might obtain above-chance scores by clairvoyance. And so, the agent thought of a symbol that did not exist as a card in a pack or as an entry on a list. He thought of five of the ESP symbols in a particular order, and the subject called aloud his guesses. The

agent made a record of each of the subject's calls and checked them for correctness as he recorded them.

In *Extra-Sensory Perception,* Rhine commented that success or failure depended very much on the conditions under which the tests were made, and he listed the following suggestions to those who might care to repeat his experiments.

1. The subject should have an active interest in the tests and be fairly free from strong bias or doubt. These would, of course, hinder effort and limit attention. An open-minded, experimental attitude is all that is required. Positive belief is naturally favorable but not necessary.

2. The preliminary tests should be entered into very informally, without much serious discussion as to techniques, or explanations or precautions. The more ado over techniques, the more inhibition is likely; and the more there is of explanations, the more likely is introspection to interfere. Playful informality is most favorable.

3. If possible to do so honestly, it is helpful to give encouragement for any little success but no extravagant praise is desirable, even over striking results. The point is that encouragement is helpful, apparently, but only if it does not lead to self-consciousness. If it does, it is quite ruinous. Many subjects begin well, become excited or self-conscious, and then do poorly.

4. Some begin more easily with PT [Pure Telepathy] and some with PC [Pure Clairvoyance]. It depends upon personality, I think, but I cannot explain it except to link sociability with PT preference. However, both conditions should be tried, following the subject's preference in the beginning.

5. It is highly important to let the subject have his own way, without restraint, at first. Later, he can be persuaded to allow changes, after he has gained confidence and discovered his way to ESP functioning. Even then it is better for him to have his way as far as experimental conditions can allow. It is a poor science that dictates conditions to Nature. It is a better one that follows up with its well-adapted controls and conditions.

6. It is wise not to express doubts or regrets. Discouragement seems to damage the delicate function of ESP. Here again no doubt personalities differ. One subject I know has worked in the face of doubt expressed; but she is exceptional in this.

7. Above all, one must not, like several investigators, stop with only 25 or 50 or even 100 trials per subject. Most of my good subjects did not do very well in the first 100. With few exceptions, the first 50 to 100 trials give the worst scores. With all my major subjects this is true. Several different occasions or sittings too should be allowed, for there is with most subjects an adjustment phase at first that may take some time.

8. It is best at first to have the subject alone with the agent in PT and in PC to leave him alone entirely. If not, he may be inhibited from the start; but, once he has a start, he can gradually work back to other

conditions. When he has observers present, the experimenter should do all he can to put the subject at ease.

9. Simple cards with 5 suits seem best as a compromise of several features of concern: easy calculation, easy recall, easy discrimination of images, etc.

10. Short runs are desirable, say 5 at a time, with a checkup after each 5. Then it is best to go casually and quietly on without too much discussion of results.

11. It is advisable not to bore or tire the subject. When he wants to stop, or even before he expressly wishes to, it is better to stop work.

12. It is best to try good friends for PT at first—or couples, single or married, who feel certain they have thought-transference; and, above all, to try those people who say they have had "psychic" experiences or whose ancestors conspicuously have had.

These are suggestions, not rules, for we do not yet know enough of the subject to lay down rules. They will help toward success, without endangering conclusions. One can always tighten up on conditions before drawing conclusions later. But any investigator must first of all get his phenomena to occur—or exhaust the reasonable possibilities in trying to.[3]

Linzmayer, the first of the high-scoring subjects, had been noticed as promising in the early 1930 tests. When tested again in 1931, he first produced a score of only 4 hits in 20 trials, which is exactly that of chance expectation. In the next series, made on May 21, 1931, he was far more successful, achieving 25 hits in 45 trials with 9 of these hits on successive cards. However, the conditions in this test could hardly be considered stringent. Rhine took a card from a shuffled pack. After first looking at it, he held it face downward under his hand and tried to visualize the symbol. He did this rather than thinking of its name so that, as he put it, the "involuntary whispering ghost need not haunt us."

Ten days later, Linzmayer was given a further 535 trials, making a total of 600. Of these, 360 were made under conditions in which the experimenter knew the symbol being guessed (described as undifferentiated ESP, Telepathy and Clairvoyance); and 240 trials were made in which the symbol was unknown to anyone (described as Pure Clairvoyance Condition). In the overall 600 trials, Linzmayer got 238 successes, and there are odds well over 10 million to 1 against this result arising by chance.

The conditions under which the tests were carried out are nowhere described in detail. The following report is, however, given of one test in which Linzmayer produced his most remarkable feat. Linzmayer and Rhine were seated in Rhine's car with the engine running. Linzmayer was leaning back so that he looked at only the roof of the car, and there were no mirrors or shiny surfaces to assist him in seeing the cards. Rhine held the pack out of sight, face down, and shuffled it several times during the series. He drew the card with his right hand, keeping it concealed as he leaned forward; then he tilted it a little, glanced at it, and laid it on a large record book resting on Linzmayer's knees. About two seconds after it was laid on the book, Linzmayer made his guess aloud. Rhine then said whether Linzmayer had been right or wrong and laid the card on the appropriate pile. The hits were counted and recorded "at the end of the 15 calls, here, and then at the end of each five calls after." On this occasion, Linzmayer was successful in 21 out of 25 trials. He also obtained 15 consecutive hits, the odds being 30 billion to 1 against the chance achievement of such a feat.

Linzmayer obtained significantly above-chance results with each of the three experimental techniques given on page 40, but he was unsuccessful when tested with the cards at a distance from him. Eventually, his results started declining until, at the finish, he was unable to score above chance.

Charles E. Stuart, the second of the high-scoring subjects, was an assistant in the psychology department. He was successful both as a subject and an experimenter with the BT technique, but this was in part due to the fact that in most of his observations he used himself as subject. He was unsuccessful when tested with the DT and PT techniques.

Following a successful result in one of the early exploratory experiments, Stuart started making ESP tests in the autumn of 1931. In a total of 7,500 unwitnessed trials carried out on himself under conditions that are not stated, he obtained 1,815 hits as compared with the expected number of 1,500. There are enormous odds against this result arising by chance.

Hubert E. Pearce, the divinity student, was by far the most versatile of all the high-scoring subjects and produced high above-chance scores when tested with each of the three techniques. He was successful with the BT and DT techniques only when seated at a table with the cards, but he succeeded in making high scores with the PT technique when at a distance of 8 to 30 feet from the agent. His most impressive result was in an experiment later known as the Pearce-Pratt experiment (see chapter 5), which was being conducted during the writing of *Extra-Sensory Perception*. Here, he obtained high scores in sitting after sitting when he was situated more than 100 yards from the cards.

The results for the remaining five high-scoring subjects were presented as a group in *Extra-Sensory Perception*. These subjects were all psychologists: George Zirkle and Sarah Ownbey being graduate assistants, while May Frances Turner, June Bailey, and T. Coleman Cooper were students in the psychology department.

George Zirkle was unsuccessful with the BT and DT techniques, but when tested with the PT technique, he averaged 11 hits per 25 trials over 3,400 trials. On several occasions he obtained 22 hits in 25 trials, on one occasion he got an unbroken run of 26 successes. Zirkle was also able to obtain high scores when at distances of up to 10 feet from the agent when PT was used.

Miss Ownbey resembled Stuart in that she was successful both as an investigator and as a subject. Like Stuart, she really succeeded as a subject only when tested by herself. She carried out the first ESP test at Duke University in which the cards were at a considerable distance from the subject.

Miss Turner, the subject in the above long-distance test, Coleman Cooper, and Miss Bailey were all successful when using BT and PT but obtained only moderate success with the DT technique.

The combined data from these last five subjects gave an average score of 8.4 hits in each run of 25 over a total of 26,950 trials. The odds against such a result arising by chance are astronomical.

WEAKNESSES IN THE EXPERIMENTAL TECHNIQUES

"Before Touching" has the obvious danger that the subject may recognize the cards by marks on their backs or sides; in addition, if he handles them, he may recognize a particular card by its feel.

In 1937, when ESP cards were first supplied to the public, it was shown that they could be read quite easily from their backs and sides (see pp. 51–53). It is thus of considerable significance that subjects could obtain above-chance scores with the basic technique only when seated close to the cards, and that as soon as they were moved away, their scores dropped to the chance level.

A second difficulty that arises with this technique is that the cards may tend to cut at a particular symbol. It was mentioned in *Extra-Sensory Perception* that some of the early cards were found to be unsatisfactory because one of the symbols was printed on a slightly larger card than the others. Such a pack would tend to cut so that the larger one would fall toward the bottom and one of the four remaining symbols toward the top of the pack. During the shuffling, cards of a particular size might also tend to come together, so that it would be possible to obtain extra hits in other positions than at the top and bottom of the pack.

With BT, the subject's score was checked, on some occasions, at the end of 25 guesses (BT25), on other occasions after 5(BT5). It is significant that in BT25, the hits tended to arise in the first five and last five cards of the pack. Details are not given of the scores on the first and last cards, but they were clearly very high, since in 60 runs of the BT25 type, Pearce got 52 of his last calls correct.

Experiments with Pearce using BT took the following form: Pearce shuffled the pack, since he claimed it gave more real contact, and the observer cut it. Pearce would then pick up the cards and remove the top one, keeping the pack and the removed card face down on the table. The observer would record the call after either 5 or 25 calls—the two conditions being used about equally. The cards would be turned over and checked against the calls recorded in the book. The subject was asked to help in the checking by laying them off. For the next run, another pack of cards would be used.

When the BT5 technique was employed, correct scores followed a cyclical pattern, being the highest for positions 2, 7, 12, 17, and 22; second highest for positions 1, 6, 11, 16, and 21; and relatively low for the remaining positions. Since, after each 5 guesses, the cards were sometimes replaced in the pack, which was shuffled and cut before the next 5 were recorded, this effect could have arisen because particular symbols tended to be brought to the top and bottom of the pack.

The down-through technique suffers from the same drawbacks as the BT25 procedure, and again it is significant that when it was employed, the subject scored most of his hits on the first and last 5 cards. Details are not given of the scoring rate at each position in the pack, but it is recorded that in 40 of Pearce's DT runs, he correctly called 33 last cards. It also appears that the DT procedure was partially originated by Pearce himself.[4]

The salient question in connection with both the basic and down-through techniques is what would happen if the cards were no longer visible to the subject? In one experiment, Pearce was tested at three distances: across a table, at 8 to 12 feet from the cards, and at 28 to 30 feet from the cards. Using both the BT and DT techniques, the scores were significantly above chance when Pearce was close to the cards, and with both techniques, scores dropped when he was at any distance from them.

The pure-telepathy technique is by far the most unsatisfactory of the three. Anyone who tries to carry out the duties of the experimenter will find them extremely difficult and tiring to perform. The possibility that errors will arise is high under these conditions, and there is no check on them if they are made.

The procedure adopted was for the experimenter to think of 5 Zener symbols in any order he liked, and then concentrate his attention on each one as its turn came while the subject made his guess. The experimenter, after signaling the subject with a key that he was to say his guess, noted down the guess and whether it was correct. After the first five targets had been guessed, another 5 would be preselected in some order, usually different from the first, and the process continued.

Under these conditions, high scores would be expected to arise owing to the manner in which people behave when they think they are generating a random series.

Also, each run of 5 trials tends to contain all 5 of the symbols arranged in a fresh order each time. Under these conditions, the subject's chances of obtaining high scores are greatly increased. In such cases there are 120 possible arrangements of the 5 different symbols, and the subject would expect to achieve 5 hits once in each 120 attempts, whereas in a true random distribution, the number of arrangements of the 5 symbols is 3,125 (5^5). If the experimenter tended to include all 5 symbols in each run, and to start his run with a symbol other than that last called by the subject, the mean score would be augmented considerably.

George Zirkle, who was able to obtain high scores only when using the PT technique and only when tested by Miss Ownbey—who later became his wife—averaged 10.7 hits per 25 guesses in 5,025 trials. An extraordinary feature of these experiments was that at no time during the 5,025 trials did anyone appear to consider the possibility that the targets generated by Miss Ownbey could be influenced by her hearing Zirkle's calls, or even that she might make mistakes in her recording. A check could easily have been made. Miss Ownbey could have been provided with a list of symbols arranged in random order. One of the faculty members could have been provided with a list of symbols aranged in random order. One of the faculty members. could have recorded Zirkle's calls. The purely academic point whether Zirkle was displaying telepathy or clairvoyance could have been forgotten for the time being, and, in any case, Zirkle had already shown that he was unable to obtain above-chance results when tested for clairvoyance.

Looking at the results of the experiments and bearing in mind the pitfalls of the techniques employed, several features cannot but strike the critic.

It was reported that placing the subject away from the cards removed high scores, except when the PT technique was used. Since the obvious weakness of BT and DT lies in the possibility of the subject receiving sensory cues from the cards, it is to be expected that subjects would be unable to maintain high scores in the event of their using such cues when placed at any distance from the cards.

In the case of PT, distance would not affect the calling habits of the experimenter. The subject and agent could be a hundred miles apart, with a telephone link for the agent to hear the subject's call, and this would not remove the inherent weakness of the experimental technique.

Rhine commented after studying the results:

> These bring out the point of the difference between PT and BT results with distance, and their similarity at close range, suggesting that while PT can clearly be done at such distances, it may be that BT may not. It is still more strongly suggested that DT may be limited to close range.[5]

The observation fits precisely with what would be expected if the subjects utilized sensory cues with the BT and DT techniques. With the DT technique, these cues would be weakest, since only the sides of the cards, other than the top card, are visible to the percipient.

A LONG-DISTANCE EXPERIMENT

While BT and DT experiments with the subject at a distance from the cards showed no evidence for ESP, one other test was reported in which the result was of quite a different nature. This was a series of runs in which Miss Turner was situated 250 miles from the cards at Lake Junaluska, North Carolina, while the experimenter, Miss Ownbey, was at the Parapsychology Laboratory in Durham.

Each day, Miss Turner was to record 25 guesses at prescribed times and to send a record of her guesses directly to Rhine. The agent was likewise to send a record of her targets each day directly to Rhine. There were 3 series of tests. In the first, 8 runs of 25 trials each were completed. The first 3 made on June 30, July 5, and July 7, 1933, resulted in scores of 19 out of 25, 16 out of 25, and 16 out of 25. The probability that these scores arose by chance is fantastically remote. Rhine states in *Extra-Sensory Perception* that it was then discovered that Miss Turner's record had not gone directly to him as planned, but that it had been transmitted through Miss Ownbey. Twelve days later, tests were resumed and further runs were made on July 19, 20, 21, 22, and 24. On these days, both records were sent directly to Rhine. but the scores were not now significantly above the chance level.

Further tests, at a distance of 300 miles, were made on August 22, 24, 29, and 31, but again the scores did not differ significantly from chance expectation.

In spite of the lapse in the experimental conditions during the first three days and the remarkable scores that emerged, Rhine did not suspect either lady of duplicity. He commented that the subject's recordings were unmistakably in Miss Turner's handwriting and in ink with no evident changes. He then came to the conclusion that the young ladies had not been deceiving him. However, it should be noted that if Miss Ownbey had wished to deceive Rhine, she would merely have written out her record of the target series after seeing Miss Turner's guesses.

GENERAL OBSERVATIONS ON THE EXPERIMENTS

The scores obtained by each of the high-scoring subjects were such that no one could deny that some factor other than chance was involved. Rhine discussed five alternative hypotheses to ESP: chance, fraud, incompetence, unconscious sensory perception, and rational inference, and came to the conclusion that he had eliminated the possibility of each of them and that ESP stood without a serious opposing hypothesis. Even a superficial examination makes it difficult, however, to understand why the alternative hypotheses should have been so summarily dismissed.

It is clear that there can be little dispute about the inapplicability of the hypothesis that the high scores were the result of chance. Some criticisms have been made of Rhine's statistical treatment, but the result is undisputed. The method he employed was suitable for randomly distrubuted targets; that is, those that would arise if the card was returned to the pack after each guess and, after shuffling, a fresh card was selected as the next target. But since the packs of cards Rhine used contained exactly five of each symbol, a *closed pack,* the distribution of targets was not random. The use of a closed pack would not, however, affect the conclusions very much. Whether the odds of Pearce's result are 10^{100} to 1 or merely 10^{90} to 1 against chance is quite irrelevant.

The question of statistical analysis does arise when the results obtained from experiments where PT was employed are considered. Here, the subject guessed at five symbols arranged in a particular order, after which he was presented with five more targets consisting of a new order of symbols. If the experimenter merely produced the symbols in different orders for each run, the subject's chances of high scores would be considerably increased when compared with the possibility of high scores when guessing a randomly generated series of symbols.

The most remarkable feature of Rhine's discussion of the fraud hypothesis was that he made no mention of the first three runs in the Turner-Ownbey experiment. Whether or not he thought that there had been any tampering with the records, it was highly relevant and should have been discussed.

Rhine considered two possibilities: fraud on the part of the subjects who tested themselves, and fraud both by subjects and experimenters. In the case of subjects who tested themselves, there was no check other than a comparison of scores obtained when they were alone with those made when witnesses were present. In most cases, the results agreed, but there was an exception in the case of Miss Ownbey, who tested herself using the down-through technique. She obtained most of her hits in the middle of the run, whereas all the other subjects who had been witnessed obtained most of theirs at the start and end of the run when this technique was used. Also, Miss Ownbey, who averaged 8.4 hits when unwitnessed, was unable to obtain a result that was statistically above the chance level when an observer was present.

When Rhine discussed the competence of the researchers and observers, he concluded that the experimental conditions had been steadily tightened up and pointed out that no adequate loophole had been discovered. His final conclusion was that the hypothesis of incompetence would find "few adherents and no justification"; but the critic cannot but be struck with the numerous occasions when a simple test on the part of an investigator would have saved a great deal of argument after the event.

It is possible that the Pearce-Pratt experiment was intended to satisfy some of these criticisms, but that does not make it any easier to understand how the investigators could have gone on for week after week blindly trusting a rather weak experimental design. When, for example, it was found that Pearce could not obtain above-chance scores with the down-through procedure when more than a yard away from the cards, why was he not tested at close range, completely screened from the cards until he had recorded all his guesses? If this was tried, no details are given. Pearce was tested with the cards *held behind a screen,* but in these tests, it transpires that Pearce himself held the cards in this position and handled each card as he guessed it.

The manner in which normal sensory cues may be employed by subjects has already been touched on. Whether such cues are used unconsciously or consciously does not affect the argument very much. Rhine raised the point that Pearce did not usually look at the pack before he called his guess, although it seems that he occasionally glanced absentmindedly at the pack. Rhine also mentioned that Pearce's favorite posture was with eyes closed, sometimes with his hand on his eyes or forehead. It should be noted that if anyone wished to look at the backs of the cards without making this too obvious, he could do so by half-shutting his eyes or by screening them with his hands. A person with half-closed eyes can be facing away from the cards with his eyes turned to them, and an observer would not necessarily be aware of the fact. A photograph of Rhine testing Pearce with the down-through technique shows that Pearce had every opportunity to study the top card and the sides of others in the pack.

Rhine also discussed unconscious whispering cues, and seemed to consider that to have a fan going or to be in a car with the motor running was sufficient safeguard against them.

The last hypothesis, that of rational inference, arises, for example, with the BT5 technique. Since the subject sees the targets after each 5 trials, he is in a position after the first 20 calls to know exactly which symbols are left in the pack He will not know the order in which they will arise, but except in the case where exactly 4 of each symbol have come up in the first 20 cards, he is in a position to obtain extra hits. Thus if the wavy-lined symbol has arisen only 3 times in the first 20 calls, the subject has merely to call it for each of the last 5, and he is bound to obtain 2 hits. Rhine himself pointed out that the subjects obtained high scores in the last 5 trials when the BT5 technique was used. He also discussed rational inference in relation to PT, but the essential points were completely missed. It can easily be demonstrated that, by employing rational inference, it is possible for a subject to obtain extremely high scores in this type of experiment.

In view of the conditions under which most of the results reported in *Extra-Sensory Perception* were obtained, it is difficult to see how the experiments can be considered as other than exploratory. The final study with Pearce at a distance from the cards was, however, of quite a different order from those previously carried out. In these tests, since he was a hundred yards or more from the cards, sensory cues were eliminated, and from the other details of the experimental conditions, it appeared that Pearce was at last having to perform under reasonably strict conditions. The Pearce-Pratt series is to this day cited as providing evidence for ESP.

NOTES

1. J. B. Rhine, "An Investigation of a Mind Reading Horse," *Journal of Abnormal and Social Psychology* 23 (1929).
2. J. B. Rhine, *Extra-Sensory Perception* (Boston: Bruce Humphries, 1964). Reprinted by permission of Faber & Faber Ltd., and J. B. Rhine. Page numbers that follow refer to the edition published in England (London: Faber & Faber).
3. Ibid., p. 229.
4. Ibid., p. 83.
5. Ibid., p. 113-14.

4

The Years of Controversy, 1934–1940

The publication of *Extra-Sensory Perception* in 1934 aroused enormous interest among the general public, and ESP became a household word; but at the same time, the book was criticized severely. It was natural that the main onslaught should come from psychologists and that some of those reading about the experiments should wish to see whether they could get the same results for themselves. Since, according to Rhine, one in five of the population could display ESP, a confirmatory test must have seemed a relatively simple matter to arrange.

ATTEMPTS AT REPEATING THE DUKE EXPERIMENTS

The first attempt to reproduce the results was reported in 1936 by W. S. Cox of the psychology department at Princeton University. Prospective subjects were told about the work at Duke, emphasis being put on the positive nature of the scores obtained there, with the aim of putting the subjects in a favorable frame of mind for the experiment. Cox noted that the majority of his subjects displayed a belief in extrasensory perception and that many of those who were skeptical about it eventually did not participate.

A total of 132 subjects produced 25,064 trials in which they attempted to guess the suits of playing cards; but there was no evidence for ESP. The data were then examined to see whether any particular persons displayed an aptitude for ESP. Cox's conclusion was:

> It is evident from the above results and computations that there is no evidence of extrasensory perception either in the "average man" of the group investigated or in any particular individual of that group. The discrepancy between these results and those obtained by Rhine is due either to uncontrollable factors in experimental procedure or to the difference in the subjects.[1]

Other psychologists attempted to confirm Rhine's findings. E. T. Adams of Colgate University reported the results of 30,000 trials in which 30 subjects were individually tested;[2] J. C. Crumbaugh of Southern Methodist University tested over 100 subjects and recorded a total of 75,600 trials;[3] Raymond Willoughby of Brown University tested 9 subjects and recorded 41,250 trials;[4] and C. P. and J. H. Heinlein of Johns Hopkins amassed 127,500 trials.[6] The results obtained at Duke University were not confirmed in any of these investigations. On the contrary, it was found that subjects could not score significantly above the chance level when sensory cues were excluded.

An attempt to repeat Rhine's experiments using his four methods of testing with a large number of subjects and experimenters was reported by Kennedy in 1939.[6] Rhine's four types of experiments, OM (Open Matching), GESP (General ESP), DT (Down Through), and PT (Pure Telepathy), were tested using the procedures laid down in a Duke publication, *A Handbook for Testing Extra-Sensory Perception.*[7] Kennedy concludes: "The results of the present experiment are certainly negative with respect to ESP in 204 subjects, 32 experimenters, and 3,094 packs of cards. The only extra-chance result was obtained under poorly controlled conditions."[8]

This last experiment used the Pure Telepathy technique with which almost any experimenter and subject will obtain above-chance results. Individuals generating what they think is a random series tend to produce fewer repeats than would be expected to arise by chance. In addition, the experimenter's choice of symbols is affected by his hearing the subject's previous guesses.

Attempts to repeat the experiments were also made in England by Britain's best-known parapsychologist, Dr. S. G. Soal.[9] Between 1934 and 1939, after testing 160 persons for telepathy or clairvoyance and recording 128,350 guesses, Soal obtained a score that was at the chance level, and only one of his subjects, Mrs. Gloria Stewart, produced a result that was in any way out of the ordinary. Her score had odds greater than 100 to 1 against chance occurrence, but as 160 persons had been tested, it was to be expected that at least one of them would produce such a score.

Further reports appeared in which Rhine's results were not confirmed, but on the other hand, several investigations were reported in which the subjects had no difficulty in displaying ESP. It is significant, however, that of the 36 experimental reports supporting the existence of ESP published in the period 1934–40, only 5 were later assessed by members of the Duke Parapsychology Laboratory as being controlled sufficiently rigorously to provide conclusive evidence.

CRITICISM OF THE ESP CARDS

In 1936, ESP cards were put on sale to the general public in the United States. On the package was printed "ESP Cards for testing Extra-Sensory Perception, developed in the Parapsychological Laboratory at Duke University, patent applied for by J. B. Rhine." It was soon noted by the psychologists R. H. Thouless, B. F. Skinner, and L. D. Wolfe, among others, that under certain lighting conditions the symbols on the faces of the cards could be seen by examing their backs. J. L. Kennedy included a photograph to illustrate this point in an article he published in 1938.[10]

In a note published in the May 1938 *Journal* of the Society for Psychical Research, C. V. C. Herbert, who was then research officer of the society, reported an investigation he had made of the cards.[11] He noted that they were of two types: the first consisted of playing-card blanks on which the symbols were impressed by means of rubber stamps or stencils; the second type was professionally manufactured. It seems that, some two years before, two packs of the first type had been sent to Thouless as examples of the actual cards used in the tests at Duke University. He found that with one pack it was possible to detect the symbol on a card's face by scrutinizing its back when it was held so that light was reflected from it. With the light from a window, 9 out of a pack of 25 cards were identified in this way, and with a 60-watt lamp hanging from the ceiling, 14 cards were so identified.

The second type was that made available to the American public. When these were held at a certain angle, it was found that the symbol on almost every card could be read easily from its back. It was further found that the pattern on the backs extended to the edges, so that the identities of some cards could be detected when the sides of the pack were inspected. Thus, four of the cards marked with a circle were identified by the white mark on their sides where the cutting machine had sliced through a particular part of the pattern printed on the back.

Replying to Herbert, Rhine commented that the cards used in the earlier years were cut from heavy, opaque stock and carefully inspected. He also stated that no conclusions about extrasensory perception were published unless supplementary tests had been made in which sensory contact with the backs of the cards was eliminated. But homemade cards cut from heavy stock are all the more likely to be recognizable from their sides, and it is difficult to see, after reading the account in *Extra-Sensory Perception,* how it can be said that sensory contact was eliminated. Screening cards with the hand, for example, hardly eliminates the possibility of sensory contact, since the back of the card that is to follow the one being held is visible.

The experiments in which subjects, after obtaining high scores when seated at a table with the cards in front of them, were moved away from the cards, merely demonstrated the manner in which ESP scores dropped to the chance level as soon as it was made difficult for the subject to utilize sensory cues. It is possible that the supplementary tests to which Rhine referred were of the pure-telepathy type, in which cards were not used, and the tests on Pearce at distances of 100 and 250 yards. These excluded the possibility of the subject directly using cues from the cards, but it must be confirmed whether they were satisfactory in other respects. In the early experiments with Pearce, his scores certainly dropped in a remarkably consistent manner as soon as he could not see or feel the cards.

J. L. KENNEDY'S REVIEW OF ESP EXPERIMENTS

In 1939, Kennedy reviewed in detail the experimental work on extrasensory perception carried out up to 1938.[12] He started by listing and discussing the known sources of experimental error. These were:

1. Minimal and Subliminal sensory cues.
   a. Kinesthetic and Tactual cues.
   b. Visual Cues.
   c. Auditory cues.
2. "Mental Habits" and preferences.
3. Recording errors.

In a separate section he discussed the statistical methods used and the effects of selection of data on the experimental results.

Kennedy concluded his review by isolating those experiments in which the experimental conditions eliminated the possibility of all the above forms of error. He was left with three "inexplicable" experiments, about which he wrote: "Eventual explanation of these results appears to the present writer to rest on an entirely different basis than the foregoing ESP data."[13]

The first of these three experiments was an investigation by Lucien Warner, a research fellow, assisted by Mildred Raible, a psychologist, both at Duke University.[14] The subject was in a ground floor room, and two experimenters were in a locked room on the first floor in an opposite wing of the same house. One of the experimenters selected the target at each trial by drawing a card from a pack that was shuffled after each trial. The subject signaled the experimenters when the next target was to be selected by pressing a key that operated a light in the experimenters' room. Only 250 trials were recorded, and the average score was 9.3 hits per 25 trials.

Kennedy noted two aspects of this experiment. First, the recording was not completely independent, since the flash of light in the experimenters' room could be varied in duration by the subject and thus provide a possible cue. Second, there were five different symbols in the target series, but the experimental record showed that two of these arose more frequently than the other three. A test showed that the observed distribution would be expected to arise by chance in one out of fifty such experiments. In view of this fact, the method by which the targets were selected was suspect. For example, if after the pack was shuffled, it had been cut before each card was drawn, a bias could easily have manifested itself if there were variations in sizes of the cards bearing the different symbols. The report did not give full details of the parts played by the two experimenters, but it would appear that further tests could have been made with little difficulty, since 250 trials would take about two hours. Even so, further results were not reported, and the subject who displayed these remarkable powers of clairvoyance sank into anonymity.

The second experiment Kennedy isolated was reported in 1937 by B. F. Riess, professor of psychology at Hunter College, New York.[15] His subject lived about a quarter of a mile from Riess's home, and the experiment was conducted between the two houses. Starting at 9 P.M., Riess exposed cards at one-minute intervals from a freshly shuffled pack lying on his desk, and the subject recorded her guesses at the same times in her home. Two packs of 25 cards were exposed each day in this manner. The very high scores obtained startled even the parapsychologists. Thus, the score in 25 trials gradually built up over successive days until over 20 hits were being obtained, and scores were consistently high day after day. The hits per pack for the last ten days were 17, 18, 19, 20, 20, 20, 19, 20, 21, and 21. Altogether, 53 runs were completed, yielding the most remarkable scoring ever observed in an ESP experiment. Then, after a break in the testing, further runs were made, and the scores dropped to the chance level. The next 10 runs yielded 2, 4, 7, 12, 7, 5, 4, 3, 5, and 4 hits per pack. Even so, the odds against the overall score arising by chance have been assessed at greater than 10^{700} to 1. Since Kennedy made his review, further information about this experiment has become available. It appears that after Riess had been openly skeptical about ESP in discussion with his psychology classes, one of his students volunteered to produce a friend with high ESP. This friend turned out to be a young woman who had the reputation of being an amateur psychic, and it was she who had acted as the subject for the experiment. After it was over, she refused to take part in further tests under more strict conditions.

Reiss kept his records of the card order in the drawer of a desk that was left unlocked during the day, and he did not receive the record of the subject's calls until the day after the session. A servant employed in Riess's home was known to the students, and the records were easily accessible to anyone in the house. Also, it seems that, at times, a period of a week or longer elapsed before the two lists were compared. Riess himself has written: "In view of the many uncontrolled factors, the data as presented are to be thought of as suggestive only."[16] Thus, this experiment cannot now be considered as in any way inexplicable.

The third inexplicable experiment noted by Kennedy was the Pearce-Pratt series, but here Kennedy was not satisfied with the information given about the method of checking the scores. At that time, very meager details of the experiment had, in fact, been revealed, and it was not until 1954 that a complete account was published.

Kennedy commented on Rhine's suggestions for experimenters as follows:

> Attitudes of expectancy of good scores, playful informality and positive suggestibility in the subject seem best to help the unnoticed or unconscious use of sensory cues. But it is these conditions at work in the experimenter or recorder which

seem to be most important in attempting to understand the production of ESP. It should be noted further that the encouragement of playful informality by the experimenter involves the condition of split attention which is a favorable if not an absolutely necessary condition for unconscious error production.[17]

He suggested that the following controls should be present in ESP experiments:

1. Distance or shielding sufficient to eliminate sensory cues.
2. Calls and cards should be recorded by two different persons and checked by comparing the two records.
3. To produce a random distribution of targets, a tested method should be used.
4. A limit to the number of trials should be established before the experiment begins, and comparisons of records might well be postponed until after the end of the experiment.
5. To assure objectivity, there should be no possibility of fraud on the part of the subject. This might involve testing high-scoring subjects in several different laboratories.[18]

In classifying experiments as inexplicable, Kennedy had not excluded the possibility of fraud: he merely implied that the experiments were not explicable in terms of the sources of error he had discussed in his article and that fraud was the only remaining explanation other than ESP.

APPRAISAL OF ESP EXPERIMENTS BY MEMBERS OF THE PARAPSYCHOLOGY LABORATORY

In 1940, the Duke parapsychologists published their own appraisal of ESP research in *Extra-Sensory Perception after Sixty Years*.[19]

The expressed aim of the authors was to survey the published reports and to assess them in terms of the criticisms that had been raised. Over the years, thirty-five counterhypotheses to ESP had been put forward to account for the scores obtained in the tests. The authors stated that the final step was to determine whether there was a remainder of evidence—an inexplicable portion of the summarized results of the ESP research—that could not be met by all the hypotheses combined.

Each of the experiments reported since 1882 was first considered in relation to each of the thirty-five counterhypotheses. Those that survived this examination were then listed, and it was pointed out how each of the counterhypotheses could be shown to be inapplicable. A total of 145 experiments carried out between 1882 and 1939 were assessed, of which the first 2 were the investigations of the Creery sisters and of Smith and Blackburn discussed in chapter 2.

Only six experiments survived after being checked against the counter-hypotheses, and these were then arranged in order of merit. Kennedy had, with reservations, included only one Duke experiment, the Pearce-Pratt, among the three he considered to be inexplicable. The Duke critics included three of their own experiments among their selected six. These three were the Pratt-Woodruff experiment (considered first in quality), which had not been published at the time Kennedy made his review (see chapter 6); the Pearce-Pratt experiment (considered third best; see chapter 5); and the Rhine-Ownbey series (considered fourth best; see below).

The other three experiments were the Warner experiment (second on the list); the Riess experiment (fifth on the list; see p. 54); and in last place, an experiment reported by Ernest Taves and Gardner Murphy, psychologists at Columbia University. This last experiment did not yield an above-chance score and will not, therefore, be discussed any further.

THE TURNER-OWNBEY SERIES

The presence of the Rhine-Ownbey series no doubt evoked some surprise in parapsychological circles, since no one had heard of it before. It is described in *Extra-Sensory Perception after Sixty Years* as follows:

> A fourth series meeting successfully all the requirements made by the combined counter-hypotheses is the following long-distance test on pure telepathy reported by Rhine and conducted by him in conjunction with Miss Ownbey (Mrs. George Zirkle) as co-experimenter. The shorter of the three distances that obtained in the three series was 165 miles. A total of 650 trials was reported in 1934 (238) under these conditions, with independent records turned over to (mailed or personally delivered to) Rhine by Miss Ownbey and the subject (Miss Turner or Mr. Zirkle).[20]

In Appendix 20, in which the scores for each session are given, it is stated only that the "Agent and Percipient mailed the records to Rhine."

From examination of the scores and dates on which the tests were made, it seems that the Rhine-Ownbey series consisted of the Turner-Ownbey series combined with a similar long-distance test in which George Zirkle acted as the percipient and Miss Ownbey as the experimenter. The tests on Zirkle consisted of 13 runs made during August and September of 1933 with a distance of 165 miles between the percipient and the cards, but the score achieved by Zirkle was not significantly above the chance level.

It will be remembered that the first three runs of the Turner-Ownbey series were sent to Miss Ownbey before being given to Rhine. The score of both percipients (Turner and Zirkle) combined in 650 trials was 177 hits as compared to the chance expectation of 130 hits; the odds are about 1 million to 1 against this result arising by chance. If, however, the scores obtained in the first three days of the Turner-Ownbey series are omitted, it is found that in 23 runs a total of 126 hits was obtained, compared to the chance-expectation score of 115 hits. Here the odds are 3 to 1, and it is unnecessary to invoke ESP to account for these scores. Thus, the result of the Rhine-Ownbey series is entirely dependent on the scores achieved during the first three days of the Turner-Ownbey series, when the conditions certainly did not eliminate the possibility that Miss Ownbey influenced the result of the experiment.

It is therefore of considerable interest to see how the authors of *Extra-Sensory Perception after Sixty Years* managed to cope, when discussing the experiments, with three of the counterhypotheses. It is remarkable that no hint was given in the discussion of the unfortunate lapse in the conditions during the first three days of the experiment, although it would appear to be difficult to provide a full discussion of the counterhypotheses without mentioning that lapse.

The reply to counterhypothesis 21, "the data must have been tampered with by the subjects, assistants, or other persons," was:

> The short series which make up this work are the only ones of their kind and are sufficiently unique to be easily remembered by both E's [experimenters]. They were summarized in record books and all data reported by one E, both to the other E and to the subject. The presence of two E's, together with the independent records, and the easy recall of such unique tests, is sufficient guarantee against these hypotheses.[21]

The two experimenters referred to are Rhine and Ownbey; the subject was either Turner or Zirkle. It is agreed that Rhine had no evidence that Miss Ownbey tampered with the records, but some mention might have been made of the fact that she could have done so, and that the experimental result was not inconsistent with her having done so.

The reply to counterhypothesis 27, "the results are due to loose conditions and poor observation by the experimenter," ran:

> Distance excludes a multitude of conceivable experimental weaknesses in telepathic tests. The only criticisms on this work bear on the questions (a) of its *p*-value, the probability of the result arising by chance, and (b) of possible pattern and preference similarity. Both are met by the data of Table 13, p. 127, giving back-check and cross-check averages on this work.[22]

The reply to counterhypothesis 30, "general untrustworthiness (moral or psychopathic) of the experimenters explains the results," was:

> If over-enthusiasm or dishonesty are back of these results, *it is difficult to account for the striking decline in scoring level.* The main extra-chance results occurred during the first few days of the series . . . and the rest of the scores

were but little above chance. *There was no change of instructions that might account for the decline:* only a shortening of the inter-trial interval from 5 to 3 minutes. *Any act of bad faith would of necessity have involved the collusion of one E with the other or with the S*[subject]. While an instance of this character is yet to be encountered in academic research, its possibility cannot, of course, be flatly denied. But again, to take the collusion hypothesis seriously throws the burden upon the group of confirmatory E's as a whole, and the mutual support of these must supply the answer needed.

That is to say, Ownbey and Turner, or Ownbey and Rhine, might be regarded as conspirators to deceive the world regarding ESP much more easily than could the combination of Ownbey and Rhine, Pratt and Woodruff, Warner and Raible, and Pratt and Rhine (to speak only of the above mentioned names). The notion of such wholesale conspiracy would be to most students more fantastic than the ESP hypothesis.[23]

These comments contain three statements, which I have put within quotation marks, each of which is misleading.

1. "It is difficult to account for the striking decline in scoring level." If the readers of *Extra-Sensory Perception after Sixty Years* had been informed that the records were not sent directly to Rhine during the first three high-scoring sessions and that they were sent directly to him after this, there would have been no difficulty accounting for the decline.
2. "There was no change of instructions that might account for the decline." But there was a change in the *procedure* after the third day that coincided with the sudden decline in the score.
3. "Any act of bad faith would of necessity have involved the collusion of one E with the other or with the S." This statement would be true if the original instructions had been followed, but in view of what happened during the first three sessions, it is not true. Miss Ownbey could have intercepted the mail and completed her record after seeing Miss Turner's record.

Subsequent published accounts of the Turner-Ownbey series make no mention of the unfortunate lapse during the first three runs. Thus, in *Parapsychology: Frontier Science of the Mind* by Rhine and Pratt, published in 1957, the series is described with reference to *Extra-Sensory Perception after Sixty Years,* rather than to *Extra-Sensory Perception,* which did note the one important point about the experiment.

In 1975, John L. Randall, in his *Parapsychology and the Nature of Life: A Scientific Appraisal,*[24] referred to the Turner-Ownbey experiment as follows: "The most staggering result of all was an average of 10.1 hits per run obtained over a distance of 250 miles in July 1933." Randall raised one criticism of the experiment, i.e., that Miss Ownbey may not have produced a random series (which is hardly very relevant) and dismissed it. He then concluded

"It therefore seems reasonable to accept the Ownbey work as evidence for the operation of ESP over large distances."[25]

He made no mention of the lapse in the experimental conditions or of the fact that above-chance results were only obtained for the first three runs of the series and fell to the chance level immediately after the experimental conditions were made more foolproof. Randall presumably knew of this criticism since he had read my earlier book—or at least he had included it in his list of references. A further feature of Randall's account is that he refers to the "staggering 10.1 hits per run achieved by the percipient," but in fact she achieved an average of 17 hits per run for those first three runs. This is one of the most remarkable performances in the history of ESP research.

NOTES

1. W. S. Cox, "An Experiment in ESP," *Journal of Experimental Psychology* 12, 4 (1936): 427.

2. E. T. Adams, "A Summary of Some Negative Experiments," *Journal of Parapsychology* 2, 3 (1938): 232-36.

3. J. C. Crumbaugh, "An Experimental Study of Extra-Sensory Perception," Master's thesis, Southern Methodist University, 1938.

4. R. R. Willoughby, "Further Card-Guessing Experiments," *Journal of General Psychology* 18 (1938): 3-13.

5. C. P. Heinlein and J. H. Heinlein, "Critique of the Premises and Statistical Methodology of Parapsychology," *Journal of Psychology* 5 (1938): 135-248.

6. J. L. Kennedy, "Experiments on the Nature of Extra-Sensory Perception," *Journal of Parapsychology* 3 (1939): 206-12.

7. C. E. Stuart and J. G. Pratt, *A Handbook of Testing Extra-Sensory Perception* (New York: Farer and Rinehart, 1937).

8. Kennedy, "Experiments on the Nature of Extra-Sensory Perception," p. 210.

9. S. G. Soal and F. Bateman, *Modern Experiments in Telepathy* (London: Faber and Faber, Ltd., 1954), pp. 135-48.

10. J. L. Kennedy, "The Visual Cues from the Backs of ESP Cards," *Journal of Psychology* 6 (1938): 149-53.

11. C. V. C. Herbert, "Experiments in Extra-Sensory Perception: 1. A. Notes on Types of Zener Cards," *Journal of the Society for Psychical Research* 30, 545 (1938): 215-18.

12. J. L. Kennedy, *Psychological Bulletin* (1938).

13. Ibid., p. 94.

14. L. Warner, "A Test Case," *Journal of Parapsychology* 1, 4 (1937): 234-38.

15. B. F. Riess, "A Case of High Scores in Card Guessing at a Distance," *Journal of Parapsychology* 1, 4 (1937): 260-63.

16. Ibid., p. 263.

17. J. L. Kennedy, *Psychological Bulletin* (1939): 91.

18. Ibid., p. 94.

19. J. G. Pratt, J. B. Rhine, Burke M. Smith, Charles E. Stuart, and John Greenwood, *Extra-Sensory Perception after Sixty Years* (Boston: Bruce Humphries, 1966), reprint of 1940 edition.

20. Pratt et al., *Extra-Sensory Perception after Sixty Years,* p. 163.

21. Ibid., p. 165.

22. Ibid.

23. Ibid., pp. 165–66.

24. J. L. Randall, *Parapsychology and the Nature of Life: A Scientific Appraisal* (London: Souvenir Press, 1975), p. 122.

25. Ibid., p. 82.

5

The Pearce-Pratt Experiment

Hubert E. Pearce had been acting as a subject in ESP experiments for more than a year before he took part in the Pearce-Pratt experiment, or Campus Distance Series as it is also known, that was started in August 1933 and completed in March 1934. Rhine has stated that the aim of the experiment was to set up experimental conditions strict enough to exclude all factors, other than ESP, that could produce above-chance scores. The experiment has been described in several articles and books, but the most complete account was provided in a 1954 article in the *Journal of Parapsychology*.[1] The description given here is based on this account of the experiment.

It was basically a clairvoyance test, in which Pearce guessed at cards in a pack controlled by Pratt, then a graduate student in the psychology department, while he was situated in another building on the campus.

THE PROCEDURE

The two men met in Pratt's room on the top floor of what is now the social sciences building on the west campus of Duke University. (At the time of the experiments this was the physics building, and the psychology department used a few rooms in it.) Both men synchronized their watches and fixed a time at which the test would start. Pearce then went across the quadrangle to the library, where he sat in a cubicle in the stacks at a distance of about 100 yards from Pratt, who from his window could see Pearce cross the quadrangle and enter the library.

THE TARGETS

Pratt sat down at a table, took a pack of ESP cards, and, after shuffling and cutting it, placed it face downward on the right side of the table. At the time fixed for the experiment to start, he took the top card and placed it, still face down, on a book in the center of the table. At the end of a minute this card was transferred to the left side of the table, and the second card in the pack was placed on the book. In this manner, each card was placed on the book at its appointed time and then transferred to a pile on the left side of the table. After a run of twenty-five cards, an interval of five minutes elapsed, and then the same procedure was followed with a second pack. Pratt did not see the faces of the cards until the end of the sitting when he turned them up to record their order. He then made a duplicate of his record, sealed it in an envelope, and later delivered it to Rhine.

THE PERCIPIENT

In his cubicle in the library, Pearce recorded his guess of the identity of each card lying on the book. After recording 50 guesses, he made a duplicate copy of his record sheet and sealed it in an envelope that was later delivered to Rhine. The two sealed records were usually delivered personally to Rhine before Pratt and Pearce compared their lists and scored the number of successes.

THE EXPERIMENTAL CONDITIONS

The above procedure was followed at each of 37 sittings held between August 1933 and March 1934. The sittings were divided into four subseries: Subseries A consisted of 6 sittings, carried out under the above conditions; subseries B was composed of 22 sittings at which Pratt carried out his part of the proceedings in a room in the medical building, which would have put him about 250 yards away from Pearce; subseries C consisted of 6 sittings with the same conditions as subseries A; in subseries D, there were 3 sittings with the same conditions as subseries A, except that Rhine was with Pratt in the room in the social sciences building.

THE RESULTS

The scores at successive sittings obtained in each subseries are shown in table 5-1.

Something other than chance was obviously operating in each of the four subseries. The odds against the overall result arising by chance are greater than 10^{22} to 1, and the result of each subseries is statistically significant.

TABLE 5-1

Scores in Each Run of the Pearce-Pratt Experiment

Sitting	Subseries A (100 yards)	Subseries B (250 yards)	Subseries C (100 yards)	Subseries D (100 yards)
1	3	1, 4	9, 8	12, 3
2	8, 5	4, 4	4, 9	10, 11
3	9, 10	7, 6	11, 9	10, 10
4	12, 11	5, 0	5, 4	
5	11, 12	6, 3	9, 11	
6	13, 13, 12	11, 9	2, 7	
7		0, 6		
8		8, 6		
9		9, 4		
10		10, 6		
11		11, 9		
12		5, 12		
13		7, 7		
14		12, 10		
15		6, 3		
16		10, 10		
17		6, 12		
18		2, 6		
19		12, 12		
20		4, 4		
21		3, 0		
22		13, 10		
Total trials	300	1,100	300	150
Total hits	119	295	88	56
Average score per run of 24 trials (hits)	9.9	6.7	7.3	9.3

ELIMINATION OF ALTERNATIVE HYPOTHESES

When discussing the experiment in 1954 in the *Journal of Parapsychology*, Rhine and Pratt stated that the only alternative to an explanation in terms of ESP would involve collusion among all three participants.

It is difficult to see how either Rhine or Pratt, unaided, could have cheated to bring about the result obtained in all four subseries; but, owing to the fact that Pearce was not supervised during the experiment, there are a number of ways in which he could have cheated to attain high scores.

Pratt saw Pearce disappear into the library; then, some time later, after the sitting was over, he met him and checked his scores. He had no confirmation, other than Pearce's word for it—if he ever asked him—that Pearce had stayed in the library. He could quite easily have walked back to where Pratt was conducting his part of the experiment. In view of this, the possibility that Pearce obtained knowledge of the targets must be carefully considered.

It would not have been necessary to obtain sight of the cards at every sitting, since the scores given in table 5-1 were only higher than chance at some of the sittings. Ten or more hits would be expected to arise by chance once in each 52 runs. If such a score is considered high, it will be seen that one was not obtained at sittings 1 and 2 in series A. In subseries B, only 9 of the 22 sittings produced high scores; in subseries C high scores were obtained only at sittings 3 and 5; and only in subseries D were high scores obtained at each of the 3 sittings. The distribution of scores shows a distinct bimodal characteristic—that is, having two maxima: one between values of 4 and 6, the other between values of 9 and 12—as if the cause of high scores was in operation on some occasions and not on others. At approximately half of the sittings, the scores reveal no evidence of either ESP or cheating. Thus, if Pearce left the library, he need only have gained sight of the cards while Pratt was recording them on those occasions when it was safe to do so.

An important point to note is that the experiment was conducted according to a strict timetable. If Pearce had chosen to cheat, he knew to the second— from the time he was supposed to start his recording to the time he was supposed to make his last guess—what Pratt was doing. He knew that he had 55 minutes during which Pratt would be fully occupied and that at the end of that time Pratt would be busy making first a list of the order of the cards in the two packs and then a duplicate of his record. Provided it was possible to see into Pratt's room, Pearce could have left the library and observed Pratt, gaining sight of the cards when they were turned up for recording at the end of the sitting or, if they could be identified from their backs, he could have inspected them while they were isolated on the book in front of Pratt. Clearly, it is essential to know something about the two rooms in which Pratt carried out his part of the proceedings and about the way in which he turned up the cards when recording their order.

From Pratt and Rhine's statement, the reader might assume that they had carefully considered every conceivable explanation, other than a trick, involving all three participants in the experiment. He may assume, since no description was given of the rooms in which the tests were carried out, that they were quite adequate for their purpose and that no one could possibly have seen into them. If he takes anything of the sort for granted, he may be led sadly astray. A first principle when assessing an experiment should be: never assume anything that is not stated in the experimental report.

THE ROOMS USED FOR THE EXPERIMENT

When I was at Duke University in 1960, Pratt showed me the rooms he used during the experiment. While doing so, he mentioned that, since 1934, structural alterations had been made to both rooms. We first visited Pratt's old room, 314, in the social sciences building. I located the position of the table as shown in figure 5–1. Pratt then pointed out that the wall beside the table had been farther back in 1933. After its original position had been located, it was apparent that the room in its original state contained a large clear-glass window that would have permitted anyone in the corridor to see into the room at the time of the experiment. I judged the window to be about 2 feet square and to be about 5 feet 10 inches from the floor at its bottom edge. Anyone looking through this window from the corridor would have had a clear view of Pratt seated at his desk and of the cards he was handling.

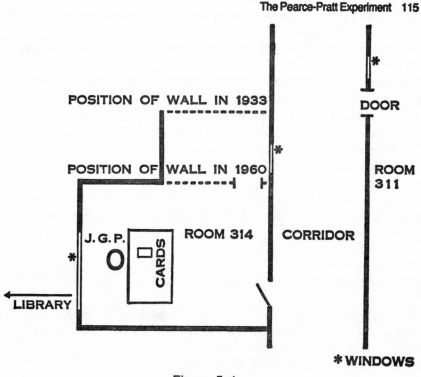

The Pearce-Pratt Experiment 115

Figure 5–1

Plan, not to scale, of the rooms in the
social sciences building, Duke University

There were similar windows leading into the office on the other side of the corridor as well as clear-glass windows above the doors of all the rooms. Later, I went into a room on the opposite side of the corridor, 311, and found that the line of vision when looking through the transom above the door was through the window into Pratt's room and down to his desk. It was impossible to be certain of this point since the wall in its new position hindered my view. However, there was a good possibility that Pearce could have returned to the social sciences building, locked himself in Room 311, and then observed Pratt with comparative safety by standing on a chair or table and looking through the transom above the door.

The room in the medical building had been changed drastically since 1934, and it was now used for making X rays. There was a transom above the door and a window, but both of these were of ripple glass, and it is doubtful whether the cards could have been identified through them. In this room there was, however, a trap door in the ceiling, measuring about 4 feet by 1½ feet and situated immediately over the position occupied by the table at which Pratt sat during the experiment. Its cover had a large hole that looked as if it had been recently made. There was also a small metal plate on the trap door that could have covered another hole, and this plate looked as if it had been there a long time.

The room was on the top classroom floor of the building, and the main staircase went up another flight to a large attic, which extended over the floor beneath it. At the time of my visit, the attic was used for storage purposes, but I was told that most of the contents had been put there well after 1934. It would thus have been possible for an intruder to have positioned himself above the trap door to see the cards on Pratt's table.

I went to the architect's office of the university and asked to see plans of the rooms as they were in 1933. I also asked for details of structural alterations that had been made to the rooms, together with the dates on which they had been made, and the persons who had asked for them. These details were to be forwarded to me, but I never received them. I wrote again requesting them, but had no reply.

FURTHER DETAILS OF THE PROCEDURE

The day after we had seen the rooms, I asked Pratt to demonstrate to me the exact procedure he used during the experiment. I was particularly interested to see how he turned up the cards to record them, whether he shuffled the packs after use, and how he left them on the table.

From his demonstration it was clear that anyone looking into the room would have obtained a clear view of the faces of the cards when they were being listed. Each was turned on its back while an entry was made on the record sheet. Pratt did not shuffle the packs after noting down their order, and after recording the first pack he moved it to the top left corner of the table. He told me that he did not lock his door during the sitting or after it was over and that he made his record on notebook paper. I also learned that the room across the corridor from the one Pratt had been in was used by students at the time of the experiment.

Pratt gave every assistance. He himself pointed out the structural alterations made to the rooms. He also emphasized, quite reasonably, that he was forced to depend on his memory of events that had taken place twenty-six years before.

THE POSSIBILITY OF VIEWING THE CARDS

Later, I asked W. Saleh, a member of the research staff at Duke, to run through a pack of ESP cards while I sat in an office farther down the corridor. He was to record the cards on a sheet of paper at the end of the run using a procedure similar to that used by Pratt during the experiments with Pearce and to keep his door closed and locked. I slipped back to Saleh's room and saw the cards by standing on a chair and looking through the crack at the top of the door. I had a clear view of them and obtained 22 hits in 25 attempts. Saleh's desk was about 15 feet from the door, and he had no suspicion of what I had done until I told him.

In a second test, I asked him to record the cards in a room in which I had left on the desk a sheet of blotting paper to take an impression of what he wrote. I then read off the identities of the cards from the impressions of his writing on the blotting paper. But by this time Saleh was tired of having his leg pulled. He had carefully written out a second list, using the blotting paper for it, so that I was given false information. It was clear, however, from these tests that knowledge of the cards could have been obtained by the use of either method, provided other factors in the situation did not eliminate the possibility.

GENERAL FEATURES OF THE EXPERIMENT

Now that information has become available about the conditions in which the experiment was carried out, it is clear that it was far from foolproof, and the result could have been brought about in a variety of ways. The conditions were remarkably loose compared to those imposed on Smith and Blackburn, and it is difficult to understand how the experiment came to be designed in such a manner that any would-be trickster could fake his scores with comparative ease. It is thus of particular interest to know to what extent Pearce participated in the design.

In *New Frontiers of the Mind,* Rhine states that after Pearce had been relatively unsuccessful in earlier distance tests, the formality and fixed routine of experimental conditions were loosened, and Pearce was allowed to suggest changes himself. "He could say 'Let's try some D. T.' or 'Let me go over to the next room while. . . .' This broke the monotony and very probably contributed to his doing successful scoring."[2]

In the Pearce-Pratt experiment the distance of 100 yards was fixed from the start, although it was, "possibly, suggested by Pearce."[3] Whether Pearce made other suggestions is not mentioned. It would be of interest to know, for example, who selected the rooms used for the experiment.

The experiment comprised some 37 sittings in all. For sitting after sitting, Pratt sat in his room slowly turning over packs of cards and recording them at the end of each day's runs. Pearce, after having failed miserably in earlier experiments as soon as he was moved more than a yard from the cards, was now suddenly obtaining very high scores at 100 yards or more. One would expect that anyone in Pratt's position would have examined the room carefully and taken elaborate precautions to insure that no one could see into it. At least he might have covered the windows leading to the corridor. Also, the cards should have been shuffled after they were recorded, and the door of the room might well have been locked during and after the tests. These experiments were not a first-year exercise. They were intended to provide conclusive proof of ESP and to shake the very foundations of science. If Pratt had some misgivings, there is no evidence that he ever expressed them. He took no precautions to ensure that Pearce stayed in the library or to prevent the cards being visible to anyone looking into his room.

Again, Rhine might well have been wary of trickery, for neither he nor Pratt were novices in psychical research. Both of them were fully aware of the long history of trickery in that area.

COUNTERCRITICISMS

I criticized the experimental conditions under which the Pearce-Pratt experiment was conducted in the *Journal of Parapsychology*.[4] Rhine and Pratt made a joint reply in the same number of the journal. Their answer was that the subseries D experiment, in which Rhine was with Pratt while it was conducted, eliminated the possibility of Pearce cheating:

> In this series J. B. R., who had remained in the background previously, came into the test room with J. G. P. and sat through a series of six runs through the test pack (150 trials) for the purpose of scrutinizing the entire procedure from that point of vantage, to ensure that it was faithfully executed. He, like J. G. P., *could see the subject from the window as the latter entered the library* (and, of course, could see him exit as well). He was in the experimental room at the end of each session to receive the independent records from both J. G. P. and H. E. P. immediately on the arrival of the latter at the close of the session. Thus the subject was obviously allowed no opportunity to enter the room alone and copy the order of the cards

or the impressions left on the record pad. Even with the somewhat imaginative supposition that H. E. P. had a collaborator, there was no time for the latter, even if he had (unnoticed by J. B. R.) observed the card-turning and recording by J. G. P., to have communicated the knowledge of card order thus gained to H. E. P. as he arrived in the building for the check-up. H. E. P. had to have his duplicate record in his own handwriting, with one copy sealed in an envelope, ready to hand to J. B. R. on entering the room. J. G. P. had to do the recording of the last run of each session after the test was over and H. E. P. was already on his way to the test room. Yet these final runs of the session were, in themselves, independently significant statistically.[5]

However, what is important here is not whether Rhine could have seen Pearce leave the library if he had been watching for him, but whether he actually did see him leave at the termination of the experiment each day. Did Rhine stand by the window watching for Pearce to leave the library? If so, how did he know that Pratt was not busy faking his record? Rhine was with Pratt to see that he did not cheat, for it was assumed that a trick was possible only if both Pearce and Pratt were in collaboration, and Pratt need only have made about five false entries for each run to create scores such as those obtained by Pearce.

Rhine could not have been watching the window leading into the corridor to see that no one was looking in and at the same time have been looking through the window on the opposite wall to see Pearce leave the library. In fact, according to the experimental report, he was watching Pratt record the cards.

That Rhine saw Pearce leave the library, or the fact that he could have seen him had he been watching for him, now appears to be a most important control feature of the experiment. But even if Rhine or Pratt had watched to see Pearce leave the library—and there is no mention in any of the reports that this was done—it would have been a simple matter for Pearce to have deceived the experimenters. He could have returned to the library without being seen. He could have left a few gaps in his record and noted them as they were turned up. He could then have completed his list after entering the social sciences building. Only ten entries, each a simple symbol, were required. The envelope addressed to Rhine could already have been prepared by Pearce while he was in the library.

It might be expected that Pearce would arrive at Pratt's room before the listing was completed, since he had merely to make copies of his record, whereas Pratt had to write down the order of the cards and then make a duplicate copy. What did Pearce do? Did he tap on the door and wait until he was called in? Did he peep through the window to see whether Pratt had finished? How long after the last run did Pearce make an appearance? Were his records checked to see that they were all in his own handwriting? He wrote down a list of symbols, not words or letters, and it would be difficult for even a handwriting expert to detect forgery.

THE FACTS OF THE EXPERIMENT

Up to this point, criticism of the experiment has been based on the account published in the *Journal of Parapsychology* in 1954 and on my viewing of the room used at Duke by Pratt. (I never saw the room used by Pearce; Pratt was unable to remember where it was located.) The 1954 version of the experiment has been used because it is by far the most complete, but when it is checked with the other descriptions provided from time to time since 1934, it is clear that it may have little resemblance to what actually took place.

The experiment was first mentioned, while in progress, in *Extra-Sensory Perception* (1934).[6] Brief accounts were later given in the *Journal of Abnormal and Social Psychology* (1936),[7] the *Journal of Parapsychology* (1937),[8] *New Frontiers of the Mind* (1938),[9] *Extra-Sensory Perception after Sixty Years* (1940),[10] *The Reach of the Mind* (1948),[11] and *The New World of the Mind* (1954).[12] Pratt has given further details in a recent book, *Parapsychology: An Insider's View of ESP* (1964).[13]

Close examination of these sources indicates that while it is likely that some sort of long-distance test was carried out on Pearce in 1933–34, the reports of the experiment may have changed with the passage of years. Completely contradictory statements appear in these various sources on the procedure adopted by Pratt, the recording of the targets, the number of sittings, and the actual scores obtained. For example, in *New World of the Mind,* the procedure adopted by Pratt when he moved the cards from a pile on the right of his desk, via the book, to a pile on his left is completely reversed. Also, there is doubt whether the experiment as reported constituted only a part of a larger series of tests.

The duplicate records made by both Pearce and Pratt were an essential control feature of the experiments. It is therefore surprising to find no mention of them in the four accounts of the experiments published before 1940.

The duplicates are first mentioned in *Extra-Sensory Perception after Sixty Years,* where the various counterhypotheses to ESP were being considered. After 1940, however, the duplicate records are mentioned in each of the four additional published accounts of the experiment.

In *New Frontiers of the Mind,* it is stated that there was to be no discussion between Pearce and Pratt until the records had been delivered to Rhine in sealed envelopes. In *New World of the Mind* the revised statement is that Pratt sealed his copy of the record in an envelope for delivery to Rhine before he met Pearce and that Pearce placed his copy in a sealed envelope before checking his duplicate with Pratt. The version in the *Journal of Parapsychology* is that the two sealed envelopes were delivered personally to Rhine "most of the time" before Pratt and Pearce had compared their records.[14]

The *Journal of Parapsychology* article discusses the recording of targets as follows: "Over in his room J. G. P. recorded the card order for the two packs used in the test as soon as the second run was finished."[15] *New Frontiers of the Mind* contains a similar statement. When replying to my criticisms of their experiment, Rhine and Pratt appeared to be implying that the recording of the targets in the first pack was made before the second run was started. "J. G. P. had to do the recording of the last run of each session after the test was over and H. E. P. was already on his way to the test room." In case there was any doubt as to the precise implication of these words, Pratt later clarified the matter in his book *Parapsychology: An Insider's View of ESP*, in which he stated:

> When all the cards had taken their turn on the book, I made a record of the twenty-five cards in the order in which they had been used. As a rule, we went through this procedure again on the same day after taking a recess of five minutes to allow time for me to make the record and shuffle and cut the cards for the next run.[17]

This new account of the procedure with the cards would invalidate a criticism I raised: that the two packs used in the experiment could have been inspected after the tests were over while Pratt was delivering his sealed record to Rhine, but it is strange that Pratt should only remember this revised procedure thirty years after the experiments were completed.

Extra-Sensory Perception states that when the cards were moved 250 yards from the percipient, there was a low-scoring adjustment period at first.

But in *New Frontiers of the Mind,* it is stated that after increasing the distance to 250 yards in subseries B, there was no falling off in the score at the first sitting and that Pearce obtained scores of 12 and 10 in the two runs. Scores for the next five days are given as follows: second day, exactly chance; third day, two 10s; fourth day, a 2 and a 6; fifth day, a 5 and a 12; sixth day, a 7 and a 5. Similar scores are given in *Extra-Sensory Perception after Sixty Years,* but these are different from those given in the *Journal of Parapsychology* and reproduced in table 5-1. Yet in *The Reach of the Mind,* we read: "For a time Pearce did as well at 250 yards as at 100; then something went wrong. . . ."[18] Moreover, the scores published in the *Journal of Abnormal and Social Psychology* disagree with those in the *Journal of Parapsychology*. They give total hits for the four subseries as: A, 179; B, 288; C, 86; D, 56. The individual scores quoted are also in a different order for subseries B and C from those given in the *Journal of Parapsychology*.

In *Frontiers of the Mind,* it is said that in six runs made on three successive days, Pearce five times made a score of 4 hits and that he scored 1 hit in the other run. This cannot be reconciled with the data given in the *Journal of Parapsychology*. According to the figures published in the *Journal of Abnormal Psychology,* there were 8 runs, and the scores obtained over four successive days were 12, 4; 4, 1; 4, 4; 4, 7.

The *Journal of Parapsychology* article states that subseries D consisted of 6 runs, and the dates are given as March 12 and 13; but the scores for subseries D are given as 12, 3; 10, 11; and 10, 10; we are told also that the division between days or sessions is marked by the use of semicolons. Thus, it appears that two of the three sessions must have taken place on one of the two days. But in *New Frontiers of the Mind,* Rhine says that he witnessed a three-day series. Thus, either the dates in the table or Rhine's memory is at fault. Rhine has remarked about subseries D: "As a matter of fact, it is not easily overlooked and would be, for most readers, quite obviously, the climax series in the paper."[19] As this subseries was the only part of the experiment in which Rhine actively participated, he might well be particularly aware of it. But in *New Frontiers of the Mind,* published three years after the experiment, Rhine completely forgot the subseries, saying that, after the tests in the medical building, "Pratt moved back to the Physics building for another 300 trials."[20] According to this account, "The next step involved a distance of two miles, and things went wrong from the start. The room arranged for the tests was not open when it should have been and for several days there was frustration in the physical details of the experiment. After things were finally straightened out, there was no appreciable success." In *New Frontiers of the Mind,* further tests are also mentioned in which Pearce went in a car to different places in the country and recorded calls, but it appears that he was not hopeful, and there was no success. By 1954, however, the tests at a two-mile distance had been forgotten. The *Journal of Parapsychology* article, after reporting subseries A, B, C, and D comprising 74 runs, states: "The 74 runs represent all the ESP tests made with H. E. P. during this experiment under the conditions of working with the subject and target cards in different buildings done at the Duke Laboratory at the time."[21]

It is stated by Rhine that, shortly after the experiment was concluded, Pearce received a letter one morning that distressed him greatly. This incident was claimed to have been responsible for his loss of ESP. In fact, the last sitting of the Pearce-Pratt experiment appears to have been the last occasion on which Pearce displayed any supposed ESP ability, although he was later tested on several occasions.

FURTHER COUNTERCRITICISMS

My account of the Pearce-Pratt experiment given above has been criticized on the grounds that my plan of the positions of the rooms in the former physics building was inaccurate. The criticisms were contained in a review by Ian Stevenson, M.D., a leading expert on reincarnation, that appeared in the *Journal of the American Society for Psychical Research.*[22]

While I was at Duke University in 1960, I drew only a rough plan of the room positions in the physics building, as I was expecting to receive more detailed plans from the architect's office. It is remarkable that Stevenson, who it happens visited the laboratories and obtained a plan, has not revealed what mistake I made.

The diagram in figure 5–1 contains one error, which does not in fact alter the argument in any way. This can be remedied by crossing out the lettering "Room 311" and writing it about 1½ inches higher up.

It should be noted that my impression, when examining the rooms, was that it was possible to view the cards from one of the rooms on the other side of the corridor by looking at an oblique angle across the corridor. But I wrote that it was "impossible to be certain." In fact, the simplest way of obtaining sight of the cards would have been from the corridor. Stevenson writes that no one could have spent "hours on a chair or on tiptoe" without drawing attention to himself. But the time at which the cards were to be recorded was known exactly—the two men had synchronized their watches (p. 61). The total time for recording the 25 cards in a pack would be about 30 seconds. The top floor of the physics building was at that time very little used except by members of the psychology department, who had a few research rooms in it. The experiments were carried out at times agreed between Pearce and Pratt but which were unlikely to have been known to others except Rhine. If Pearce had wanted to use a trick, he would have arranged times when other students were not likely to be in the corridor.

SUMMARY

The Pearce-Pratt experiment cannot be regarded as supplying evidence to support the existence of extrasensory perception for the following reasons:

1. The various reports of the experiment contain conflicting statements, so that it is difficult to ascertain the precise facts.
2. Essential features of the experimental situation were not reported. Readers of the reports have been led to assume that the experimental conditions were foolproof and that every possibility of trickery had been considered and guarded against when this was not so.
3. A number of aspects of the experimental design enabled the result of the experiment to be brought about by a trick. These features were: the subject was left unobserved; the rooms used by Pratt were not screened to make it impossible for anyone to see into them; Pratt recorded the targets at the end of each sitting in such a manner as to expose their faces to anyone looking into the room.

NOTES

1. J. B. Rhine and J. G. Pratt, "A Review of the Pearce-Pratt Distance Series of ESP Tests," *Journal of Parapsychology* 18, 3 (1954): 165–77.
2. J. B. Rhine, *New Frontiers of the Mind* (London: Faber & Faber, Ltd., 1938), p. 154. Reprinted by Penguin Books (London, 1950).
3. Ibid., p. 155.

4. C. E. M. Hansel, "A Critical Analysis of the Pearce-Pratt Experiment," *Journal of Parapsychology* 25 (1961): 87–91.

5. J. B. Rhine and J. G. Pratt, "A Reply to the Hansel Critique of the Pearce-Pratt Series," *Journal of Parapsychology* 25 (1961): 92–98.

6. J. B. Rhine, *Extra-Sensory Perception* (Boston: Bruce Humphries, 1964).

7. J. B. Rhine, "Some Selected Experiments in Extra-Sensory Perception," *Journal of Abnormal and Social Psychology* 31 (1936): 216–28.

8. J. B. Rhine, "The Effect of Distance in ESP Tests," *Journal of Parapsychology* 1 (1937): 172–84.

9. Rhine, *New Frontiers of the Mind,* pp. 155–59.

10. J. B. Rhine, J. G. Pratt, C. E. Stuart, B. M. Smith, and J. Greenwood, *Extra-Sensory Perception after Sixty Years* (Boston: Bruce Humphries, 1940). Republished in 1966.

11. J. B. Rhine, *Reach of the Mind* (London: Faber & Faber, Ltd., 1948).

12. J. B. Rhine, *New World of the Mind* (New York: Sloane, 1953).

13. J. B. Pratt, *Parapsychology: An Insider's View of ESP* (London: W. H. Allen and Company, 1964).

14. Rhine and Pratt, "Review of the Pearce-Pratt Distance Series of ESP Tests," p. 170.

15. Ibid.

16. Rhine and Pratt, "Reply to the Hansel Critique of the Pearce-Pratt Series," p. 94.

17. J. G. Pratt, *Parapsychology: An Insider's View of ESP* (London: W. H. Allen and Company and Doubleday and Company, Inc.), p. 49.

18. Rhine, *Reach of the Mind,* p. 50.

19. Rhine, *New Frontiers of the Mind,* p. 93.

20. Ibid., p. 157.

21. Ibid., p. 168.

22. Ian Stevenson, "An Antagonist's View of Parapsychology: A Review of Professor Hansel's *ESP: A Scientific Evaluation,*" *Journal of the American Society for Psychical Research* 67 (1967): 54–67.

6

The Pratt-Woodruff Experiment'

THE OHIO SYMPOSIUM

In September 1938, during its annual meeting at Columbus, Ohio, the American Psychological Association held a symposium on the methods of ESP research. This was attended by members of the Parapsychology Laboratory including J. B. Rhine and J. G. Pratt. Criticisms raised in the past were discussed and the experimental methods being used at that time at Duke were considered. A list of recommendations for the conduct of experiments was formulated. Each point was discussed in considerable detail. Some of these are summarized below.

1. The subject must not be permitted to see the cards, faces, or backs at any time during the tests. This period of concealment, as a minimum, covers the time from the beginning of a shuffle to the completion of the record of the distribution.
2. The cards must not at any time be handled by the subject. All shuffling and dealing are to be done by the assistant or assistants, or by one of the supervisors of the experiment.
3. During a test the faces of the cards must not be visible to an assistant or to any other person.
4. No information shall be given to any subject concerning his successes, or his scores, in the experiment until after the termination of the service as subject.
5. Scores should be withheld from the subject throughout the research.
6. No computation of scores should be made until the end of the experiment.
7. Each subject as far as possible should have the same number of tests as every other subject.
8. Work periods should be of uniform time length; they should contain the same number of runs and have the same distribution throughout the week.

9. Subjects should not use ESP cards in any other connection during the course of the experiment.

10. The experiment should be set up under the superintendence of three psychologists, each from a different university. In addition the experiment should be under the direction and control of two or more psychologists who are regarded as competent in the experimental field by members of the profession generally; one of these psychologists is to be on duty during every work period.

After the meeting a committee was set up under the chairmanship of Professor S. B. Sells of Columbia University. It included a number of well-known psychologists including Lillian Dick, J. J. Gibson, E. R. Hilgard. J. L. Kennedy, and R. R. Willoughby. The intention was that research to be reported in the *Journal of Parapsychology* be vetted by this committee prior to publication.

Before the Ohio symposium an experiment had been conducted at Duke by J. L. Woodruff, a graduate student in the psychology department, under the supervision of Dr. J. G. Pratt. After the meeting Pratt returned to Duke and a further series of tests was carried out incorporating as far as thought desirable points raised at the symposium. The earlier set of results obtained by Woodruff was called series A. The new tests were called series B. The two series of tests were published together and have since become known as the Pratt-Woodruff experiment.[2]

THE PRATT-WOODRUFF EXPERIMENT

The Pratt-Woodruff experiment was carried out at Duke University between October 1, 1938, and February 28, 1939. It was originally intended as a test to determine the effects of the size of stimulus symbols on clairvoyance, but owing to the results obtained, the care taken in the experimental design, the precision of its execution, and the careful account of the procedure contained in the report, it has remained as the classic ESP experiment. Rhine and Pratt, when discussing conclusive test methods some fifteen years later, commented: "Those who wish to acquire a reading acquaintance with the highest standards of controlled psi testing may, for example, consult the Pratt and Woodruff report."[3] Rhine made even stronger claims: "The experiment was designed for the express purpose of meeting all the criticisms that came up in the years of controversy. In the entire history of Psychology no experiment has ever been carried out with such elaborate controls against all possible error."[4]

THE PERSONS TAKING PART

Three persons were present at each sitting: a main experimenter, J. L. Woodruff; a second experimenter, J. G. Pratt; and a subject. Pratt's task was to ensure that the experiment was carried out efficiently and that all the controls were observed; he will therefore be referred to as the "observer." In addition, one of the laboratory secretaries was responsible for seeing that all the score sheets, which were serially numbered in advance, were completed and included in the final analysis so that all tests would be contained in the final result and that only the predetermined number of runs would be made.

THE EXPERIMENTAL PROCEDURE

The experimenter and the subject sat at opposite ends of a table. Between them, across the width of the table, was a screen 18 inches in height and 24 inches in breadth. This screen had a gap 2 inches high and 20 inches across along its bottom edge so that five blank cards placed on the table beneath it were visible to both the subject and the experimenter. A smaller, sloping screen attached to the main one on the experimenter's side permitted the experimenter to see the five blank cards, but ensured that the subject could not gain sight of the experimenter or of a pack of ESP cards that he was handling.

On the subject's side of the screen, five "key cards," each bearing one of the five different ESP symbols, were hung on pegs above the gap at the bottom of the screen. Each card was then directly above one of the blank cards lying on the table. Before each run of 25 trials, the observer took the key cards from the pegs and handed them to the subject who changed their order and replaced them.

The experimenter, on the other side of the screen, could not see their positions on the pegs, and only the five blank cards were visible to him. He shuffled and cut a pack of ESP cards and then gave the signal to start. Thereupon the subject attempted to guess the top card in the pack. He indicated his guess by pointing with a pencil to the blank card beneath the key card with the appropriate symbol. The experimenter, seeing the end of the pencil through the gap at the bottom of the screen, laid down the top card from the pack, face downward, opposite the blank card the pencil pointed to. The subject made 24 more guesses in the same manner, and the experimenter put the cards in five piles in accordance with the positions indicated by the pencil. At the end of the run of 25 trials, with the screen still in position, the experimenter made a record of the cards in each of the piles on one of the serially numbered forms. At the same time, the observer recorded the order of the key cards, the subject's name, and the date of the sitting on a form bearing the same serial number as that used by the experimenter. When these two records were completed, they were clipped together and put through a slot into a locked box. The observer was careful to ensure that his record was not seen by the experimenter until the latter had recorded the five piles of cards.

The screen was then laid on its side. The cards in each pile were compared with the key cards, and the observer placed the hits together, next to the key card. The number of hits was counted and checked by the three persons present. It was then recorded by both the experimenter and by the observer in their personal notebooks. Thus, the scores as later determined from the serially numbered forms could be checked with these two other records.

Before the start of the next run, the screen was placed back in position. The key cards were "rearranged on the pegs," and the observer returned to his seat about 6 feet behind the subject and slightly to his right. The experimenter shuffled and cut his pack. He then gave the signal to begin the next run.

On average, each run of 25 trials, including scoring, took two minutes. The experiment included 2,400 runs of which 2,000 were conducted in the above manner (called the STM procedure). In the remaining 400 runs, a modification was introduced: before each run the key cards were removed from the screen by the observer and replaced by him in different positions with their faces toward the screen (BSTM procedure).

THE RESULTS

The 32 subjects who took part in this experiment obtained a total of 12,489 hits in 60,000 trials. This constituted an excess of 489 hits over the score expected to arise by chance. The mean scoring rate for the group was, however, only 5.204 hits per run as compared with the chance expectation of 5.0 hits per run. Thus, only 1 extra hit need have arisen in each 100 trials to account for the scores. Even so, the odds against the observed result arising by chance are greater than a million to one, and this provides an example of the way in which a mean score only slightly above the chance-scoring rate can assume enormous significance provided it is based on a sufficient number of trials. Such a result must be treated with caution, since even the slightest laxity in the experimental conditions or the presence of weak sensory cues can make itself manifest.

Closer examination of the results of this experiment shows, however, that the explanation is unlikely to be in terms of such forms of error. The subjects varied considerably in their performance, but one subject in particular achieved scores at some sittings that, merely by inspection, can be seen to involve much more than chance. Even though the high scores of this subject, designated P.M. in the report, arose mainly in three out of eight sittings, her overall score of 947 hits in 4,050 trials had odds greater than 20 million to 1 against arising by chance. Four other subjects also obtained scores having odds greater than 20 million to 1 against their arising by chance. Thus, there are clear indications that something other than guesswork or experimental error was involved in this experiment and also that its effects were by no means negligible in the case of at least one subject.

ANALYSIS OF THE EXPERIMENTAL CONDITIONS

If the experimenter had carried out his duties efficiently, it would have been extremely difficult for the subject to have achieved high scores in the absence of ESP. The following criticism of D. H. Rawcliffe's should, however, be noted:

> When we hear that the screened touch-matching technique involves the personal handling of a face-down pack of cards by the experimenter who is sitting only a couple of feet away from the percipient, the claim to have imposed the strictest experimental controls must raise a smile.
>
> The only value of a screen between the percipient and the experimenter is that it probably prevents direct visual cues from reaching the percipient. If, in the absence of a screen, the possibility of direct visual cues reaching the *percipient* is admitted, then plainly the same possibility exists in regard to the experimenter; for he can not only see the backs of the cards but he can also touch the backs of the cards and probably the faces as well. Any information he may get from the cards, perhaps subconsciously, may be readily transmitted by unconscious articulation or *endophasic enneuoris,* by an auditory code of ideomotor movements, by intonations and variations in breathing, or by involuntary reactions to any tentative movements of the percipient's pointer over the exposed "key cards."[5]

While it has been established that individuals are capable of responding to minute auditory, visual, and tactile stimuli as mentioned by Rawcliffe, it is unlikely that the result of the Pratt-Woodruff experiment could have arisen in this way. The time taken to make the 25 guesses during each run was about 20 seconds. The experimenter was watching the fast-moving pointer and sorting the cards into five piles. It would have been difficult for him at the same time to have looked at the backs of the cards unless he was bent on identifying them. In that case, he could quite easily have turned them over and looked at their faces. It is difficult to understand why the experimenter and the subject should have been placed in such close proximity, particularly after Pearce's results at more than 100 yards, but if the experimenter had carried out his duties efficiently, it is unlikely that high scores could have arisen either through the unconscious utilization of cues or by deliberate cheating on the part of the subject. If, on the other hand, the experimenter had any knowledge of the positions, or likely positions, of the key cards, and wished to influence the result of the experiment, he was clearly in a position to do so. He was completely screened from the other persons present and had ample opportunity, either while distributing the cards or while recording them, to change the positions and numbers of the cards in the five piles.

While at the Parapsychology Laboratory in October 1960, I inspected the apparatus used in the experiments and found that, when acting in the role of experimenter, it was quite a simple matter for me to detect the positions at which cards were being replaced on the pegs on the other side of the screen before the start of a run. I obtained the assistance of Michael Sanders, who at that time was a research fellow in the Parapsychology Laboratory, and asked him to remove the cards from the pegs in order from left to right and then to replace them in different positions. Having noted the symbol occupying the left-hand position among the key cards while the screen was turned on its side at the end of the previous run, I was able to detect the position in which it was replaced. Thus, in the role of the experimenter, I would have been able to place cards in a position where they would secure extra hits during the following run.

If the experimenter had wished to influence the results of the experiment in this manner, he could have adopted the following procedure. When the screen was turned on its side during the scoring at the end of a run, he could have noted the symbol occupying position 1 (or position 5) in the row of key cards. After the screen was placed back in position, and when the key cards were removed from the pegs by the observer, he could have noted the order in which they were removed. When the subject changed their order and replaced them, he could assume that the last card replaced would be the one that occupied position 1 or 5 in the last run, depending on whether they had been removed from the pegs from left to right or from right to left. If, on the other hand, the positions of the key cards were changed by moving them about on the pegs, he could keep track of a particular card during this process, getting to know the position of the one key card. He would allocate the cards to one of the piles during the run and then, after turning up the cards to record them at the end of the run, he would move cards bearing the appropriate symbol into the position where they would result in hits.

A trick of this type would cause a high score to arise frequently on a key-card symbol that had occupied one of the outside positions (1 and 5) during the *previous* run. The effects of such a procedure would also manifest themselves with the best possibility of being detected in the records of the highest-scoring subject (P.M.). The following preliminary analysis was, therefore, carried out to check whether this was so.

All runs made by the high-scoring subject yielding a score of 8 hits or more were considered. The symbol that secured the maximum number of hits in each run was noted. Where two or more symbols secured an equally high number of hits, that run was rejected for the purpose of the analysis. Having identified the symbol that secured the maximum number of hits in a run, its position was checked among the key cards in the previous run.

It was found that in the 22 runs considered, the high-scoring symbol had occupied either position 1 or 5 among the key cards in the previous run in 17 cases. Most of the cases in which high scores involving preceding positions 1 or 5 did not arise were in the last two sittings. These were the two sittings in which the BTSM procedure was used and in which the key cards had their faces to the screen. When considering the first six sittings, in which the STM procedure was employed, it was found that in only one case out of eighteen had the high-scoring symbol occupied a position *other* than 1 or 5. Thus, it was clear that something had happened during the experiment to cause hits to arise in this remarkable manner.

The analysis was then extended to include all runs in which more than 5 hits were obtained. The result is shown in table 6–1.

The number of hits arising on a particular symbol should be independent of the position of that symbol in the key cards in the previous run. Thus, the highest score should arise on a symbol previously occupying positions 1 or 5, 40 percent of the time, and it should arise on symbols previously occupying positions 2, 3, or 5, 60 percent of the time.

However, of the 55 cases considered in table 6–1, there are 39 in which the high-scoring symbol occupied positions 1 or 5 in the previous key-card order, and 16 where it had occupied positions 2, 3, or 4 during the previous run. The contingency table 6–2 (p. 83) is obtained. A statistical test indicates that the numbers of cases observed in the two categories would be expected to arise by chance in only 1 in 100,000 similar experiments.

TABLE 6-1

Positions that High-Scoring Symbols Occupied
in the Row of Key Cards Used for the Previous Run

(S = Star, R = Rectangle, P = Plus, W = Waves, C = Circle)
Subject P.M.

Date and type of sitting	Run	Score on run	Highest-scoring symbol	Position of symbol in previous run
Nov. 21, 1938	3	6	S	1
STM	5	6	P	1
	6	6	R	5
	12	10	W	5
	14	8	S	5
Nov. 28, 1938	2	7	P	5
STM	3	8	W	5
	4	6	C	5
	5	6	R	5
	6	6	C	2
	8	9	C	3
	9	9	S	5
	10	9	W	5
	11	7	W	1
	12	11	R	5
	14	11	P	1
	15	6	P	2

TABLE 6-1 (cont.)

Date and type of sitting	Run	Score on run	Highest-scoring symbol	Position of symbol in previous run
Dec. 12, 1938 STM	6	10	S	5
	7	7	R	5
	8	11	W	5
	10	6	C	5
	12	10	C	5
	15	8	R	5
Jan. 9, 1939 STM	2	6	C	5
	3	7	P	1
	6	10	C	1
	8	7	C	4
	12	6	S	1
	18	6	C	1
	19	10	W	1
	20	7	C	5
	22	9	R	1
Jan. 31, 1939 STM	3	10	W	5
	4	6	C	3
	5	7	S	5
	7	8	P	1
	11	7	S	1
	13	6	W	3
	15	6	R	1
Feb. 3, 1939 STM	2	6	C	1
	7	6	P	2
	10	7	W	1
	15	7	R	1
Feb. 10, 1939 BSTM	2	7	S	4
	15	7	P	2
	16	9	S	2
	17	7	R	3
	22	8	R	3
	24	7	S	5
	27	10	S	4
Feb. 17, 1939 BSTM	8	8	R	2
	9	6	C	2
	11	12	P	1
	16	7	C	5
	25	7	W	4

The high-scoring subject obtained 946 hits in 4,050 trials. Table 6–3 (p. 84) shows the number of *hits* arising on symbols that, in the previous run, occupied positions 1 and 5 among the key cards compared with the number of hits on symbols that occupied the remaining positions. The first run cannot be included in this analysis; therefore, it relates only to the remaining 4,025 trials in which 941 hits were scored.

Thus it will be seen from table 6–3 that the above-chance scores are accounted for entirely in terms of hits made on symbols that occupied positions 1 or 5 in the previous run. The odds on the scores achieved on symbols that occupied positions 2, 3, and 4 in the previous run are nearly even, whereas the odds on the scores achieved for positions 1 and 5 are greater than 100 billion to 1.

THE RANDOMIZATION OF KEY-CARD ORDER

It would have been impossible for such a trick as described above to have been carried out by the experimenter if the observer had thoroughly shuffled the key cards before they were replaced on the pegs. There is no mention of the cards having been shuffled in the experimental report, but when I was at the Parapsychology Laboratory, Pratt told me that he remembered shuffling them. However, a study of the key-card order of many runs of the second highest-scoring subject (D.A.) shows little evidence of shuffling. At the first sitting, comprising 14 runs, the order of the key cards remained unchanged for the last 7 runs. At the second sitting, comprising 18 runs, the order of the key cards remained unchanged from one run to the next on six occasions. On three occasions the order of the cards was simply reversed; another time, two cards were interchanged and then put back to their original positions on the following run. These effects are confined to the first two sittings in which the STM procedure was used. In the third sitting, using the BSTM procedure, the order of cards appears to have been randomized effectively.

TABLE 6-2

Positions Occupied, During Previous Run,
by Symbols Securing Maximum Number of Hits in Present Run

Position that highest-scoring symbol occupied in previous run	Cases observed	Cases expected
1 or 5	39	22
2, 3 or 4	16	33
Totals	55	55

Unless the cards were systematically shuffled after every run, a trick could have been employed, and the experimental report makes it clear that the investigators had not seriously considered the necessity of such shuffling. It is stated that Woodruff shuffled the pack of cards that he used, but the word "shuffle" is at no time used with reference to the key cards.

THE REMAINING HIGH-SCORING SUBJECTS

Five of the thirty-two subjects obtained scores significantly above the chance level, at odds greater than 20 to 1. The number of cases in which the high-scoring symbol occupied each of the five positions in the key-card order for these subjects, when the STM procedure was used, is shown in table 6–4 (p. 85).

The total expected frequency is 25.2 for each position, and the observed values have odds greater than 1 million to 1 against arising by chance. When only subjects C.C., D.A., D.L., and H.G. are considered, their result is also significant, having odds greater than 100 to 1 against arising by chance.

TABLE 6–3

Analysis of Scores Arising on Symbols that Occupied Positions 1 and 5
on Previous Runs Compared with Scores Arising on Symbols
that Occupied Positions 2, 3, and 4

Subject P.M.

Position of symbol in previous run	Trials	Hits obtained	Hits expected to arise by chance	Odds against score arising by chance
1 and 5	1,670	453	336.6	greater than 10^{11} to 1
2, 3, and 4	2,355	488	471.0	less than 2 to 1

COUNTERCRITICISMS RAISED BY PRATT AND WOODRUFF

When replying to my criticism of their experiment in the *Journal of Parapsychology*,[6] Pratt and Woodruff objected that I selected the data used in my analysis.[7] They stated that out of P.M.'s series of 4,050 trials I selected a relationship that depended upon only 55 observations. The data given in table 6–1 included 55 runs, which were isolated from a total of 162 made by this subject in which an above-chance score was obtained. It was selected in this manner to save time and to give reasonably high sensitivity.

TABLE 6–4

Positions Occupied by High-Scoring Symbols During Previous Run

STM Procedure

Previous position of symbol	C.C.	D.A.	D.L.	H.G.	P.M.	Totals
1	13	2	2	13	16	46
2	3	1	4	5	3	16
3	6	2	2	5	3	16
4	3	0	3	6	1	13
5	5	0	5	3	20	33
Totals	30	5	16	32	43	126

Pratt and Woodruff provided an alternative form of analysis in which the effect I had pointed out was confirmed. It should be noted that their own analysis also involved selection of data. They took all runs in which a score of more than 5 hits was obtained. They then counted the number of hits and misses secured by each symbol in relation to its position among the key cards during the previous trial. This form of analysis also involves selection, however, and is rendered relatively insensitive because attention is confined to those runs in which an above-chance score is obtained. If all runs are included, it becomes much more sensitive than my original analysis. Thus, the data given in table 6–3, which was not included in my report published in the *Journal of Parapsychology*, shows how marked the effects become when account is taken of all the observations.

The second point raised by Pratt and Woodruff was the assertion that the effect present with P.M. was absent in the other high-scoring subjects. This is not so. It is only absent when the relatively insensitive analysis that they used is applied to the data. When the data for subjects C.C., D.A., D.L., and H.G. are taken together (see table 6–4), the effect is certainly present, and in the case of subject D.A., his results given in table 6–5 (p. 86) show an effect similar to that of the high-scoring subject P.M.

If the results of the three other high-scoring subjects were analyzed in a similar manner, it is likely that they would show the same effect.

Three alternative explanations were put forward by Pratt and Woodruff to account for the effects present in the scores of P.M. They wrote:

1. Actually, one can offer a consistent and reasonable ESP hypothesis, as follows: For the subject P.M., the run began, in the psychological sense, when she rearranged and placed the target cards. The ESP task being a difficult one, she dealt with it by a "narrowing of attention" procedure. For her the task became one of attempting to identify only *some* of the cards in the deck: those with the particular symbols which had become salient because of their prominent end positions in the preceding run.

2. There may be an alternative ESP interpretation, such as a differential rate of scoring on the five symbols, coupled with some habitual tendency in the placement of the symbols on the pegs.

3. Finally, as stated above, this may be a selected, meaningless, statistical effect, for statistical oddities are a dime a dozen. To take one seriously it is necessary to confirm it. The data of other subjects in our series fail to support this oddity, whereas they do support the significant scoring level of the experiment. Therefore the Hansel effect is still unconfirmed and unexplained, and it certainly could not explain the Pratt-Woodruff result.[8]

TABLE 6–5

Analysis of Scores Arising on Symbols that Occupied Positions 1 and 5
on Previous Runs Compared with Scores Arising on Symbols
that Occupied Positions 2, 3, and 4

Subject D.A.

Position of symbol in previous run	Trials	Hits obtained	Hits expected to arise by chance	Odds against score arising by chance
1 and 5	491	126	98.2	0.002
2, 3, and 4	734	162	146.8	0.200

Their first explanation is difficult to consider seriously. First, it assumes ESP; moreover, it describes a new salience effect that arises in more than one subject. It is difficult to see how the second explanation works. While at the Parapsychology Laboratory, I did investigate P.M.'s results to see whether they could be accounted for in terms of the tendency of the subject to assign more cards to one pile than another, coupled with a tendency to replace key cards in particular positions. There was no evidence that any such effects could account for the result. If this second explanation is to be taken seriously, it must be described more clearly, and further data should be provided from the record sheets.

The third explanation can hold no water whatsoever. The effect in P.M.'s data is so definite that it emerges with any analysis that is applied. The fact that it is not present with all the other subjects is quite immaterial. If any of the subjects did shuffle the key cards before replacing them a trick would not have been possible. If, in an experiment of this type, just one of the subjects did not perform this operation, the effects should then only appear in the records of that one subject. If some subjects omitted shuffling the cards on a small number of occasions before replacing them, the overall score for the experiment could easily give a result that was statistically significant without the result for any single subject displaying any evidence that a trick had been used.

Having worked out what seemed to me the only possible way in which the result could have been brought about in the absence of ESP, it came as a considerable surprise to find such clear-cut evidence for it in the records of the highest-scoring subject.

Pratt and Woodruff also asserted that the effect was only present in the case of one subject (P.M. in the report) and was absent in the case of other high-scoring subjects. For this reason I showed that it was also present in the case of subject D.A. when taking into account *all* the trials made by that subject under the STM condition. The effect was also present when taking the four high-scoring subjects—other than P.M. In this case, I had taken into account only the runs in which a score of 8 or more was obtained. The particular statistical analysis employed is unlikely to have affected the findings very much, but it was not possible to answer criticisms raised by Pratt and Woodruff owing to the nonavailability of the record sheets. (These were in my possession for only a fortnight while at Duke University and had to be returned after I refused to sign a form that would have made publication of my findings dependent on the consent of the laboratory.)

Dr. Ramakrishna Rao, of the Parapsychology Laboratory, in a book *Experimental Parapsychology* published in 1966, disposed of my criticisms of the experiment more succinctly, writing: "This is, of course, the disgraceful argument of the dogmatic goat and has no merit as scientific criticism."[9]

EVIDENCE PROVIDED BY SCOTT AND MEDHURST

Christopher Scott and R. G. Medhurst, thinking that confirmation of the effect on high-scoring subjects other than P.M. was of paramount importance, obtained the record sheets from the Parapsychology Laboratory. They carried out an analysis of the result for these subjects, which showed the effect to have odds of 1 in a 100 of arising by chance. This finding was reported in the *Journal of Parapsychology* in 1974.[10]

It should be noted that if a trick was employed, it was entirely at the discretion of the trickster whether he employed it with one subject or with a number of subjects. The evidence from the records supports the conclusion that a trick was employed with more than one subject.

Medhurst and Scott suggested that such a trick might not have been consciously employed. They suggest that the experimenter might have been able to identify the cards from their backs owing to the fact that the cards had been used many times over and that he might "occasionally misplace one unconsciously into the pile where he knew it ought to go."[11]

But, to do this, he would have had to learn where "it ought to go," and, in addition, he would have had to learn to identify cards from their backs. He would hardly do this through continued use of the cards, since he merely placed them into piles without learning their identities until they were turned up at the end of the experiment. In any case, an alternative explanation of this type implies that the result of the experiment cannot be accepted as providing evidence for ESP.

REEXAMINATION OF THE PRATT-WOODRUFF EXPERIMENT

Further examination of the Pratt-Woodruff experiment, taking into consideration the fact that any sources of experimental error were not checked by the use of a control series, raises the possibility that the small excess of hits obtained from a large number of trials may have arisen without there having been cheating on the part of anyone involved, or even awareness of the cards in the pack by Woodruff, as suggested by Medhurst and Scott.

In Coover's experiment sources of error were both eliminated and revealed by the use of a control series. The main form of error was probably due to the use of a pack of playing cards that tended on a small number of occasions to cut at particular cards, causing these to arise more frequently in the target series than others, together with the fact that subjects tend to display preferences for particular cards, as demonstrated later in Woolley's broadcast experiment.

Coover's experiment was the first in which a large number of subjects were tested, each making a large number of attempts at identifying a target. His reason for using a large number of different subjects was that at that time there were two possibilities being discussed regarding the nature of telepathy: first, that particular individuals had the ability to receive telepathy; second, that some such ability was distributed throughout the general population. To cover both possibilities Coover took a large sample of subjects and in addition tested ten professional psychics who claimed to have telepathic ability. Consideration of his results makes it clear how small sources of error can account for antichance results at low levels of significance.

Coover's control series was sufficient to check for telepathy owing to the fact that telepathy could be eliminated in the control series by ensuring that no one knew the identity of the target card. After the experiment was completed, it was possible to eliminate the possibility of clairvoyance by checking guesses against targets for which they were not intended.

If Coover's target series had been random, i.e., generated by a process that would give each target a 1 in 40 chance of arising at each selection, guessing habits of the percipients would not have increased their chances of success. High scores could only arise if card preferences on the part of the percipients had some correspondence with targets as they arose in sequence after the cards had been shuffled and cut before each run.

The possibility has to be considered of nonrandom features being present in the pack of target cards handled by Woodruff, coupled with the use of information acquired during the tests by the subjects.

FURTHER DETAILS OF THE EXPERIMENTAL CONDITIONS AND PROCEDURES

The original aim of the Pratt-Woodruff experiment was to see whether ESP scores were dependent on the size of the symbols being guessed. For this reason four different packs of cards were employed. One of these contained the normal 1 1/2-inch Zener symbols on manufactured cards similar in size to playing cards. The other three sizes (1/16 inch, 1/4 inch, and 2 1/2 inch) contained symbols drawn in Indian ink on cards of the same size.

Series B consisted of eight subseries, each of 300 runs. In the first subseries packs containing the 1/16-inch, the 1/4-inch, and the 1 1/2-inch symbol sizes were selected "subjectively" by Woodruff. In the next two subseries, i.e., 600 runs, the same symbol sizes were used, but the choice of size for each run was determined by the cast of a die. In the next 300 runs only the regular 1 1/2-inch symbols were used. During the last four subseries, i.e., 1,200 runs, the 1 1/2-inch and 2 1/2-inch packs were used alternately.

In the description of the procedure used in the experiment, it is stated that Woodruff shuffled and cut the pack of cards after the screen had been placed back in position before starting the next run. Later under special points of procedure it is stated that during the last 830 runs of the experiment, the cards were shuffled by Pratt and cut by Woodruff using a paper knife.

In an earlier account of the experiment given by Pratt he stated that "The cards to be guessed are shuffled five times by the second experimenter (Pratt) and are given a final cut with a paper knife after the screen is placed back in position for the run."[12]

THE TARGET SEQUENCE

At the end of each run the cards were in piles opposite the relevant key-card positions. The cards in each pile were then turned over and displaced, making their faces visible and maintaining the order in which the cards had been placed on the pile. After the cards had been recorded by Woodruff, Pratt moved cards that had secured hits to positions next to the screen. The cards were later gathered together into a pack by Woodruff and presumably placed aside while he took the second pack to use in the run that was to follow. This second pack was presumably resting either on his side of the table or on the other side of the screen, i.e., on the subject's side of the table or on a second table at which Pratt sat during the run. The screen was then placed back in position. The pack was shuffled and cut and the next run started.

In the last 830 runs it is likely that Pratt would take the pack to his desk so that he could shuffle it and have it ready for use when it was required. This pack would have been visible to the subject before the screen was placed back in position. If the subject knew the symbol on the top card and pointed to that position on the rearranged key cards at his first guess on the following run, he would score a hit in the event of the pack not having been cut.

Little attention appears to have been paid to screening of the target pack before the run started. Rhine's earlier experiments indicate that subjects can obtain high scores if a pack is visible to them, and that these scores arise at the start and end of the run. This is what Rhine called a salience effect. The high-scoring subjects in the Pratt-Woodruff experiment also scored at above-chance level only in the first and last five trials. This effect was shown by Pratt who, being unable to obtain the target order for each pack, got an estimate of it by taking the first and the last cards in each of the five piles at the end of the experiment. He argued that these targets were most likely to have arisen at those positions. There was a very strong effect even with the estimation that had been made of the card order.

It is not clear from the report whether Woodruff collected the cards together in view of the subject or not. Since there was little space in which to lay out the cards in the five piles at the end of the run in order to record them, they are likely to have extended on to the screen. They would then have had to be moved before the screen was put upright preparatory to starting the next run.

If Woodruff assumed that the pack was to be both shuffled and cut by Pratt, this situation would arise. If on the other hand there were lapses in the procedure owing to the boring and repetitive task being carried out week after week by the experimenters, the final cut behind the screen could have been forgotten.

INFORMATION GAINED AFTER THE RUN

If cards were gathered together from left to right, pushing each pile together and adding it to cards already forming the deck, the last cards collected (i.e., opposite position 5 among the key cards) would be the hits achieved in that position followed by other cards in the pile. Similarly, other ways of gathering the cards together could cause the last card collected to fall at the top of the pack.

The pack so formed would be stacked to some extent since hits in each pile had been gathered together. Normally only one or two hits would be expected in a pile, but in a series of successful runs further cards could come together in the event of inefficient shuffling. Woodruff's method of shuffling is described as follows: "Woodruff used the method of shuffling in which the pack is held in one hand while cards are slipped out of it and reinserted into the pack with the other."[13]

During series B of the experiment Woodruff should have cut the cards 2,400 times. In series A preceding the main experiment he had already cut the packs 1,840 times. It is possible that shuffling and cutting were perfunctory or omitted altogether at some sessions. If there were any cutting tendencies owing to slight differences in size, adhesion at the face because of the printing of the symbols, or wear caused by repeated shuffling, particular symbols could tend to arise at the bottom—or top—of the pack.

THE SUBJECTS' MOVEMENT SEQUENCE

Subjects signified their guess by moving a pencil to point at a position between 1 and 5. They did this at high speed, taking an average of 15 seconds to complete the 25 movements of the pencil for each run. The method employed by the subject is not stated but presumably he would either move his pencil in a haphazard way over the five positions or he might select a symbol and allot several guesses to it before passing on. If a subject were guessing it might be expected that particular tendencies—for example, lack of repeats and runs— would be present in the guess sequence. If he selected a symbol and made repeated guesses at it before passing to another symbol, the effect would be reversed, i.e., similar to stacking.

The subject would acquire information about the position of the last card from the target pack when the cards were exposed at the end of the run. He could also learn about the positions of other cards by experimenting. For example, if he only pointed to a position once for the first target in the pack, he would discover the identity of the first card at the end of the run.

Subjects also had some control of the experiment since they replaced the key cards onto pegs before each run started. If they observed that their last card in the previous run had scored a hit, they might elect to point to it at the start of the next run in whatever position it occupied among the key cards.

The table on which the screen rested was about 2-feet square judging from the photograph published in the original article. The screen was about 10 inches from the subject, leaving 14 inches on Woodruff's side, but the additional sloping screen was set back about 3 inches. This would leave about 11 inches of table on which Woodruff turned up the piles of cards to reveal their identities before the screen was turned over from its vertical position. Thus, the cards when turned up would have to overlap in their piles since there would be an average of five cards in each row.

It is reported that the average number of runs per hour was 30. Subjects worked by appointment for from 30 to 45 minutes at a session. Several subjects were usually tested at each experimental session. Subjects had a lengthy and boring task. They might complete 16 runs mostly by moving a pencil about just as rapidly as they could do so. Many subjects completed between 200 and 300 runs of 25 guesses during the course of the experiment. One subject completed 313 runs. Precise instructions given to the subjects are not stated, but they would presumably learn in the first run of their first session that they were supposed to get the cards from the pack to land opposite the appropriate position shown by the key card. Eight of the subjects had also taken part in the earlier series-A experiment.

At least a few of the subjects are likely to have developed a strategy to improve scores, or they may have modified their selections after seeing where the cards fell in the previous run. Many such strategies may be completely useless, but some may result in extra hits arising. Going through run after run a subject has the opportunity of trying a variety of strategies and he may be fortunate in discovering one that appears to work, or he may merely get extra hits and not notice it.

At the end of each run the subject first sees the target cards as laid out by Woodruff opposite the key cards. At this point the subject will learn the symbol at which he last pointed since it will be at the top of the pile opposite the key-card position at which he has last pointed. He will also learn whether it made a hit or not. Over a long series of runs, say 150, at the rate of about 30 per hour in which each run takes about 15 seconds, the subject has ideal opportunities for testing out strategies until he finds one that gives promising results.

Subjects were students and members of the department steeped in the lore of ESP research. They would have been drilled in Rhine's "salience effect," i.e., that hits tend to arise at the beginning and end of a run. Some may have been highly skeptical of the research, as indeed was one subject, D.A.—the highest-scoring subject in terms of scoring rate.

CONCLUSIONS

In the original paper by Pratt and Woodruff the experiment is described in far more detail than was the custom at Duke at that time. This was probably due to the requirements listed at the Ohio symposium. Had the requirements been fully met most of the possibilities discussed above would not have arisen.

Since above-chance scores could have arisen in the Pratt-Woodruff experiment through the use of a trick, it cannot be considered as providing conclusive evidence for ESP. Whether or not a trick was used is a secondary matter. There is no reason why the experiment should not be conducted again under conditions similar to those used originally but with additional precautions to eliminate the possibility of a trick. It is remarkable that, in spite of the great claims made for the experiment and its relative simplicity, it was never repeated at the Parapsychology Laboratory itself.

NOTES

1. Symposium on ESP methods, Southern University for Philosophy and Psychology, Chairman J. B. Rhine, held at Duke University and the University of North Carolina, April 7 and 8, 1939. Published in full in *Journal of Parapsychology* (1940).

2. J. G. Pratt and J. L. Woodruff, "Size of Stimulus Symbols in Extrasensory Perception," *Journal of Parapsychology* 3 (1939): 121–59.

3. J. B. Rhine and J. G. Pratt, *Parapsychology: Frontier Science of the Mind* (Oxford: Blackwell, 1956), p. 39.

4. J. B. Rhine, *New World of the Mind* (London: Faber and Faber, 1954), p. 55.

5. D. H. Rawcliffe, *Illusions and Delusions of the Supernatural and the Occult* (New York: Dover, 1959), p. 388.

6. C. E. M. Hansel, "A Critical Analysis of the Pratt-Woodruff Experiment," *Journal of Parapsychology* 25 (1961): 99–114.

7. J. G. Pratt and J. L. Woodruff, "Refutation of Hansel's Allegation Concerning the Pratt-Woodruff Series," *Journal of Parapsychology* 25 (1961): 123.

8. Ibid., pp. 126–27.

9. R. R. Rao, *Experimental Parapsychology. A Review and Interpretation* (Springfield: Thames, 1966), p. 18.

10. R. G. Medhurst and C. Scott, "A Reexamination of C. E. M. Hansel's Criticism of the Pratt-Woodruff Experiment," *Journal of Parapsychology* 38 (1974): 163–84.

11. Ibid., p. 164.

12. J. G. Pratt, "A Further Advance in Methods of Testing Extra-Sensory Perception," *Journal of Parapsychology* 3 (1939): 98.

13. Pratt and Woodruff, "Size of Stimulus Symbols in Extrasensory Perception," p. 130.

7

Group Experiments

Before 1934, investigators at Duke University had no difficulty finding subjects who could consistently obtain high scores in ESP tests. But such subjects became increasingly scarce as experimental designs were made more rigorous. Then following the discussions at the meeting of the American Psychological Association in 1938 and publication of Kennedy's criticisms in 1939, high-scoring subjects became extinct. Since 1939, not a single subject has appeared who can consistently obtain high scores guessing ESP cards.

HUMPHREY'S EXPERIMENT

After 1940, many of the experiments on ESP carried out in the United States relied on a new technique introduced by Betty Humphrey at the Duke Parapsychology Laboratory. She first used it to test the relationship between ESP ability and personality characteristics.[1] In her experiment ninety-six subjects were first classified by means of a test into "compressive" and "expansive" types. After this, the subjects were given a test for clairvoyance, and the mean ESP score of the compressives was compared with that of the expansives. It was found that the expansives scored significantly higher on the test, the odds being greater than 300,000 to 1 against the difference in scores arising by chance. The overall score for the ninety-six subjects was, however, not significantly above the chance level, nor was the score of any one subject significantly above chance.

The personality test used in the experiments required the subjects to draw anything they pleased on a blank sheet of paper. Subjects who filled the area of the paper with a bold drawing were classified as expansives, while those who used only a part of the paper were classifed as compressives. Thus, while ignoring any assumptions that related the manner in which a person draws to other personality characteristics, Miss Humphrey's experiment seemed to indicate that people who fill a sheet of paper when drawing on it tend to obtain high scores in ESP tests and that people who make small drawings covering only a part of the paper tend to obtain low scores. A further remarkable result reported by Humphrey was that when telepathy tests were used instead of clairvoyance tests, the result was reversed: compressives got high scores and expansives, low ones.

J. Fraser Nicol and Betty Humphrey (now Mrs. Nicol) carried out two further experiments of the same type. The first of these gave scores that tended in the same direction but were not statistically significant.[2] The second has not been published, but Nicol informed me in correspondence that the result was "pure nullity" and that the whole affair needs to be reexamined. Dr. D. J. West of the Society for Psychical Research also repeated this experiment and found no difference in the scores of the groups and no signs of ESP.[3]

SHEEP AND GOATS

Since 1940, several investigators have divided their subjects into two groups, but they have used different criteria from those of Humphrey. In most of the research the results have the same general characteristics as in Humphrey's experiment.

The most extensive of these tests were those conducted by Dr. Gertrude R. Schmeidler of the City College at New York.[4] She divided her subjects into sheep and goats, a sheep being a person who believed in ESP and a goat being one who did not. She then found that sheep scored above chance and goats below chance. Again, the overall score did not differ significantly from the chance level, and again repetition of the test by other investigators did not confirm the original result.[5]

EXPERIMENTS IN THE CLASSROOM

A similar technique was employed in a number of experiments carried out in classrooms with the aim of seeing whether pupils who had good feelings toward the teacher displayed ESP. Margaret Anderson of the biophysics department at the University of Pittsburgh, and Rhea White, a research fellow in the Parapsychology Laboratory, employed a questionnaire to determine children's attitudes toward the teacher and the teacher's attitude to the children.[6]

The children were then given a clairvoyance test, and it was claimed that where there was mutual good feeling between teacher and pupil, the scores tended to be above the chance level, where there was lack of good feeling scores were below it. Repetitions of these experiments by other investigators have again failed to confirm the original result, and a repetition by White herself also failed to achieve any confirmation.[7]

TARGET MISSING

A peculiar feature present in the results of the group experiments is that above- and below-chance scores obtained by the subgroups balance out so that the overall score is at the chance level. In the event of any weak ability being present in a population, which is more evident in certain types of individual, say men, than in others, say women, there would be a point in confining the sample to men, as scores from the women would lower the average value obtained. The group experiments do not, however, show less ability in one subgroup than the other—or even complete lack of any ability. They show *negative* ESP ability, i.e., the subjects, when attempting to identify targets, tend to identify them wrongly. It is as if when they are attempting to identify a target something makes them miss it.

In order to obtain scores consistently below the chance level, the subject has to receive information just as he does to obtain above-chance scores. But equal amounts of information will not produce equal numbers of hits and misses. Let a subject obtain information sufficient to enable him to obtain H hits in 100 attempts. He will then obtain H hits through receiving this information and on the remaining cards $(100 - H)$ he will score at the chance level. His score denoted by S_H is then equal to $H + (100 - H)/5 = 20 + .8H$.

If, using the same amount of information, the subject is to avoid securing hits, he can achieve this on H cards but will score at the chance level on the remainder. His score denoted by S_H is then equal to $(100 - H/5 = 20 - .2H$.

Thus if ESP were being employed by equal-sized subgroups, the overall score would not be expected to be at the chance level.

It may be objected that ESP does not operate in this manner to cause low scores. But whatever its way of operating, it is remarkable that scores should invariably balance between subgroups so as to give an overall score at the chance level.

PRECAUTIONS NECESSARY IN GROUP EXPERIMENTS

Provided adequate precautions are taken in its design and execution, the group experiment has several advantages over one testing a single subject. A high-scoring subject may lose his ability, making it impossible to verify the original result by further tests; but in the group experiment, subjects selected at random from the population should give the same average score as other similar-sized groups within the limits indicated by statistical theory. None of the subjects need by himself display any significant signs of ESP. Anyone can repeat such an experiment by drawing a group of subjects from the same population.

The type of group experiment in which two subgroups are compared does, however, introduce further hazards into the experimental situation. There are two potential sources of error that need to be carefully guarded against. It is necessary to take as stringent safeguards against spurious high scores as in experiments with single subjects, but extra precautions are necessary to ensure that the experimenter himself cannot unwittingly influence the result. (In the earlier types of experiments, the main aim was to keep the subjects from getting any information about the targets; in the new group experiments, it is, in addition, necessary to ensure that the scoring of the tests and the classification into groups are completely independent and exact.) In a split-group experiment, the lack of confirmation of a result in which one subgroup has scored above chance and the other subgroup below chance while there is an overall result at the chance level at once points to some form of error in allocating individuals to their groups. Ideally, the groups should be decided and the result made public before the ESP tests are carried out, so that there can be no possibility of the original classifications being changed after the scores of the ESP tests become known.

It is also necessary that the nature of the test and the number of trials to be given to each subject be standardized before any tests are made. It would be quite easy to obtain a spurious result when dividing people into believers and disbelievers in ESP if the number of trials to be given to each subject was not decided from the start. The skeptical goat might otherwise carry on with run after run until he had proved his point by getting a total score below the chance expectation. In this way, he would influence the outcome of the experiment. If some goats, after obtaining high scores, decided that they did believe in ESP after all and change their classification, this again would result in a lowered score for the goats and a higher one for the sheep.

In the card-guessing experiments carried out by Rhine and Soal, the aim was to design the experiment so that above-chance scores could not be attributed to anything other than ESP. Emphasis was placed on the accurate recording of targets and guesses, the isolation of the subject from normal sensory contact with the targets, and accurate checking of the guesses against the targets. In a group experiment, at least as much emphasis must be paid to maintaining the groupings into which subjects are placed before the testing starts. Whereas in the early card-guessing tests, emphasis was placed on controlling the activities of the subject, in the group experiments it is of even greater importance to control investigators in order to maintain independence.

The group experiment, if its results can be trusted, provides the ideal way of giving repeatable results. Its failure to do so implies that lack of efficient control of the investigators is the determining factor.

Experiments giving differential-scoring rates between two groups of subjects provide a new source of error unforeseen by the early investigators. The most obvious source of such error is present if the assessments for each subject's ESP scores and his categorization into one type or the other are not entirely independent.

By the time the first differential-scoring ESP tests were conducted it had been generally agreed by Rhine and by other leading parapsychologists that the records of a subject's guesses and of the targets had to be maintained independently, the two lists only being brought together at the end of the run—

or of the experiment. This essential requirement of the experimental conditions had also been stressed at the Ohio symposium. In the Pratt-Woodruff experiment the two records showing targets and guesses were clipped together and placed through a slot into a sealed box for scoring by an independent person before either Pratt or Woodruff could become aware of the other's list.

In a group experiment just as stringent precautions are necessary to maintain separate records of the subject's categorization—e.g., sheep, goats, and ESP performance—as are required to maintain independence of recording of targets and guesses. Thus at least two investigators are needed to ensure independence of targets and hits, and at least a third experimenter to ensure independence of categorizations. The investigators should, ideally, have no knowledge of each other's data or of the subject's until the experiment is completed.

Records should be copied and brought together only at the final stage, after all subjects have been tested and their results tabulated. The Ohio committee had also agreed that the number of subjects and the number of trials undertaken should be stated in advance, and that all subjects tested should be included in the final assessment. These are only some of the requirements laid down by the Ohio committee in respect of the straightforward types of experiment carried out earlier at the Parapsychology Laboratory.

By the time the group experiments appeared on the scene the precautions and experimental rigor that had been used to make Rhine's early experiments more reasonable brought about a marked change in results. High-scoring subjects had disappeared from the scene, and it was becoming increasingly difficult to obtain any result to provide evidence for ESP. The committe set up at the Ohio symposium reported on a few papers appearing after 1938 but then the committee appears to have been abandoned. Its main effect, coupled with the mounting criticism of Rhine's research methods, was to make it increasingly difficult for parapsychologists to obtain positive results. The group experiment with differential scoring gave results that were not dependent on the actual ESP test but on the selection of subjects for one category or the other. As a result a whole new area of research opened up in which it became possible to demonstrate, at least to the satisfaction of the investigators, a host of new properties of ESP.

NOTES

1. Betty M. Humphrey, "Success in ESP as Related to Form of Response Drawings: Clairvoyance Experiments," *Journal of Parapsychology* 10, no. 2 (1954): 78–106.

2. J. F. Nicol and Betty M. Humphrey, "The Exploration of ESP and Human Personality," *Journal of the American Society for Psychical Research* 48, no. 4 (1953): 133–78.

3. D. J. West, "ESP Performance and the Expansion-Compression Rating," *Journal of the Society for Psychical Research* 36, no. 660 (150): 295–308.

4. G. R. Schmeidler, "Separating the Sheep from the Goats," *Journal of the American Society for Psychical Research* 39, no. 1 (1945): 47–50.

5. W. R. Smith, E. F. Dagle, M. D. Hill, and J. Mott-Smith, "Testing for Extrasensory Perception with a Machine," *Data Sciences Laboratory Project 4610,* AFCRL–63–141 (May, 1963); and S. D. Kahn, "Studies in Extrasensory Perception," *Proceedings of the American Society for Psychical Research* 25 (October, 1952): 1–48.

6. M. Anderson and R. White, "Teacher-Pupil Attitudes and Clairvoyance Test Results," *Journal of Parapsychology* 20, no. 3 (1956): 141–57.

7. M. E. Rilling, Clare Pettijohn, and John Q. Adams, "A Two-Experimenter Investigation of Teacher-Pupil Attitudes," *Journal of Parapsychology* 25, no. 4 (1961): 257–59; and R. White and John Angstadt, "A Resume of Research into Teacher-Pupil Attitudes," *Journal of the American Society for Psychical Research* 55 (October, 1961): 142–47.

8

The Soal-Goldney Experiment

In Britain, Dr. S. G. Soal of Queen Mary College, London University, dominated research on ESP much as Rhine did in the United States. Soal first became interested in psychical research through meeting Mrs. Blanche Cooper, a well-known medium, in 1922. He took part in Woolley's 1927 radio tests of telepathy as one of the agents, and he repeated Ina Jephson's clairvoyance experiment. In neither of these early tests was any evidence found for ESP.

During the thirties, when Soal was carrying out extensive tests to check the claims made by Rhine, Soal's attitude was skeptical, and he was extremely critical of Rhine and his experimental conditions. At that time, Soal's investigations revealed no evidence to support Rhine's claims, and only one of his subjects obtained above-chance scores regarded as significant. He stated that, until the autumn of 1939, he believed that it was practically impossible to find persons, at any rate in England, who could demonstrate extrasensory perception by guessing cards.

However, in November 1939, according to Soal, it was suggested to him that he should reexamine the record sheets of his unsuccessful ESP tests to see whether any of the subjects were scoring, not on the target card but on the card one ahead or one behind in the target series. After doing this, he found that his most promising subject in the early tests, Mrs. G. Stewart, displayed significantly above-chance scores, both for the target one ahead and for the target one behind. He also claimed that, after checking the score sheets of the remaining subjects, a second subject, Basil Shackleton, a professional photographer, displayed similar high scores. Mrs. Stewart had been introduced to Soal in 1936, and in that same year Shackleton had first called to see him at the offices of the Society for Psychical Research in London. Shackleton had read an account of Soal's investigations in a Sunday newspaper, and he declared that he had come, not to be tested, but to demonstrate telepathy. J. Alfred, a barber by profession and an old friend of Soal's, happened to be present when Shackleton called, and he acted as agent. Shackleton did not succeed, at the time, in convincing Soal of his ability to guess the card being seen by some other person. The high displacement scores that Soal alleges he found three years later were the first indications of any striking effects in Shackleton's score sheets.

In 1941, with the collaboration of a council member of the Society for Psychical Research, Mrs. K. M. Goldney, Soal started a new investigation to test the telepathic abilities of Shackleton. The investigators aimed at designing a completely foolproof test, and the Soal-Goldney experiment of 40 sittings, held during the London blitz between January 1941 and April 1943, was to become the most extensive and best known of all experiments on extrasensory perception carried out in Britain.[1]

THE PROCEDURE

One basic procedure was used throughout the experiment, but it was not always enforced in full, and changes were introduced at some of the sittings. The first 38 sittings were held at Shackleton's studio on Shaftesbury Avenue; the remaining two, in the rooms of the Society for Psychical Research.

Shackleton guessed the identity of cards bearing drawings of animals seen by only one other person, the agent, situated in an adjoining room. The door between the two rooms was slightly ajar so that Shackleton could hear an experimenter (EA) in the other room call out when he was to record his guess, but the subject was seated in a position where he could not see the agent.

THE AGENT

The agent and the EA sat at opposite sides of a table. A screen, 31 by 26 inches with an aperture 3 inches square in its center, was placed across the table and screened the agent from the EA. Resting on the table, on the agent's side of the screen, was a rectangular box, about 16 inches wide by 10 inches high by 10 inches deep, with its open side toward him. Before each run of 50 guesses, five key cards, each bearing a different symbol, were shuffled by the agent or by an observer and placed face downward in a row in the box so that while they could be seen by the agent, they were screened from the view of other persons in the room. The key cards bore on their faces pictures of five animals: an elephant, *E;* a giraffe, *G;* a lion, *L;* a pelican, *P,* and a zebra, *Z.* The agent was instructed to lift one of the key cards, look at the symbol on its face, and then replace it during each trial.

The EA indicated to the agent which key card he was to look at by holding up a card bearing one of the numbers 1 to 5, so that it could be seen by the agent through the hole in the screen. Thus, if the number 3 appeared at the hole in the screen, the agent raised the key card occupying the position third from the left among the five cards that lay in the box before him, and after looking at the symbol on its face, he replaced it face downward in the box. The experimenter also called out the serial number of each trial so that it could be heard by Shackleton in the adjoining room, thus indicating when he was to record his guess.

The number that the EA displayed to the agent at the hole in the screen during each trial was decided by consulting a record sheet, which was composed of two columns of 25 entries each (see p. 103). Each column had two sections, *A* and *G*. Before each sitting, Soal entered one of the numbers 1 to 5 in random order 50 times in the *A* sections of the columns on a number of record sheets. These sheets were then kept under lock and key until brought to the sitting in a suitcase that was never out of his sight. At the start of each sitting, Soal produced these sheets of prepared random numbers, which were then serially numbered 1 to 50 to show the order in which they were to be used by the EA. The same number of blank record sheets were serially numbered. These were to be used by the percipient, Shackleton, who recorded his guesses in pencil in section *G* of the columns. Shackleton's guesses were not of the number of the key card but of the letter identifying the symbol shown.

THE PERCIPIENT

After hearing the serial number of the trial, Shackleton wrote down the initial letter of the animal which he guessed was depicted on the card being seen by the agent. He was watched throughout by a second experimenter, EP, to ensure that he wrote his guesses on the correct lines of the sheet.

RECORDING THE ORDER OF THE KEY CARDS

After each run of 50 trials, the five key cards in the box in front of the agent were turned up by the EA who was watched by the agent and by any observers present. The code showing which number each symbol occupied was then entered on the sheet of prepared random numbers that had been used by the EA during the run. Before the next run, the key cards were shuffled and replaced by the agent or observer. Eight or more sheets of 50 guesses were completed in this matter at a sitting.

SCORING

At the end of each sitting, the two sets of record sheets were brought together in the presence of the experimenters and any observers. The letters written down by the percipient on his record sheets were converted into numbers according to the positions that the key cards had occupied during the run and entered in the *G* column of the sheet of prepared random numbers used by the EA.

The percipient's guesses were checked against the targets for straight, 0, hits and for +1, +2, -1, and -2 hits. Plus two hits signified that the percipient's guess at, say trial 4, agreed with the target that arose at trial 6, that is, 2

FIGURE 8–1

Type of Record Sheet Used in the Soal-Goldney Experiment

SCORING SHEET

NAME ________________
DATE ________________

	G	A		G	A
5			5		
10			10		
15			15		
20			20		
25			25		

TOTAL CORRECT ____ TOTAL CORRECT ____

trials ahead. A duplicate set of records was then placed in a stamped envelope and posted, in sight of three persons, to C. D. Broad, Professor of Philosophy at Trinity College, Cambridge.

The main modifications to the basic design used at some of the sittings can be classified as follows:

1. *Experiments with counters.* In some experiments, instead of using sheets of prepared random numbers to decide which key card the agent should look at, the EA drew a counter from a bowl containing equal numbers of five different-colored counters. Each color denoted a position of one of the key cards. Soal, who acted as recorder, sat near the agent, where he could see the counters as they were displayed at the hole in the screen. After mentally converting the color into the appropriate number, he recorded it in the blank column of the record sheet. These records were later checked with Shackleton's guesses, using the same procedure as when prepared random numbers were employed to decide the targets. To carry out the above procedure, considerable skill is required, particularly when the calls are being made at a rapid rate.

2. *Clairvoyance experiments.* At some sittings, runs of 50 guesses were recorded under clairvoyance conditions. In these runs, the agent did not see the faces of the key cards either before or during the run; he merely touched the backs of the cards in accordance with the numbers that appeared at the hole in the screen.

3. *Prepared random numbers compiled independently.* At three of the sittings, to avoid any possibility that Soal was in collusion with either the percipient or agent, the sheets of prepared random numbers were prepared by someone other than Soal.

4. *Outside observers.* At some sittings, observers were present. They included C. E. M. Joad, a well-known philosopher, and C. A. Mace, professor of psychology, both at Birkbeck College, London University; H. Habberley Price of New College, Oxford University; and Sir Ernest Bennet, a member of Parliament.

FINDINGS OF THE SHACKLETON EXPERIMENT

Shackleton obtained high above-chance scores with three agents. In 3,789 of the +1-type trials with one agent, Miss Rita Elliott, in which prepared lists of random numbers were used, he scored 1,101 hits compared with the chance expectation score of 776 hits. The odds against such a score arising by chance are greater than 10^{35} to 1.

In the 1,578 +1 trials with this agent, in which the random series was obtained by drawing counters from a bowl at the normal rate, Shackleton obtained 439 hits compared with a chance expectation of 321. This gives odds against chance occurence of 10^{11} to 1.

In experiments using counters at the rapid rate of guessing, Shackleton scored at the chance level on +1 targets but greatly exceeded the chance score on +2 targets. That is to say, he now scored on the card that the agent would be looking at two trials after he was recording his guess. In 794 trials at the rapid rate, with Miss Elliott as agent, Shackleton obtained hits on 236 +2 targets, compared with the chance-expectation score of 159. The odds against this score arising by chance are more than 100 million to 1.

The clairvoyance experiments in which the agent did not look at the letter cards gave scores that did not differ significantly from those to be expected by chance. Cross-checks were also made by comparing the targets intended for the second 25 guesses on each sheet with the guesses made for the first 25 targets, and the targets intended for the first 25 guesses with the guesses of the second 25 targets. These cross-checks in no case showed significant deviations from chance scores, thus showing that the results were not due to characteristics of the number series or the manner in which the percipient made his guesses.

Shackleton was also highly successful during nine sittings in which Aldred acted as agent. With Aldred, he scored at above-chance levels both on the +1 and the -1 targets at the normal rate and on both the +2 and the -2 targets at the rapid rate. Thus, in 720 trials at the normal rate he obtained 203 hits on +1 targets and, at the same time, 207 hits on -1 targets. The odds against this result arising by chance are greater than 10^{11} to 1. At the rapid rate, his scores on +2 and -2 targets were equally impressive. With this agent, Shackleton scored significantly below chance on 0 targets.

Significantly above-chance results were also obtained at 2 sittings in which Mrs. G. Albert acted as agent, and at sitting 5, at which Mrs. Goldney acted as agent. She was not, however, very much impressed by her own abilities as a transmitter and did not act as agent again until sitting 12, two months later. On that occasion, over three runs, scores were low, and Mrs. Goldney never acted as agent again.

Shackleton's rate of scoring with the successful agents was such that his results at most of the individual sittings had extremely large odds against arising by chance. He was, however, unsuccessful with ten other agents.

After the experiments were over, Shackleton's powers waned. He emigrated to South Africa and was tested there for extrasensory perception, but he displayed no ability to obtain high scores. In 1961, he returned to England, but further tests again revealed no evidence for his precognitive abilities.

EVALUATIONS OF THE EXPERIMENT

In an extensive review of the experiment, C. D. Broad wrote:

> There was already a considerable mass of quite good experimental evidence for telepathy, e.g., in the work of Dr. Rhine and his colleagues at Duke

University, but Dr. Soal's results are outstanding. The precautions taken to prevent deliberate fraud or the unwitting conveyance of information by normal means are described in great detail, and seem to be absolutely water-tight.[2]

G. Evelyn Hutchinson, professor of biology at Yale University, wrote concerning the experiments: "they appear to be the most carefully conducted investigations of the kind ever to have been made," and that "Soal's work was conducted with every precaution that it was possible to devise."[3] Rhine spoke of the experiment with approval and compared it favorably with the best of the Duke experiments.

A research can be so carried out that no errors can be made to favor any theory or mislead anyone. All such safeguards should be included in the design of the experiment. As already demonstrated, in the Pearce-Pratt and the Pratt-Woodruff series the experiment was to set up that these precautions were included. Similar provisions were made against error in the Soal and Goldney experiments.[4]

The public has to take statements such as those made by Broad, Hutchinson, and Rhine on trust. However, it is reasonable to ask whether all thirty-five alternative hypotheses to ESP discussed by Rhine and his colleagues in 1940 were adequately eliminated in the Soal-Goldney experiment, whether the precautions against fraud were absolutely watertight, and whether the Soal-Goldney experiment, in fact, was conducted with every precaution that it was possible to devise as was claimed by the investigators.

By 1939, Soal had shown himself to be a careful and critical investigator. Unlike Rhine he had no overwhelming faith in the reliability of his fellows, and from the start it was stressed in the Soal-Goldney report that the investigators were aware of the necessity of adequate safeguards against trickery on the part of any participant. In their report, Soal and Goldney stated that they had given much thought and discussion to the question of making the conditions of the experiment "proof, so far as was humanly possible, against even the possibility of fraud, on the part of percipient and experimenters alike."[5] To decide whether the experiment supports the hypothesis of precognition, a critical examination must ensure that Soal and Goldney were successful in accomplishing their aim. In the event of some alternative explanation being found, the experiments cannot be regarded as providing *conclusive* evidence for precognition. They could then just as well be said to provide conclusive evidence for an alternative explanation.

SENSORY CUES

Any possibility of Shackleton's score having arisen through sensory leakage appears to have been eliminated by the fact that he scored on the symbol not yet seen by the agent and, in the experiments with counters, not yet decided by a process of random selection.

During the first 8 sittings, however, Shackleton called "right" immediately after he had recorded his guess. He was thus in a position to transmit information of what he had written back to the agent and others present. Thus, if Shackleton called "right" in a certain manner, such as by imposing a particular emphasis or delay, after he had written down one symbol, or even if the manner in which he said "right" was affected involuntarily by the symbol he had just written down, the agent could have been given information to enable him to move the appropriate key card for the following trial so that it occupied the position designated by the number card displayed by EA, thus securing a +1 hit. This possibility, however, was present after the eighth sitting on only one occasion.

It should also be noted that the speed at which the EA had to manipulate the cards was such that he would almost certainly have had to look ahead to the next symbol on his list at the time he was displaying his number card at the hole in the screen. The EA was thus in a position, consciously or unconsciously, to transmit information concerning the number series when he called out the serial number of the trial. The fact that the order of the key cards was unknown to the EA ensured, however, that he could not provide cues relating to the target, but merely to the number shown at the hole in the screen.

A TRICK ON THE PART OF AGENT AND PERCIPIENT

It is clear that the percipient could not have brought about his high scores by means of a trick unless he was aided by either the agent or the EA.[6] In considering the possibility of Shackleton having been aided by the agent, it becomes quite clear that above-chance results could have been obtained and that this possibility was not eliminated in the experimental design. I suggested one such system to Dr. Soal when he visited Cambridge University in 1949.

The percipient memorizes a series of five symbols, say *P, G, L, Z, E,* that he will write down on lines, say 5, 10, 15, 20, and 25 of his record sheet when listing his guesses. The agent memorizes the same information. During the experiment, whatever random number comes up at trial 5, the agent places card *P* into the position designated by the number that appears at the hole in the screen. The percipient thus scores a hit on trial 5. On the tenth trial, the agent attempts to place card *G* in the position designated by the random number that appears at the hole in the screen. He may not always be able to do so as the same random number may arise as at trial 6. If the percipient and agent have memorized five different symbols, they can expect to obtain, on the average, 3.36 hits in the 5 trials by means of this trick. In the remaining 45 trials, they should obtain an average of 9 hits, thus giving a total of 12.36

hits in 50 trials. Higher scores can be obtained by memorizing more symbols, but the trick then becomes difficult to implement. In order to produce precognitive +1 hits in the above example, the percipient writes down his guesses one trial ahead, that is, on lines 4, 9, 14, and so on.

There has been considerable discussion over the possibility of such a trick having been used, and during it Soal has pointed out that it is impossible to account for the high scores achieved at some sittings by its application. In addition, it is difficult to believe that the percipient and agent would go to the effort of memorizing long lists of symbols and their positions on the score sheets for week after week. The fact that such a trick could have been employed constitutes, however, a weakness in the experiment, and it is difficult to see how Soal and Goldney could claim that their design completely eliminated the possibility of fraud.

THE CRITICISMS OF GEORGE R. PRICE

In 1955, George R. Price, a research associate in the Department of Medicine at the University of Minnesota, in a brilliant analysis of ESP research dealt with the problems of trickery in considerable detail. One statement that must have impressed parapsychologists and their critics alike was:

> Surprisingly, it is not only believers who are reluctant to imagine fraud, but virtually all skeptics as well will prefer almost any other type of explanation. It would be tedious for me to cite statistics to show that "the knavery and folly of men" are indeed "common phenomena," for everyone is aware of this—in an intellectual way. But when we try to imagine knavery and folly in connection with a particular individual, we encounter a surprising emotional blockage, and the possibility seems unreasonable. And thus we find skeptics searching for every other conceivable sort of explanation. While the one explanation that is simplest and most in accord with everyday experience is dismissed as inconceivable.[7]

Price pointed out that if Soal himself had wished to cheat and had got others to collaborate with him, he could have faked high scores in a number of ways. He then described six methods that could, he thought, have been employed. In the following quotation Price is assuming that he is taking the part that Soal had in the experiment and that he is bent on trickery.

> (1) The percipient and the agent are "in the trick." The agent arranges the code as previously directed by me, and the percipient writes down a memorized sequence or takes a list from a drawer if no outsider is watching him. (This would be preferred procedure in most experiments except when an outsider determined the order of the code cards. It would succeed with outsiders as the EA and the EP.)

(2) The percipient and the agent (or the EA or an observer) are "in the trick." The code-card order is determined by an outsider. The agent (or the EA or an observer) notes this order, classifies it into 1 of 6 groups, and signals the group number to the percipient before or after the run. Only 2.6 bits of information are needed to designate a choice of 1 out of 6. For example, the agent glances at the backs of the cards and then says "Ready," "All ready," "Yes, I'm ready," "Yes ready"—and so forth. The percipient then takes from a drawer the designated guess sheet, which is already filled out in his hand-writing. (If the agent is an outsider, the EA or an observer can note the card order when it is recorded at the end of the run and signal it in the conversation then.)

(3) The percipient and the agent are "in the trick." The agent notes the card order and signals it (6.9 bits for 120 possible permutations) before the start of the run. The percipient has memorized a number sequence, and he uses the card order to encipher each number mentally. (This can work with outsiders watching both the agent and the percipient and shuffling the code cards; or if the agent is an outsider, the signaling can be done by an observer who shuffles the cards.)

Next consider some of the procedures that could be used even when the number sequence was not known to me in advance:

(4) The percipient and the agent are "in the trick." They have copied or memorized the same lists of letter symbols. During the run the agent records (concealed by the box) the numbers corresponding (precognitively) to the letters that he knows the percipient is guessing, and at the end he rearranges the code cards to give the desired degree of success. For example, with a record like that shown in figure 8–1 [a contingency chart compiled by the agent showing the number of times each symbol arose in each position], the agent could see that card arrangement *LEGZP* will yield a large number of hits. (This procedure would be particularly useful when the EA was an outsider.)

(5) The percipient and the EA are "in the trick." The EA learns the order of the code cards and signals information to the percipient during the run. The percipient has memorized a random sequence of letter symbols. The EA, in calling out the serial numbers, slightly alters his voice or timing a few times during each run (5 times per 50 trials to give 14 hits). Ordinarily the percipient is to guess at random, but at each signal he writes down the next letter on the memorized sequence. (I would use this method particularly in experiments when an outsider who wore glasses served as agent. Then the preferred experimental arrangement would be that in which the cards are turned face up for 30 seconds, the screen aperture would be located as it was in the Stewart sittings, and the lighting would be so arranged that the EA could see the cards by reflection in the agent's glasses.)

(6) The percipient plus the EA, the recorder, or the agent are "in the trick." In runs where the number sequence is generated by counters, I would

have the EA draw counters of the needed color at particular points, or the recorder could keep false records of counters drawn. And in some experiments, procedures 1, 4, or 5 could be used. . . .

The procedures that could give the highest degrees of success, and that thus would be chosen when I wanted simultaneous "-1" and "+1," or "-2" and "+2" successes, are procedures 1 and 3. Any of the others would be more than adequate for scores of 12.68 hits per run of 50, or 13.77 hits in 48 trials. For long-distance experiments, procedures 1 and 4 would work. Or I could employ procedure 2 by telephoning the percipient after the sitting to tell him which lists to mail in.[8]

Price pointed out that many other procedures were possible, but the six chosen for description were selected as examples of what could be done by simple means. He concluded:

[T]hus it should be clear that Soal's work was *not* conducted with every precaution that it was possible to devise. The work would have been enormously more nearly fraud-proof if Soal, instead of employing his highly complex arrangements, had simply had many different agents send directly from lists prepared by outsiders and given directly to the agent at the start of each run.[9]

Some time after Price's criticism of the experimental conditions, it was revealed that Mrs. Albert, one of the three agents with whom Shackleton obtained above-chance results, had stated after one sitting that when glancing through the hole in the screen, she had seen Soal, while acting as the EA, altering figures on the score sheet.[10] Whether Soal was in fact altering figures or merely tidying them up is immaterial. But, looking back at the records of the experiment, it is clear that this incident had a considerable effect on the duties allocated to the experimenters during subsequent sittings. The allegations were made after sitting 16 held on May 25, 1941, and from the detailed list of sittings in the Soal-Goldney report, it is found that until sitting 16, Soal had acted as the EA on all occasions when prepared random numbers were used to decide the targets. After that sitting, he never again acted as the EA but, at all sittings where prepared random numbers were used, he took the role of EP. (There was one sitting at which Soal was not present, but then the regular agent was also absent, and Shackleton scored at only the chance level.)

FURTHER INFORMATION ABOUT THE
SOAL-GOLDNEY EXPERIMENTS

Further information about Mrs. Albert's allegations that she had seen Dr. Soal altering figures on the record sheets was revealed in an article by R. G. Medhurst.[11]

He pointed out that the published details of the charge of fraud made by Mrs. Albert were incomplete. Three documents relating to the fraud episode were held by Mrs. Goldney, Soal's co-experimenter at the sitting in question, and in one of these, which had not been published, Mrs. Albert stated that she had seen Soal altering Figures 1 to 4 or 5 not once but four or five times.

CHECKING ALLEGATIONS OF FRAUD

Medhurst first showed that there was an excess of hits on target numbers 4 and 5 at the sitting in question (number 16), having odds of 70 to 1 against chance occurrence. He then investigated the random numbers employed.

It will be recalled that during the experiment, sheets containing 50 prepared random numbers (1–5) were used for each run of 50 targets. The identity of the target was then dependent on the animal card occupying the particular position (1–5) among the five animal cards under the box in front of the agent, indicated by the random number.

At the end of each run of 50 targets the order of the five animal cards was recorded on the sheet of random numbers. At the sitting in question, after the first four runs the checkup was made. The letters signifying Shackleton's guesses were converted into the relevant numbers according to the code for the animal cards and entered in the "guess" column of the record of prepared random numbers that had been employed during the run. Medhurst concluded that the alterations must have been made on the list of numbers identifying the target sequence during the checkup and probably after the second half of the sitting.

Medhurst also reported that a computer search revealed that the lists of random numbers had not been prepared in the manner stated by Soal and Goldney in their report.

THE METHOD OF FRAUD

In 1974 Christopher Scott and P. Haskell gave details of further findings.[12] They calculated that if target 1s were changed into 4s and 5s in order to score hits, this would lead to (1) a deficiency of 1s among the targets; (2) an excess of 4s and 5s among the targets; (3) a deficiency in the number of cases where a guess 4 or 5 arose against a target 1; and (4) an excess of hits on 4s and 5s. The data at sitting 16, when Mrs. Albert made her allegation, did not conform completely with these predictions. In particular the deficiency of 1s could not account for the overall score.

They then examined an alternative procedure, which was that an excess of 1s had initially been placed in the list of prepared random numbers together with a deficiency of 4s and 5s. The data should then display effects

(1) to (4) above and they also predicted two further effects: (5) A high-scoring rate on "4s" and "5s" together with the above chance score on 1s (since a 1 would only be changed to a 4 or 5 if it was a miss); (6) no tendency for the number of cases where Shackleton called 1 against a target 1 to exceed cases where he called 2 or 3 against a target "1." This would arise, since when a 1 arose in the target sequence it might be altered to "4" or "5" when the subject had called 4 or 5, but if he had called 1, 2, or 3, it would not be altered.

TABLE 8-1

Targets Remaining on the Score Sheets and Hits for Each Target Number Sitting 16 and All Relevant Sittings (nos. 8, 16, and first 3 sheets of 17)

| Target number | Sitting 16 | | Sittings 8, 16, and first 3 sheets of 17 | |
	Targets on score sheet	Hits on score sheet	Targets on score sheet	Hits on score sheet
1	59	20	142	46
2	78	20	156	38
3	77	19	167	40
4	64	33	158	79
5	58	26	143	62
Totals	336	118	766	265

All six effects were found to be present, both in the sitting where Mrs. Albert had made her allegations of fraud and in two other sittings (see table 8-1) at which two different agents took part. These included sittings in which the list of targets was written down by Dr. Soal when he was watching the colored token that appeared at the hole in the screen. Scott and Haskell showed that all the observations including the significant ESP score could be accounted for in terms of their proposed procedure by producing an example to fit the data.

They assumed the numbers of targets originally present at sitting 16 to be 1, 100; 2, 78; 3, 77; 4, 43; 5, 38 (the values for 1, 4, and 5 being arbitrarily selected to give a good fit when 41 targets were changed into 21 4s and 20 5s.

CONFIRMATION OF FRAUD

The calculated values will be seen to agree closely with those observed at the sittings. Since sitting 16 consisted of 7 sheets, each containing two columns of 25 guesses, it was only necessary to change a 1 into a 4 or 5 about three times in each column to bring about the observed scores.

After noting the fit of the data to their six principles, Scott and Haskell asked the question, ". . . can these findings be attributed to the capricious behavior of ESP?"[13] They pointed out that such a hypothesis faces several difficulties: (1) The observed anomalies appear in terms of *digit* symbols whereas the ESP task was defined in terms of *letter* symbols, the code linking the two being changed after each 50 guesses. (2) The anomalies are present in consistent form at three different sittings and with two different agents. (3) The effects are entirely those that Mrs. Albert's observations would lead one to expect, and they arise at the sitting in which she reported it.

Shackleton's guesses were converted into numbers—according to the position of the letter he called among the key cards—and these numbers were written in the "guess" column of the sheet of prepared random numbers employed for the run.

The effects noted by Scott and Haskell were not present in the letters written down by Shackleton; i.e., there was no tendency for high scores to arise on particular letters. It was only present in relation to the numbers—changed each 50 guesses—into which the subject's guesses were converted. The effects were, therefore, not related to Shackleton's guesses or to particular animal cards, but to the numbers allotted to the animal cards.

The effects would be expected to arise if Shackleton tended to score above chance only on the target numbers occupying particular positions under the box in front of the agent, but it would then be difficult to explain why there is a precise relationship between the score on target 1 and on targets 4 and 5 combined. Thus, Scott and Haskell could have put forward a seventh principle of the form

$$S_{45} = \frac{T_{45} + 20S_1 - 4T_1}{5}$$

There was a considerable dispute about the truth of the allegations made by Mrs. Albert. It is remarkable, however, that this keen-eyed lady made a specific observation—i.e., that 1s had been changed to 4s and 5s—and that if what she claimed to have seen did take place, it would have led to precisely those features in the record sheets that are in fact present. Mrs. Albert's observations led to testable hypotheses about the record sheets and these were confirmed.

THE MARKWICK FINDINGS

Further dramatic evidence that irregularities had arisen in the conduct of the experiment was provided by Betty Markwick in 1978.[14] Following up Medhurst's investigation of the prepared random numbers, she confirmed his findings that Soal had not followed the stated procedures. But also she discovered some remarkable properties present in the target numbers that clearly indicated that they had been tampered with.

First, she found two sequences of nineteen digits from two different sittings that matched. A further case was then found, involving the same two sittings where a run of twenty-four digits was involved. In other cases, two series matched when one of them was taken in reverse order. Eventually, following a computer search, it was found that there were frequent cases of matchings of this nature, many of which were not exact, but in which one of the series had extra interpolated digits. These interpolated digits almost invariably secured hits.

One such case is shown below where a bracketed number denotes a hit.

Sitting 24   [5] 1 [4] 3   2 5 3 [2]   5 4 3 [2] 5 [1]   1 4 2 3 2 1 5 4
Sheet (1a)

Sitting 24   5 1 4 3 [1] 2 5 3 2 [2] 5 4 [3] 2 5 1 [3] 1 4 2 [3] 2 [1] 5 4
Sheet (1a)

Markwick observed that, in one run of sitting 23, five single extra digits were present at five-digit intervals, and each of the five extra digits secured a hit. Overall, three out of four of the extra digits secured hits. When the targets corresponding to the extra digits were omitted, scores were at chance level.

Miss Markwick concluded that Soal might have left gaps when preparing the target lists (in ink) and then have penciled in 1s for future manipulation. This, it will be noted, is not inconsistent with Scott and Haskell's finding or with the finding that hits tended to arise at particular positions on the score sheets at some of the sittings. Miss Markwick interpreted these features as showing that there had been manipulation of the score sheets. She concluded that all the experiments reported by Soal had thereby been discredited.

Thus, when making sheets of prepared random numbers, particular locations would be filled with 1s in order to obtain extra hits when these were later changed. The remaining spaces would then be filled with "random numbers" taken from old sheets. This would confirm Scott and Haskell's findings that extra 1s were placed on the sheets before these were changed to secure hits. Soal was only in a position to perform this type of trick during sittings 1 to 16. For the remaining sittings, 17 to 40, he did not act as EA and, if the record of the experiments is exact, would have been in no position to change the record sheets.

Markwick's data show repeated runs with interpolated hits at the first seven sittings and then at sittings 12 and 16 (where Mrs. Albert made her allegations). After that they are present again in sittings 21–26, 29, and 36. At these sittings Mrs. Goldney was EA and had charge of the sheets of random numbers, while Soal was in the room with Shackleton. It is significant, however, as stated earlier, that at sitting 20 Shackleton called aloud his guesses so that they could be heard by Soal. This would have permitted the agent to change the positions of the key cards to suitable positions in accordance with the agreed positions on the score sheet. Shackleton need not have been in the trick, since Soal was recording the guesses and could have done this on a marked sheet.

It is now generally accepted, following Markwick's findings, that Soal indulged in trickery at some sittings. If the experimental report is accurate and the observers acted as more than dummies, it is difficult to see how Soal, unaided, could have cheated so as to give above-chance results at some of the later sittings where he had not compiled the lists of random numbers and where, according to the report, the target sheets were maintained and scored by other persons. It is now, however, generally agreed that the experiments cannot support the hypothesis of precognition.

CONCLUSIONS

Looking back at the Soal-Goldney experiment, it is clear that a great deal of time could have been saved had the original experimental report been accurate and complete. Soal did not work by himself as experimenter, but had a collaborator, Mrs. K. M. Goldney, and a most important feature of the experiments stressed in the report was the presence of observers who were there to ensure that nothing untoward took place. But on the one occasion when an observer reported witnessing a trick, this was not mentioned in the report or in the chronicle of the experiments. It was only subsequently reported following some pressure exerted by R. G. Medhurst.

Furthermore, since Soal was able to make changes on the sheets throughout the experiments, it is established by Markwick's findings that any attempt made to control his activities must have been ineffective. It is also clear that unless the accounts of the experiments are completely inaccurate, persons in addition to Soal must have assisted in the deception at some of the sittings.

The long history of events following the Soal-Goldney experiment indicates that, even in cases where a second experimenter or observers are present, they have little effect on a determined trickster. It is likely that if Soal had not been careless in filling in the random numbers around his interpolated digits, or if he had been more careful in changing digits, the Soal-Goldney experiment would still be claimed as providing conclusive evidence for precognitive telepathy. It is seen that its meticulous experimental design was an illusion. It tended to be too complicated in design, and insufficient attention was paid to the really important point—the targets being guessed. While independent observers were invited to attend the experiments, they at no time had control of the arrangements, and as a check on the experimental conditions, they were useless. If above-chance scores had been obtained when all the regular investigators were absent, or if a critical observer had been left free to change the experimental conditions imposing his own safeguards, a positive result would have been vastly more impressive.

NOTES

1. S. G. Soal and K. M. Goldney, "Experiments in Precognitive Telepathy," *Proceedings of the Society for Psychical Research* 47 (1943): 21–150.

2. C. D. Broad, *Philosophy* (1944): 261.

3. G. E. Hutchinson, "Marginalia," *American Scientist* 26 (1948): 291.

4. J. B. Rhine, *New World of the Mind* (London: Faber & Faber, 1954), p. 59.

5. S. G. Soal and K. M. Goldney, "Experiments in Precognitive Telepathy," p. 80.

6. C. E. M. Hansel, "A Critical Review of the Experiments with Mr. Basil Shackleton and Mrs. Gloria Stewart," *Proceedings of the Society for Psychical Research* 53 (1960): 1–42. (This number includes a reply by Dr. Soal.)

7. G. R. Price, "Science and the Supernatural," *Science* 122 (1955): 362.

8. Ibid.

9. Ibid.

10. S. G. Soal and K. M. Goldney, "The Shackleton Report," *Journal of the Society for Psychical Research* 40 (1960): 378. Dr. Soal's answer to Mrs. Albert's statements is noted in the same article.

11. R. G. Medhurst, "The Origin of the Prepared Random Numbers Used in the Shackleton Experiments," *Journal of the Society for Psychical Research* 46 (1971): 44–45.

12. C. Scott and P. Haskell, "Fresh Light on the Shackleton Experiments," *Proceedings of the Society for Psychical Research* 56 (1974): 43–72; also C. Scott and P. Haskell, "Normal Explanation of the Soal-Goldney Experiments in Extra-Sensory Perception," *Nature* 245 (1974): 52–54.

13. Scott and Haskell, "Normal Explanation of the Soal-Goldney Experiments," p. 53.

14. Betty Markwick, "The Soal-Goldney Experiments with Basil Shackleton: New Evidence of Data Manipulation," *Proceedings of the Society for Psychical Research* 56 (1978): 250–80.

9

Factors Relating to Card Guessing

The majority of ESP experiments carried out between 1915 and 1950 required subjects to guess the identities of symbols from among a known number of symbols depicted on cards. After 1932, the number of choices became standardized at five. This was probably due to the success of J. B. Rhine after he started using Zener cards. In view of the failure of subsequent investigators to confirm any of Rhine's results, this limitation of the number of targets may have been premature.

In addition, subjects were placed in a forced-choice position. They were not allowed to pass if they had no idea of the target. (It had been accepted on the basis of very little evidence that subjects did not know when they had been successful and when not.) Except under the most lax of conditions, subjects in card-guessing experiments are wrong more often than they are right. If a subject identified Zener symbols correctly on 5 occasions in 25 trials and passed on the remaining trials, he would achieve antichance odds of more than 3,000 to 1.

In one of his early experiments at Stanford, Coover tested to see whether a subject did better when he stated his degree of confidence at each trial. Results were compared for those trials in which the subject felt confident of success and others in which he had no confidence. Coover found no difference in the scoring rates under these conditions, but both sets of values were at the chance level.

MULTIPLE GUESSING

It might be expected that a high-scoring rate could be achieved by having a large group of subjects guess at the same series of targets. At each trial, the symbol among the five securing the most guesses, i.e., the mode, would then be taken as the identity of the target.

If this were the case, it would be a simple matter to demonstrate ESP to a skeptic by having him think of a symbol when screened from a large audience. Each member of the audience would identify his choice by pressing one of five buttons. The symbol selected by the most members of the audience would then operate an indicator to inform the skeptic of the symbol involved.

Similarly, having a subject repeatedly guess at the same list of targets might be expected to enable him to identify the targets with greater success than with a single attempt. Taking a high-scoring subject such as Hubert Pearce obtaining 10 to 12 hits per run of 25 trials, it may be asked what would happen if, having obtained 8 to 10 hits with a particular pack of cards, he is given the same pack again in the same order a few runs later. Would he obtain 8 to 10 or so hits again and would these be mainly on the same cards among the 25 as before or on other cards in the pack? In either case it becomes possible to identify targets in the pack to a level approaching 100 percent, given enough runs through the pack.

If the subject's performance changed, resulting in a below-chance score when, unknown to him, the original pack was used, this would reveal a further remarkable property of ESP known as psi-missing, in which subjects display ESP by scoring below chance. It may be noted that if a subject is a psi-misser, it is possible to change each of his guesses systematically to some other symbol in order to achieve above-chance results. Thus a subject obtaining n hits will obtain $(25-n)/4$ hits in each run of 25 guesses after changing his guesses as above. If n is less than 5, he will now score at above the chance level.

DECISION TIME

Given a length of time to make a decision at each trial, rather similar effects to those of multiple guessing might be expected. Coover's subjects were given 15 to 20 seconds to decide on their choice of symbol. In the Besterman, Jephson, and Soal experiment, subjects could take their own time and make as many guesses at each target as they wished before coming to a decision. In neither case were results at above-chance level. In some later experiments, subjects guessed at a rate approaching 0.5 seconds per card, i.e., almost as fast as the cards could be manipulated.

TELEPATHY AND CLAIRVOYANCE

Rhine decided that subjects were as successful under clairvoyance conditions as under telepathy conditions and that under the two conditions subjects showed no difference in their scoring rates. This is what might have been expected if above-chance scores in both cases were due to error and not to ESP. But since it was not possible to confirm the results obtained by Rhine using his methods of experiment, it was premature to make any such claim. It should be easier to design and conduct an experiment on clairvoyance than on telepathy since the activities of an agent do not have to be considered. The clairvoyance experiment carried out by Besterman, Jephson, and Soal was simple and sufficiently foolproof for most purposes. It is remarkable that the methods it employed were dropped almost completely in subsequent work. This may have been due to the fact that it was sufficiently well designed to have eliminated the main forms of error and reduced results to the chance level.

THE REPEATABLE EXPERIMENT

The main emphasis in parapsychology has been on providing a repeatable demonstration of ESP. In the absence of such a demonstration, there would be little point in investigating the properties of a hypothetical process before it has been made available for investigation.

The research at Duke University started with *exploratory* experiments, i.e., attempts to get some sort of result in loose conditions with the idea that once the experiment got a result, the method could then be tightened up. The difficulty was that as conditions were tightened up the results changed and the experiment no longer provided any evidence for ESP.

Eventually it was claimed that there was an "experimenter effect." Rhine and Pratt commented on the fact that some experimenters obtained only chance results after going through the standard testing procedures. Rhine and Pratt wrote: "Another major difficulty can be seen in the fact that some experimenters after a period of earlier success in obtaining extra-chance results in psi experiments have proved less effective in their later efforts. In such instances something apparently has been lost that was once a potent factor."[1]

In much scientific investigation the aim is to improve an experiment until anyone can confirm the result. At Duke the approach seems to have been to try method after method until a result was obtained. Thus the subjects in Rhine's first experiments were unsuccessful, possibly because they consisted of groups in a classroom who were thus at a distance from the cards. The methods that Rhine found successful in the main necessitated the subject being close to the cards.

DISTRIBUTION OF ESP ABILITY IN THE POPULATION

The early investigations were of individuals who were thought to have special abilities. Coover used a sample of 100 subjects and found none with ESP ability. Rhine, after testing groups of subjects, found no ability at the start of his research, but then after using Zener cards found the ability to be present in almost every psychology student whom he tested. He later claimed that ESP ability was present in a fifth of the population.

CONFIRMATORY TESTS

Before reporting an experiment it might be expected that a sufficient number of observations would be made so that the investigator could check his own results and demand high antichance odds before making any claims for his findings. This was done by S. G. Soal, whose experiments consisted of sitting after sitting at which high antichance odds were observed at most sittings.

With the disappearance of high-scoring subjects, reliance was placed on obtaining large numbers of guesses from groups of subjects. The scoring rate in these experiments was often such that about one extra hit was obtained in each 200 trials. Eventually, these experiments were less successful, following criticism of the methods employed.

By 1940, the main stages at which error could arise had been identified. The Pratt-Woodruff experiment at Duke University was intended to take account of these forms of error. The investigators sought to avoid error arising through selection of data. Error could arise if all observations were not included in the final assessment of results. The plan of the experiment was prepared in advance. All forms used to record details of the subject, guesses, and targets were registered in an office beforehand and had to be returned to the office after data had been collected and before the score was measured by counting the correspondence between targets and hits. The number of subjects and the number of trials to be carried out were planned before the experiment started and not changed thereafter.

The experiment was designed so that neither experimenter could bring about high scores unless aided by the other. One experimenter recorded the guesses, the other the targets on preregistered forms that were placed in a sealed box before the hits were counted. Separate records were also kept by each experimenter.

After the Ohio symposium (see p. 75) it had been generally accepted that in the initial planning stage the number of observations must be specified beforehand. This had to include the number of subjects to be tested, the number of trials to be made by each subject, and the conditions under which these trials were to be conducted. It is also clear from the study of recent experiments that the experimental plan must include safeguards to ensure that all points of procedure are carried out.

A pack of cards may be employed in two ways. In Coover's experiment, a pack of 40 cards was shuffled and cut before each trial; Rhine's pack of Zener cards was usually shuffled and cut before each run. In Coover's case, the possibility of error was present in the manner the cut was made, which could affect each target in the run. With Rhine's method, only the first and last trials in the run were likely to be affected.

Coover's control series allowed for any cutting tendency. In Rhine's laboratory a method of cutting using a paper knife was eventually introduced that was intended to remove error arising through the cut.

A further possible source of error arises if the subject sees the pack of cards before a run starts. Coover had his subjects at distances of from 1 to 10 meters from the cards, which were screened from the subjects. Rhine's subjects were close to the cards and had full view of the back of at least the top card of the pack and the sides of those just below it or at the bottom of the pack. Under these conditions, high scores were observed that were due to hits mainly arising in the first and last 5 trials.

DIFFERENTIAL SCORING

In the forties, the differential-scoring type of experiment was introduced in which one subgroup scored high and the other low. A feature of these experiments was that the average score of the whole group was usually at chance level, raising the possibility that the division of subjects into subgroups was not made independently of the ESP test scores. It should have been apparent that as much attention was necessary to maintain independence of the test scores and the division into subgroups as was paid to the maintenance of independence between guesses and targets in ESP tests.

INTERPRETATION OF RESULTS

Since the time of Sidgwick's pronouncement on the investigation of the Creery sisters, parapsychologists have tended to make excessive claims for their findings.

In the case of the Soal-Goldney experiment, C. D. Broad, professor of philosophy at Cambridge University, came to the conclusion that it provided evidence "which is statistically overwhelming for the occurrence not only of telepathy but of precognition."[2] Broad appears to have assumed that the result could only have been achieved if the percipient possessed powers of precognitive telepathy. If, however, there is any possibility—no matter how small—of some other explanation, the results of the experiment support that explanation as much as they support the probability of precognitive telepathy. The probability of 10 obtained in the experiment is that of the score having arisen by chance. It tells us nothing about the probability of precognitive telepathy.

To provide statistically overwhelming evidence for the occurrence of ESP in experiments of this nature requires satisfaction of two conditions: (1) the scores achieved by the subject must be such as are very unlikely to arise by chance, and (2) the experimental conditions must be such that only ESP could account for them.

The first condition is quite simple to assess. The percipient's score is compared with one expected to arise by chance. The frequency with which such a score would be expected to arise in a large number of such experiments if the guesses were purely random is calculated. In the case of Shackleton, it was found that his score would be expected to arise only once in about 1,034 similar experiments.

The second condition causes the difficulties. Any hypothesis for why the experimental result differs significantly from the chance expectation is dependent on what is known about the conditions under which the experiment was carried out. A low probability that a certain result will occur, as noted in the first condition, reveals nothing about the probability that ESP does or does not exist. It is entirely dependent on the second condition.

The weight attached to an experimenter's supposed proof of ESP is entirely dependent on how certain one can be that any alternative explanations of the result are entirely eliminated. The subject's score and the probability of its arising by chance serve merely to indicate whether an assessment of the experiment should be made at all.

NOTES

1. J. B. Rhine and J. G. Pratt, *Parapsychology: Frontier Science of the Mind* (Oxford: Blackwell, 1956), p. 132.

2. C. D. Broad, "Discussion: The Experimental Establishment of Telepathic Precognition," *Philosophy* 19, no. 74 (1944): 261.

Part Three

Contemporary Research

10

Testing ESP with a Machine

By 1965, card guessing was almost a thing of the past, and the repeatable experiment had failed to materialize. In that year, J. B. Rhine retired from the Parapsychology Laboratory, and in the same year Duke University withdrew its support. A new organization, The Institute for the Study of Man, was set up by Rhine outside the campus.

Since 1965, new developments have arisen in ESP research, the most important of which is the use of machines and automated procedures.

AUTOMATIC RECORDING

Although it is a simple matter to randomize targets, present them to a subject, and record his successes and failures, it is remarkable that few attempts were made to use machines until recent times. A machine constructed by Tyrrell in 1936 employed automatic randomization, presentation of targets, comparison of guess and target, and registration of hits and trials made.[1] When all these features were operating so that the testing was completely automatic and the targets were decided by the randomizer, subjects' results were consistently at the chance level. As soon as any human element was present, e.g., when Tyrrell compiled random numbers with his randomizer and then used these in an experiment without further use of the machine, the subject obtained above-chance scores.

VERITAC

The first full-scale investigation using automation was conducted at the United States Air Force Laboratories in 1963.[2] The investigators, William R. Smith, Everett F. Dagle, Margaret D. Hill, and John Mott-Smith, approached their

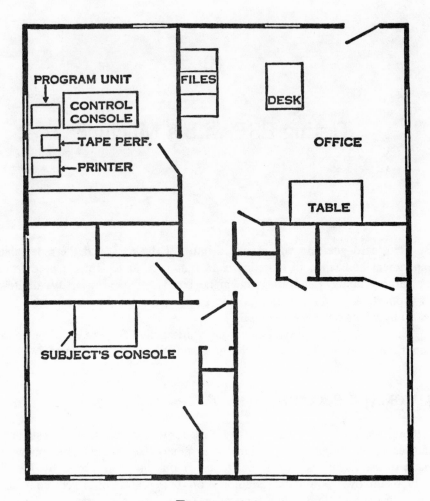

FIGURE 10–1

Layout of Rooms Used with VERITAC

research with the idea that it was a waste of time to conduct further experiments merely to demonstrate the occurrence of ESP and that it was more important to discover how ESP worked. The apparatus they used was called VERITAC. It automatically generated random targets, registered the subjects' guesses, compared them with the targets, and registered scores. There were two consoles in different rooms: the subject's console at which he indicated his guess at each trial by pressing a button, and a control console on which the targets were generated (figure 10–1) together with a printer to record targets and subject's responses.

The targets, consisting of the digits 0–9, were created by means of a random-number generator. The number selected by the generator at each trial appeared on an indicator tube on the control console. The subject's console contained two electromechanical counters that indicated to him the number of trials he had made and his number of successes. In addition, a light flashed on the console each time he secured a hit. Thus, the subject had partial knowledge of the result after each trial. Provision was made for the automatic recording of the targets, the number selected by the subject, and the time at which each trial was made. In addition, the total numbers of trials and hits were recorded. A record was also maintained to show the response time of the subject at each trial.

The rooms in which the consoles were situated were separated by a third room, and the doors between the rooms were kept closed during tests. VERITAC was checked for operational effectiveness, and several pilot studies were run to ensure that the apparatus was reliable in operation. The numbers generated by the randomizer were checked and found to meet rigorous statistical criteria for randomness.

Each subject had been given an indirect, probing interview that classified him as a sheep or a goat. The thirty-seven subjects each then completed 5 runs of 100 trials for each of three types of experiment:

1. *Clairvoyance.* At each trial the subject depressed the button representing the digit he thought had been selected, and it was indicated but not seen by anyone on the control console in the other room.
2. *Precognition.* Here the subject had to select the number he thought would be generated on the next trial. He started and stopped the random-number generator, and the numbers so generated were presented on the control console but were not shown to the subject or to anyone else.
3. *General extrasensory perception (GESP).* The subject indicated the number he thought had been selected. The target was shown on the control console in the other room where it was seen by one of the experimenters.

The group of thirty-seven subjects completed a total of 55,500 trials. It was found that neither the group as a whole nor any member of it displayed any evidence of ESP. The difference in scores between the sheep and the goats was also not significant.

The apparatus used in these tests was carefully designed and could be standardized and used by parapsychologists for testing extrasensory perception. A feature of VERITAC was that the subject was informed of the correct result after each guess. In most of the earlier card-guessing experiments, the subject completed at least 25 trials before learning how he had scored, and he had no means of knowing whether he had made a hit or a miss at each trial. If ESP is possible and exists to a small extent in most subjects, as some parapsychologists claim, performance would only be expected to improve if subjects are given the chance to learn from knowledge of results in previous trials.

THE EXPERIMENTS OF HELMUT SCHMIDT

In his 1975 review of ESP research, John Randall commented that in 1969 "an extraordinarily brilliant piece of work was being performed in the U.S.A. which was to lift parapsychology out of the doldrums and raise it to a position of respectability never before achieved."[3] According to Randall, this research confronted the critics with the most powerful challenge they had had to face so far, and parapsychology "was now about to enter the space age." Randall was referring to experiments carried out by Helmut Schmidt, a physicist at the Boeing Research Laboratories, employing a machine for randomization of targets and checking of scores.

Randall quoted a statement made in my earlier book about VERITAC in which I wrote that "an acceptable model for research has been made available by the investigators at the United States Air Force Research Laboratories." He then claimed that Schmidt's machine "satisfies all the requirements laid down by Hansel." This is certainly not the case. A machine may be well designed, foolproof, and accurate, but "an acceptable model for research" consists of more than a piece of apparatus. The words "model for research" were based on the report published by the VERITAC team in which they wrote: "A design of a scientifically rigorous experiment in ESP is presented as an acceptable model for work in this field."[4] While automatic generation of targets and scoring are desirable in an ESP experiment, the design and conduct of the experiment are of paramount importance. The use of a machine—however foolproof—does not permit the experimenter to drop other experimental safeguards.

It is necessary to examine in detail the apparatus and the experimental procedures employed by Schmidt to see whether they can be considered to be as adequate as those employed by the VERITAC investigators.

THE RESEARCH OF HELMUT SCHMIDT

In 1969, Dr. Helmut Schmidt published details of research carried out at the Boeing Research Laboratories,[5] in which he claimed that subjects, when tested on a machine, were able to predict a target before its identity had been established by a process of random selection. His results were, thus, contrary to those obtained with VERITAC. Schmidt had constructed a machine for use in the experiments that generated a random sequence of four targets and gave automatic recordings of the number of hits and trials. The subject attempted to predict which of the four targets would arise during each trial.

The targets consisted of four lamps (blue, green, orange, and red). The subject signified his selection of a particular lamp by pressing one of four buttons. Before each trial, the lamps were unlit. After the subject had pressed a button indicating his guess, the correct lamp lit up so that he became aware of whether he had predicted correctly or not.

Randomness was achieved in the following manner. An oscillator generated pulses at the rate of a million a second. These operated a two-bit counter and decoder giving four outputs that ran in a repeating (A B C D A B C D A B . . .) sequence. After the subject had pressed a button, a circuit was completed, stopping the counter and permitting the output present to light up the lamp.

The random nature of the target sequence was achieved by utilizing the unpredictability of quantum processes, i.e., the unpredictability of the time at which an electron is emitted by a strontium-90 source. This source was arranged so that electrons arrived on a Geiger-Müller tube placed near to it at an average rate of 10 per second. The oscillator was continually running, but it was gated so that the counter was only operated after the subject pressed his button. The four possible outputs then arose in rapid sequence during the interval between the subject pressing a button to signify his choice and the next electron emitted by the strontium-90 source arriving at the Geiger-Müller tube. Randomness was dependent on the unpredictable time at which the electron was emitted. Following a delay of 1/10000th of a second, the relevant lamp then lit up. Thus the target had not been decided at the time the subject pressed his button.

When the subject had pressed his button, a lamp lit showing him the correct answer, and when he released his button there was a delay of half a second, after which the counter again started running. The half-second delay enabled external recording equipment to be operated, which indicated the target selected by the machine and the button pressed by the subject.

Electromagnetic counters in the machine registered the number of attempts and the number of hits. In each case two counters were provided. One gave a running total and could not be reset. The other one could be reset when required. These counters could be switched in or out of circuit and, thus, did not record every trial made on the machine.

The following safety features were built into Schmidt's machine:

1. More than one button could not be pressed at the same time and also operate to give a hit.
2. A millionth of a second after a button was pressed the other buttons were made inoperative until the cycle of operations was completed and all buttons had been released. If two were pressed within a millionth of a second, the mechanical counters became blocked, and the trial was not registered.
3. Mechanical reset counters were located on the front panel, but nonresettable counters provided a check on these. The machine could also be connected to a paper-tape puncher, which recorded details of buttons pressed and targets generated.

The resettable counters were usually reset after 100 trials, and the results written down by the experimenter. The nonresettable counters could be read at the beginning and end of a series of trials and compared with the readings recorded from the resettable counters. They could also be switched out of operation when not required.

Initially, Schmidt tested a large number of people—"perhaps 100"—the number is not specified. The subject sat in front of the machine, the front panel of which contained the four pushbuttons and four corresponding lamps. The subject then tried to predict which lamp would light at each trial by pressing the relevant button. One of the four lamps then lit indicating the correct target, and the counters advanced to show the total number of trials made and the number of hits achieved.

Schmidt found that only a few persons seemed to be "outstandingly successful in predicting random numbers."[6] Three of these persons took part in the first experiment.

THE FIRST MAIN PRECOGNITION EXPERIMENT

The tests were carried out in the subjects' homes. During tests the paper-tape puncher was connected and the electromechanical reset and nonreset counters for hits and trials were switched on. Between tests, the paper-tape puncher and the nonreset counters were disconnected, and the subjects were allowed to play with the machine.

It had been decided in advance to evaluate all the events recorded on tape and no others. The total number of trials to be made was specified in advance as being between 55,000 and 70,000. It is not clear why a precise number was not specified for each subject. In fact, 63,066 trials were made.

Great care was said to be taken to work only under what seemed to be "psychologically favorable conditions."[7] The number of trials to be made each day was determined by the subjects' and experimenters' mood and "availability." A single experimenter, Dr. Schmidt, took part. He was present at most of the tests, but in certain cases the subjects worked without an experimenter being present.

The paper punch was employed during all tests, and it was pointed out in the report that record forging by the subject would have been extremely difficult, as it would have required advancing the nonreset counters by electrical impulses and the punching of properly coded holes into the paper tape.

The first subject (Mr. O.C.) was tested on eleven days between February 20 and March 9, 1967. Over this period there appear to have been consistently above-chance scores. In all, O.C. gained 5,928 hits in 22,569 trials as against the chance-expectation score of 5,642.25 hits. The odds against chance of such a score are about 1,000,000 to 1.

The second subject (Mrs. J.B.) was tested on five days and produced 4,153 hits in 16,250 trials. This represents 90.5 more hits than expected by chance (odds about 8 to 1). The third subject (K.M.R.) achieved 6,377 hits in 24,247 attempts. This represented 315.25 hits above the chance level with odds against chance occurrence of around 100,000 to 1. Combining the results for the three subjects gave 16,458 hits in 63,066 trials. Such a result had odds against chance greater than a million to one.

The results for the three subjects are shown in table 10-1 where it will be seen that the scoring rate for the three subjects combined was such that about 1 extra hit above the chance level was obtained in every 100 trials.

TABLE 10-1
Hits and Above-Chance Odds Achieved by
Three Subjects in First Main Experiment

(Chance-occurrence figures corrected for optional stopping)

Subject	Trials	Hits	Hits above chance	Odds against chance occurrence (approx.)
O.C.	22,569	5,928	285.75	27,000:1
J.B.	16,250	4,153	90.5	6.5:1
K.M.R.	24,247	6,377	315.25	94,000:1
Total	63,066	16,458	691.5	10^8:1

THE SECOND MAIN PRECOGNITION EXPERIMENT

In the second main experiment[8] one of the subjects (K.M.R.) was replaced by S.C. (the sixteen-year-old daughter of O.C.). In these tests the subject had the option either to predict which lamp would light next or to try to select a lamp which would not light, thus aiming at a low score on the machine. Whether to try for a high or low score was decided at the beginning of each session, and the two modes of guessing were recorded on the tape in different codes (details of which are not given) so that the computer could separate the two types of test.

Four sessions were held with subject O.C., who only tried for high scores, eleven sessions with J.B., who tried for both high and low scores, and six sessions with J.C., who only tried for low scores. It was decided in advance to make a total of either 20,000 or 40,000 trials. In fact 20,000 were made. The number of trials in which high or low scores were to be attempted was not specified in advance. The results were as in table 10-2.

It will be seen that while the total hits—i.e., where the button depressed agreed with the target—were 23 below the chance-expectation level (a purely

TABLE 10–2

Hits Above Chance Level and Successes Achieved by
Three Subjects in Second Main Experiment

Subject	Aim of subject	Trials	Hits above chance expectation	Successes above chance expectation
O.C.	High score	5,000	+66	+66
J.B.	High score	5,672	+123	+123
J.B.	Low score	4,328	−126	+126
S.C.	Low score	5,000	−86	+86
Totals		20,000	−23	401

chance result), the successes—i.e., including cases where the hits belwo chance were regarded as successes when the subject was aiming at scoring low— were 410 above the chance level (a result having odds of greater than 10^{10} against chance).

PRECAUTIONS NECESSARY WHEN USING A MACHINE

While the use of a machine eliminates some of the obvious causes of error in ESP research—e.g., nonrandomness of targets and errors in recording hits and misses—its use does not mean that all other experimental precautions can be dropped. Assuming for the moment that the machine was foolproof, there are several obvious features of the experiments that require investigation. In particular the use of a system in which the subject tried for high or for low scores requires special experimental safeguards.

Given a satisfactory machine with nonresettable counters permanently in circuit sealed up within it, that machine should show a significant excess of hits (or a deficiency, if it is used exclusively for attempts at low scores) after a period of use, provided it is only used either for the high- or for the low-score condition. If, for example, the score registered on the machine after a period of use had a probability of 10^{-6} of having arisen by chance, such a result would be much more striking than the type of data so far produced by Schmidt.

In his second experiment the significance of the result was not revealed by the nonresettable counters inside the machine, since these showed only a surplus of 23 hits in 20,000 trials. The odds of ten thousand million to one, claimed as those appertaining to the result of the experiment, apply to data extracted from the machine on the print-out but selected according to whether the subject was trying to secure hits or misses.

While the tape-punch recording showed which type of attempt was being made, the data was not, so far as the report indicates, obtained on a continuous tape, nor were precautions taken to ensure that all those tapes were employed in the final analyses and checked against other records of counter readings. The presence of observers (or a second experimenter), the use of separate machines for high- and low-score attempts, the fixing of the exact dates and numbers of trials to be made by each subject, and the counterchecking of all records, were precautions that should have been included.

CLAIRVOYANCE EXPERIMENTS

Rather than proceed further with the investigation of precognition or even to substantiate his data with the use of independent investigators, Schmidt next turned to clairvoyance.[9] He used the same type of machine, but this time the target—rather than being decided by a random-number generator after the subject made his choice—was obtained from a prepared list of randomized

TABLE 10-3

Clairvoyance Experiments

Hits Above Chance Level Obtained
Under High- and Low-Aim Conditions for Three Subjects

Subject	Aim	Trials	Hits above chance level
D.W.	High	3,687	+56
V.H. and M.K.	High	542	−10
J.B. and R.L.	High	718	+8
O.C.	High	2,144	+54
Total		7,091	+108
D.W.	Low	2,381	−60
V.H. and M.K.	Low	2,576	−48
J.B. and R.L.	Low	250	+5
O.C.	Low	2,702	−49
Total		7,909	−152
Overall totals	High and low combined	15,000	−44

targets punched on tape, one such target being available for each trial. The target had, therefore, been determined before the subject recorded his guess, although the preselected lamp remained unlit until a button was pressed.

The results shown in table 10-3 had a remarkable similarity to those in the second precognition experiment. The total of 15,000 trials was specified, but the total number of attempts using each condition (high or low scores) was not specified. Again subjects aimed at either a low or a high score, but the number of attempts using each subject was not specified in advance.

The overall deficiency of hits recorded on the counters in the machine was 44 in 15,000 trials—indicating that the built-in counters did not provide any evidence that the users of the machine had displayed any ESP ability. The subject was not obtaining a significant number of hits on the correct target. Only when positive and negative deviations were combined as "successes" from data recorded on the external recording equipment were any peculiarities observed in the result.

WEAKNESSES IN DESIGN

A machine could be constructed that would carry out a complete test procedure. The subject would have to "beat the machine." This was not the case with either Schmidt's machine or VERITAC. They each consisted of a tool that the investigator could use to enable a randomized series of targets to be generated and to provide automatic checking of guesses against targets. The precautions necessary for shuffling cards adequately when using them and independently recording guesses and hits are catered to by the machine. But other precautions that are of equal importance are left to the investigators. It would have been a simple matter to ensure that the safeguards listed at the Ohio symposium were observed together with other safeguards the necessity for which has become apparent since that time.

The first question that arises is whether the machine was reliable. Unlike VERITAC, Schmidt's machine was constructed from discrete components to provide a custom-built test apparatus. Schmidt states that soon after it was built a physicist demonstrated that he could "beat" the device.[10] After this a new apparatus with additional safety features was built. This is stated to have been "electronically and statistically checked."[11]

The statistical checks were made by letting the apparatus run for long periods and testing outputs for randomness. It is possible, however, that electronic defects were linked with nonrandomness. In a machine of this type that incorporates solid-state switching, electromagnetic counters, and manual ON and RESET switches, electronic irregularities are most likely to arise at the start and finish or when the electromagnetic devices are in operation. Defects may also be time dependent, for example, the power-supply arrangements may be such that interference via the main supply may arise at particular times of the day when other apparatus is in use.

Full details of the apparatus and the manner in which it was used are not given. It is clear that the paper-tape recorder and the mechanical counters could be disconnected and that switches could be adjusted to switch mechanical counters on and off. Checks for randomness could have been made by incorporating a control series during each run, or with adequate maintenance of records from an analysis of recorded targets and responses. The main form of bias that is likely to be important is in the lengths of the runs of symbols in the target series. This arises owing to the tendency of most people to display prediction tendencies of a systematic nature. A simple way to test for such tendencies is to incorporate a "control guessing system" within the machine. In its simplest form this changes its guess to something else in the event of its guess being similar to the preceding target.

EXPERIMENTS AT SRI

Experiments using a machine performing essentially the same functions as that of Helmut Schmidt have been conducted by Russell Targ, Phylllis Cole, and Harold Puthoff at the Stanford Research Institute (SRI).[12] They have not published details of their investigations in a journal although the intention of doing so is stated in the report. Details of the experiments together with a critical evaluation have, however, been published by Martin Gardner in the *Scientific American*.[13] It appears that the research was funded by an $80,000 grant from NASA. Gardner comments: "The story of the failure of this expensive experiment is almost a paradigm of what has happened numerous other times in ESP research. High-scoring subjects are first identified by loosely controlled screening, then as their testing proceeds, under better (that is, more complex) controls, their psi powers mysteriously fade."

In these experiments, the aim was both to use a machine that would provide automatic generation and checking of targets and to give training on ESP recognition by providing knowledge of results after each trial. As stated in connection with VERITAC, such feedback cannot affect the success rate provided the target series is random. But it may be argued that if there is some degree of ESP ability present in the population, as suggested by Rhine and others, then subjects should learn to use this ability through knowledge of results so that their scoring rate becomes improved.

The machine showed four targets represented on 35-mm. slides. After the subject had signaled his guess by pressing a button, the relevant slide lit up so that he could see whether he was correct or not, and in addition a bell sounded following a correct choice. The total hits and trials for each run were shown on counters on the front panel. The subject could also, if he desired, press a "pass" button and proceed to the next target without the machine recording a trial.

The machine was used to test clairvoyance by changing the target after the subject had made his choice and before he made his next attempt. Each run consisted of 25 trials. A record of runs, hits, and misses was maintained on special score sheets or, on some occasions, by employing a print-out. Four series of experiments were reported in which the experimental conditions were varied.

PHASE 0 (PILOT STUDY)

After about 100 trials had been run on the device by friends and fellow employees, two individuals were asked to act as subjects. Subject A_1 worked at home. The scores for each run were recorded on prepared score sheets by his father. Subject A_2 recorded his own data on the prepared score sheets, working the machine in the SRI Laboratory.

Under these conditions, A_1, in making 9,600 guesses, averaged 26.06 hits per 100 trials (as against the chance-expectation value of 25). The odds against this score arising by chance are about 120 to 1. Subject A_2 achieved a scoring rate of 30.5 with odds against chance of 500,000 to 1. Each subject's scoring rate improved as the tests proceeded.

PHASE 1 EXPERIMENTS

Phase 1 was intended to screen 145 volunteer subjects consisting of adults and children. They worked unsupervised in one of three laboratories, either at the institute or in a school. During these tests the machine provided a print-out on paper tape.

The group as a whole produced 105,890 hits in a total of 423,000 trials. This is not significantly above the chance-expectation value of 105,750 hits.

One subject (A_3), however, had a scoring rate of 29.57 per 100 trials with odds against chance of greater than a million to one. One other subject had a scoring rate having odds of 200 to 1 against chance, and a further nine subjects had scores with odds of greater than 20 to 1 against chance. Except in the case of A_3, the results are not unexpected in view of the fact that 145 subjects were tested.

PHASE 2 EXPERIMENTS

The aim of Phase 2 was to carry out further, more rigorous tests with successful subjects. The conditions here were tightened up by having the printer located in the experimenter's office, remote from the subject. Twelve subjects who had done well in earlier experiments were tested (including subject A_3).

Under these new conditions, none of the twelve subjects who had been outstandingly successful in the previous experiment obtained a result that was significantly above the chance level. The investigators did not interpret the difference between this result and the earlier tests as indicating that anything untoward had occurred in the less rigorously conducted experiments. They thought that the difference in results might have been due to the fact that in the second experiment the subjects were aware that they were in a test situation. They state that their subjects uniformly complained that in the revised experimental conditions "it all felt different, being connected to a computer."[14] However, in the Phase 2 experiment the print-out was not in the same room as the subject, and he need not have been aware of its use. In the Phase 1 experiment the print-out was creating a great deal of noise and was located in the room with the subject.

PHASE 3 EXPERIMENTS

Here the investigators stated that they wished to examine the hypothesis "that the more complex the observation system of a subject's performance, the more gross is the perturbance of his perceptual channel."[15]

They thought that an unfamiliar experimenter, or the presence of a print-out apparatus would have adverse effects on the subject. In Phase 3 they attempted to rehabilitate selected subjects' high scores by returning to the experimental conditions of subject A_1 in Phase 0. Here, it is stated, an observer seated with the subjects recorded the score at the end of each run of 25 trials. (In fact, in the earlier part of the report discussing Phase 0, *data collection*, it is stated that one of the two subjects "recorded his own data on the prepared score sheets.")[16]

Seven subjects who had achieved significantly above-chance scores in the pilot study and Phase 1 (screening) experiments acted as subjects. A new subject also took part. In the Phase 3 experiments, there was an experimenter with the subject in sessions carried out both in his own home and in the SRI Laboratory.

Seven of these subjects now produced scores at the chance level (odds less than 20 to 1). The eighth subject (A_3) worked under different conditions. He, it seems, expressed a desire for "practice sessions at various points during the experiment."[17] He specified, prior to any set of trials, when he wished to practice. His results are shown in table 10–4.

TABLE 10–4

Scores Obtained by Subject A_3 in Practice and Test Sessions

	Presentation	Hits	Surplus	Odds against chance
Trials	2,500	697	+72	2,000 to 1
Practice	4,500	1,143	+8	4 to 1
Total	7,000	1,840	+90	148 to 1

WEAKNESSES IN THE EXPERIMENTS

In general, these experiments show that in Phase 0 and 1, where the experimental conditions were relatively loose, a significant above-chance result was obtained that was mainly dependent on one subject (A_3). When conditions were tightened up, as in Phase 2, by placing the subject in another room and presumably under the supervision of an experimenter, the high scores were no longer obtained. After relaxing the conditions, subject A_3 again achieved a score having a low probability of chance occurrence. This was not the total score recorded by the machine, but the score obtained after removing the scores made under practice conditions.

These experimental results are again of importance in showing that a testing machine in itself will not eliminate the possibility of error or trickery. Since subject A_3, and possibly others, obtained above-chance scores under Phase 1 conditions but not under those of Phase 2, a reasonable suggestion would be that the difference in the conditions was responsible for the difference in results obtained.

Targ and Puthoff state that one change made in Phase 2 was to place the "fairly noisy printer" where it was remote from the subjects.[18] They thought that the clatter of the printer might have been a distraction. The result after moving the printer to another room was, however, to reduce scores to the chance level.

It should be noted that there was only one outstanding subject, referred to as A_3 in the report. Under Phase 1 conditions, when he worked alone in the room with the print-out, he obtained high scores. He was unable to maintain his impressive performance when the print-out was moved to another room.

Since he was a scientist employed at SRI, he may have been familiar with the operation of the print-out apparatus. It would thus be essential to ensure that when he worked alone with the apparatus and obtained high scores, it was not possible for him to interfere with the apparatus or with the print-out record.

Discussing Martin Gardner's criticisms in the *Scientific American* article, Targ and Puthoff point out that subjects made runs of 25 trials and that these trials were automatically printed on continuous fanfold paper tape, which carried a permanent record of every "trial, machine state, and trial number from 1 to 25 for each run." They state that after 8 to 10 runs the subject "would bring the continuous fanfold tape to one of the experimenters for entry into the experimental log."[19] They claimed that the tapes were always delivered intact with all runs recorded.

An essential control feature of any experiment is to ensure that all records are preserved in the final assessment. With cumulative unresettable counters inside the machine, it is possible to take precautions to ensure that this is done. With a print-out this is possible, provided there can be no selection of sheets handed to the experimenters—or included in the final report. This requires that all recording is done on a single, continuous uncut tape or that every run in the machine has a serial number that is preserved on a nonreset-table counter within the machine and that it is marked on the tape. This counter must indicate the serial number of every run made on the machine after it is initially constructed and put into use. The final report must show that these serial numbers are continuous and account for all runs made on the machine. In the Pratt-Woodruff experiment (chapter 6) this precaution was taken by having standard score sheets serially numbered in the office and maintained there after each subject had been tested. In the experimental session each subject's score sheet was inserted through a slit into a locked box by an experimenter and checked by the second experimenter at the end of each run. A further independent record was kept by each experimenter.

Targ and Puthoff appear to have been blissfully ignorant of the need for precautions to ensure that experimenters could not select data. It is necessary not only to embody such precautions in the experiments but also to have checks to ensure that any such features are rigorously adhered to during the course of the experiment. This requires that each experimenter is checked by a second experimenter and a record made each time a check is made.

Targ and Puthoff state, in reply to Gardner's criticism, that the tapes were always delivered intact and not torn into "disconnected bits and pieces."[20] But from their own descriptions, subjects took along the tape after they had torn it off the remainder of the reel contained in the machine. What precautions were taken to ensure that all runs made by the subject were included on the tape, that all tape torn off was handed in, and that it was all included when arriving at the final figures? In the absence of a predetermined number of runs, the subject could ensure that his record started and (or) finished with an above-chance score. The machine printed a cumulative trial number from beginning to end of a session. But switching the machine off and on again would presumably ensure that the subject could reject an unsatisfactory initial run or initial guesses and restart, since the counters were electronic, i.e., they would at that time have reset at switch off. The subject need not have included his first run until he had achieved one that was above chance.

In general, the criticisms of experimental procedure expressed in connection with Schmidt's experiments also apply to the SRI experiments. Although three investigators prepared the report, they do not appear to have been involved together in each test in a manner that would provide an adequate check either on each other or on the subjects.

NOTES

1. G. N. M. Tyrrell, "Further Research in Extra-Sensory Perception," *Proceedings of the Society for Psychical Research* 44, no. 48 (1936): 99–116.

2. W. R. Smith, Everest F. Dagle, Margaret D. Hill, and John Mott-Smith, "Testing for Extra-Sensory Perception with a Machine," *Data Sciences Project 4610* (May, 1963).

3. John Randall, *Parapsychology and the Nature of Life: A Scientific Appraisal* (London: Souvenir Press, 1975), p. 121.

4. Smith et al., "Testing for Extra-Sensory Perception with a Machine," p. 140.

5. Helmut Schmidt, *Anomalous Prediction of Quantum Processes by Human Subjects,* Boeing Scientific Research Laboratories Document D1.82.0821, Plasma Plastics Laboratory (February, 1969).

6. Ibid., p. 11.

7. Ibid., p. 22.

8. Ibid., p. 28.

9. Helmut Schmidt, "Clairvoyance Tests with a Machine," *Journal of Parapsychology* 33 (1969): 300–306.

10. Schmidt, *Anomalous Prediction of Quantum Processes by Human Subjects,* p. 21.

11. Ibid.

12. R. Targ, Phyllis Cole, and H. Puthoff, "Development of a Technique to Enhance Man/Machine Communication," obtainable from Stanford Research Institute, Menlo Park, California 94025. Final report covering period from April 15, 1973 to May 15, 1974.

13. Martin Gardner, "Mathematical Games: Concerning an Effort to Demonstrate Extra-Sensory Perception by Machine," *Scientific American* (November, 1975): 113-18.

14. R. Targ et al., "Development of a Technique to Enhance Man/Machine Communication," p. 34.

15. Ibid., p. 35.

16. Ibid., p. 18.

17. Ibid., p. 38.

18. Ibid., p. 31.

19. R. Targ and H. Puthoff, *Mind-Reach* (New York: Delacorte, 1977), p. 181.

20. Ibid.

11

Telepathy in Dreams

The possibility of dreams being affected by telepathy has been investigated since 1960 by Dr. Montague Ullman, a New York psychiatrist. His work eventually led to the setting up of the Dream Research Laboratory at the Maimonides Medical Center in Brooklyn, New York. Experiments conducted there by a team of investigators are claimed to provide conclusive evidence for ESP arising during dreaming.

The dream research reported in 1973 by Ullman, Stanley Krippner, and Alan Vaughan in their book *Dream Telepathy*[1] has been said, in the appendix to that book by Dr. Berthold Eric Schwarz, a consultant psychiatrist at the Brainwave Laboratory, Essex County Medical Center, New Jersey, to herald "the long awaited breakthrough and the beginning of a new era in parapsychology."[2]

In their summary of experiments, Ullman, Krippner, and Vaughan give details of some ten investigations. Two of these were screening studies in which twelve subjects were tested for one night each in the attempt to find successful subjects for later research. In a single night's test the dreams of the subject were compared with a target viewed by another person to see whether there were signs of ESP. The main results reported in *Dream Telepathy* were obtained by eleven subjects, each tested for several nights. Of the ten experiments, seven are reported as having given a result with odds of up to 250 to 1 against arising by chance. Two of the experiments were conducted on subjects who had done well in screening tests but who then failed to give a significant result when retested. As the experiments proceeded, changes were introduced into the design, procedures, and the statistical analysis to make them more watertight, but the main features of the experiments are as described below.

THE BASIC METHOD

An agent concentrated on a picture and attempted to influence by telepathy a sleeping person so that his dreams would display features in common with the picture.

The subject slept in a special room situated at a distance of 96 feet from the room occupied by the agent. Electro-oculogram (EOG) electrodes were attached to the subject's head. The EOG measures the potential difference between the retina at the back of the eye and the cornea. By placing electrodes on each side of the eye, its movements may be detected through the changes in potential arising between the electrodes. It affords a measure that can detect about 1° of lateral eye movement. Rapid eye movements have been found to arise during dreaming. Thus, by observing the subject's EOG, an experimenter in an adjoining room detected when he started to dream. He then alerted the agent so that he could concentrate on a randomly selected target picture. When the eye movements ceased, indicating that dreaming had ended, the experimenter was able to awaken the subject through an intercom system and obtain details of his dreams. The subject might be asked questions by the experimenter, after which he could go to sleep again. He might be re-awakened several times during the night in this manner. Next morning additional information was obtained from the subject in an interview conducted by the experimenter. Both the reports of the subject about his dreams and the interviews were tape-recorded.

The results were evaluated in two ways. In the first method the subject was given eight pictures, one of which was the target picture that had been employed. He then compared each of these pictures with the dream material and decided which one fitted best, giving it the rank 1. Second best was given rank 2, and so on, until the eight pictures had been ranked 1 to 8 according to their correspondence to the dream.

The second method was to send transcripts of the dreams, together with the eight pictures used on the eight different nights, to independent outside judges who ranked, in order, each of the eight targets against the set of eight dream materials. Ranks 1 to 4 were then considered as hits, and ranks 5 to 8 as misses. If the dreams over an eight-night investigation were assessed in this manner, the chance expectation of hits was 4, since each target had an equal chance of being a hit or a miss. The odds against any score arising by chance could then be calculated.

Other methods of evaluation employing various forms of statistical method were employed in the earlier experiments. These were of dubious validity and will not be discussed further. The claims made for the experiments do not depend on these earlier types of evaluation, and the conclusions reached through their use are, in fact, unlikely to be very different from those when the method described above is employed.

THE EXPERIMENT ON ROBERT VAN DE CASTLE

In the most successful of the experiments, originally reported by Stanley Krippner and Montague Ullman,[3] the subject was Dr. Robert Van de Castle, a clinical psychologist and parapsychologist who had performed well in earlier exploratory tests. Over a series of eight nights, his dreams, when assessed against the targets by the independent judge, gave a hit against the target on each occasion, yielding a result having odds of 256 to 1 against arising by chance. The main features and the procedure employed in this experiment are described below.

The targets employed were postcard-sized prints of famous paintings. One of the Dream Laboratory staff members (name not given) was designated the "Recorder" (R). He had the task of preparing sets of targets in the following manner. He collected together 72 pictures and divided these into 9 target pools, each containing 8 pictures. Each picture was given a separate number for later judging purposes. Recorder placed each art print into an opaque envelope, which he sealed and signed across the flap. He then covered his signature with transparent adhesive tape. The eight envelopes in each pool were then randomly assigned numbers 1 to 8. Recorder placed the eight envelopes for each pool into a large opaque envelope, which was again signed and sealed as above. It was also marked with a code number. He then had a set of nine envelopes, each containing a target to be used by the agent during the experiment and also a second duplicate set of the targets to be used when checking the subject's dreams for their correspondence with the targets. Recorder had no contact with the subject and returned to college shortly after the experiments started.

The aim of this part of the procedure was to ensure that the target pictures to be used with any subject were unknown to the subject, the agent, or the two experimenters.

The subject slept in the Dream Laboratory on eight successive nights. Three agents were employed for these eight sessions, the subject being allowed to choose the agent he was to work with on each night.

At the start of a session, the subject and agent engaged in informal conversation while the electrodes were being attached to the subject by one of the investigators (E). The subject then went to bed, and immediately afterwards, the agent, together with an experimenter, entered an office and selected a "random number." The agent then counted down through the stack of large envelopes containing the nine target pools until he reached that number. He then selected another "random number," and, after opening the large envelope, counted down through the eight smaller envelopes inside it in order to obtain the target. He gave the code number of the large envelope containing the pool of targets to the experimenter, who was with him, so that the duplicate pool of targets could be located for judging purposes in the morning.

The agent then went to his room which was situated 96 feet from the room in which the subject was sleeping. There he opened the envelope and extracted the target. According to the report, "he was encouraged to write down his associations, to visualize the picture, to concentrate upon it and to treat it in any other manner which would make its contents a dynamic part of his conscious processes."[4]

During the night the experimenters in an adjoining room to the subject monitored the subject's sleep. When the rapid-eye-movement stage was reached, an experimenter signaled the agent by means of a one-way buzzer, so that he awakened and concentrated on the target. When rapid eye movements stopped, indicating that the dream had ended, the subject was awakened by means of the two-way intercom. He then gave an account of his dreams after which he was asked a number of specific questions about them. The subject might be awakened several times in this manner during the night. After the final awakening, a postsleep interview with the subject was carried out in order to elicit any additional information.

When this was completed, the subject was shown the pool of eight pictures and asked to try to identify the target. He then ranked each picture against his dreams in the manner already described. The tape recordings of the dream reports and interview were mailed to a transcriber, and the transcripts were used by an outside judge for a supplementary evaluation.

The outside judge ranked each of the eight target pictures used on the eight nights with Van de Castle against the set of eight nights' dreams. The target was, in fact, placed in the top half of the rankings for each night's dreams. This result has a probability of $(\frac{1}{2})^8$ of arising by chance, yielding odds of 256 to 1 against chance occurrence. The overall result of the experiment was thus claimed to provide evidence that the subject's dreams had been influenced by ESP.

It was important that only the agent should know the identity of the target and that its identity should not be revealed to anyone until both the subject and the judges had made their evaluations. But an experimenter appears to have been with the agent when he opened his target envelope. In the report it is stated that, before opening the envelope containing the target, *he was encouraged* to write down his associations, etc., and then *once this was done,* there was no way that A could communicate with E or with S without leaving his room and *breaching the conditions* of the experiment. (Italics mine.)[5]

ATTEMPTED CONFIRMATION OF THE EXPERIMENT

Replication of the experiment was attempted by Edward Belvedere of the Maimonides Laboratory and David Foulkes of the University of Wyoming.[6] Foulkes had not worked in parapsychology before but was well known for his work on orthodox aspects of dream research.

Five experimenters, E_1 to E_5, took part. They employed the same subject— Dr. Robert Van de Castle—as had taken part in the original experiment. The method employed was basically similar, but additional safeguards were introduced into the procedure. Only the essential differences in procedure will be described.

The material consisted of pictures from magazines. Ten groups of eight pictures were collected together and placed in small, sealed envelopes as in the earlier experiment. A duplicate set was also made. The small envelopes containing the target pictures were "randomly numbered" 1 to 8, and each pool of eight such targets was placed in a larger envelope, thus forming ten target pools, which were labeled A to J. This part of the procedure was carried out by E_1, who handed over one set of ten envelopes (each holding its pool of targets contained in smaller envelopes) to E_2. It was not completely clear what he did with the duplicate set at this point, since he is merely reported as handing over ten envelopes to E_2.

E_2 acted as "security officer." He stored these envelopes off the premises. On the evening of each experiment, he randomly selected one of the larger envelopes containing a target pool and took it to the laboratory.

At the laboratory the subject selected his own agent each night from a group of three young ladies. (The subject appeared to prefer female agents.) After the participants arrived at the laboratory, the agent watched E_3 attach the electrodes to the subject. E_4 then conducted the subject to his bedroom. When the subject was in bed, E_3 received the target pool from E_2—who only came to the laboratory after he had been given a signal from E_3 that the subject was in bed. E_3 *verified the signature and seal* and held the envelope for delivery to the agent when he was locked in his room for the night. E_3 then conducted the agent to her room, where he gave her the large envelope containing that night's target pool. The agent was instructed not to open the envelope until E_5 had delivered a slip bearing a randomly selected number indicating which of the eight potential targets (contained in the smaller numbered envelopes inside the large envelope) was to be the night's target. E_5 did not enter the room but pushed the slip under the door and then left the building. He retained a duplicate for each night's number, and *it was later* checked that the agent had opened the right envelope. E_5 selected his number with replacement so that the same number could arise more than once. E_2's numbers were selected without replacement so that a target pool would only be used once. (This feature could affect the statistical evaluation, but it is not of importance in the present discussion.)

The agent was situated in a suite of rooms well away on a different floor from the subject's room. The building was locked, the agent's door was locked, and tape seals were attached to the windows and door by E_3. Therefore, the agent could not leave her suite and return without detection.

The subject was locked in his room, and continuous polygraph monitoring was made, as well as monitoring through the intercom system. E_3 monitored the polygraph recordings from a control area next to the subject's bedroom. At the start of each period of rapid eye movements he signaled the agent via a one-way buzzer so that she could concentrate on the target. The agent indicated that she had received the signal by turning on a switch that put on a light in the control room. At the end of the period of rapid eye movements, E_3 signaled E_4, who was in a room adjacent to the control area so that E_4 could awaken the subject. He also signaled the agent so that she would know that the dream period had ended. The agent indicated receipt of the message by turning off the switch that controlled the signal lamp in the control area. Details of dreams as reported by the subject were tape-recorded and postdream interviews were carried out by E_4. After each report the subject was free to indicate any idea he had concerning the nature of the target.

The subject was awakened at 7 A.M. E_4 disconnected the electrodes from the subject. Meanwhile, E_2 had delivered the duplicate pool of targets to E_3, *who verified that the seal and signature were intact.* E_4 took these materials into the subject's room and placed the tape recorder there. The subject then ranked the targets for their similarity to his dreams—he could play back, if necessary, from the tape his own reports of the dreams which he had made during the night.

The agent was not released from her suite until the evaluations had been completed and the judgments were in E_4's hands. E_3 *checked the seals of the agent's suite* and also *checked that only one of the eight envelopes in the target pool had been opened.* He also *checked that the envelope opened corresponded to the number on the slip delivered by E_5 to the subject.* He then conducted the agent to the subject's room, where, in the presence of E_2, E_3, and E_4, the target was ascertained. *E_3 and E_5 later verified that the agent's random number sheets corresponded to those held by E_5.*

The correspondence between dreams and targets was assessed using the ranking procedure by the subject and also by independent outside judges.

RESULTS

The finding was that neither the subject nor the judges matched the dreams with targets at significantly above the chance level. The subject himself assigned three hits and five misses (i.e., one hit fewer than would have been expected to arise by chance). Judge 1 also assigned three hits and five misses. Judge 2 assigned two hits and six misses when judging only on the basis of the dreams, and four hits and four misses when also taking into account the subject's associations.

Foulkes and Belvedere concluded that their failure to confirm the result of the original experiment led to "two lines of enquiry." First, they asked, if ESP does not influence dreams, why did the original study produce above-chance results? Second, if the attempt at repetition was to be rejected as unsatisfactory, what features of the original study had been altered or omitted so as to interfere with the demonstration of a telepathic influence?

Approach I: If ESP Does Not Exist Why Did the First Experiment Produce Evidence for Its Existence?

Foulkes and Belevedere concluded that there were no flaws in the design of the original study. But this conclusion may be questioned. To the reader it may appear that a large number of additional and necessary precautions were taken in the second study, and insofar as these were not taken in the original study, it contained flaws. The most likely reason for a positive result in the first study in the absence of a positive result in the more controlled study was surely the presence of a loophole in its design. It is, therefore, of interest to see what additional precautions were present in the second experiment and how the absence of these could have affected the freedom of action of those taking part in the investigations.

Consider the essential precautions necessary to ensure that no one taking part in the experiment, either intentionally or otherwise, could influence the result.

The Agent

Completely satisfactory methods of selecting the target and of isolating the agent should ensure that neither the subject nor experimenters could influence the result. Selection of the target had to be completely random—i.e., carried out in such a way that no one could predict which of the pool of targets would be selected. The experimenters had to be ignorant of the target and of anything about it, since they had contact with the subject.

It is unlikely, but not impossible, that a subject should be in collusion with one or more agents to fake the experiment. It is much more likely that an experimenter, through having some information about the targets, should unwittingly influence the subject when communicating with him during the night or during the matching of dreams and targets the following morning. In the repetition study, elaborate precautions were taken to ensure that the agent could not leave her room until the session was complete and that only the agent should know the target for the night. It is not evident, from the experimental report, that sufficient attention was paid to this aspect in the original experiment.

In the original experiment, a great deal depended on the activities of the two experimenters in charge. Since they were in two-way sensory contact with the subject, it was essential that they should be isolated from the agent. A separate person was employed for creating the target pools, who, it was stated, had no contact with the subject or agents, but it is not clear whether he maintained contact in any way with the experimenters.

The Subject

It is claimed that the subject displayed knowledge that would normally only be available to him through transmission of information. It is, thus, necessary to ensure that the subject is isolated in such a manner that information cannot reach him through normal sensory channels.

This can be achieved in two ways:

1. by isolating the subject
2. by arranging for selection of the target and viewing of the target by the agent to be done in such a manner that information about the target is confined to the agent, who is isolated from all sensory contact with other individuals

Isolation of the subject was not complete in either experiment since the investigators communicated with him through an intercom system before and after he reported his dream. It was thus essential for the experimenters to be as carefully isolated as the subject. There would, in fact, appear to be little point in permitting discussion with the subject during the experiment or of having any form of communication with him other than the EOG monitor and a signal (such as a bell) to awaken him.

Target Selections

Precautions need to be taken when allocating targets to envelopes.

1. Envelopes should be completely "opaque," so that a target cannot be seen by strong light or by rendering the envelope transparent.
2. The envelopes to be used by the agent should be randomly numbered *after* the pictures are sealed inside by some other person who could have no knowledge of the contents. (These numbers were not required for the duplicate set.) This other person merely saw eight similar envelopes and assigned numbers 1 to 8 to them at random. It was essential to ensure that the agent did not decide which of the eight targets was used. It was only for this reason that it was necessary to number the envelopes containing the targets.

It should be noted that a target can easily be concealed so that no particular person can have knowledge of it. If there are five investigators, the first investigator places the targets into eight similar envelopes, shuffles them, and seals them. He hands these to the second experimenter, who places them at random into eight slightly larger envelopes, and so on. Each of the investigators can ensure that none of his fellows or himself has any information as to the location of the targets. Numbers 1 to 8 may then be placed randomly only on the outside envelopes, or omitted, and the agent left free to choose any one envelope. (It would be quite evident if the agent opened more than one envelope.)

During the experiment it was not essential, in view of the assessment procedure employed, for the eight possible targets to be unknown to the subject. The experimental procedures might have been simplified by letting him know the targets since this has been done in most other ESP tests. For example, both Rhine's and Soal's subjects knew the identities of five possible targets from which the target was selected for each trial.

The experimental conditions would have been improved if the same precautions had been taken to isolate the two experimenters, E_3 and E_4, from each other and from the subject, as were employed with the agent. The experimental report does not make it clear, in fact, whether communication between E_3 and E_4 was limited to the signal with which E_3 signaled E_4 to initiate the awakening of the subject at the termination of rapid eye movements.

The agent signaled to the experimenter E_3, by means of a switch, to show that she had awakened after hearing the buzzer telling her to concentrate on the target. This signaling system might have been omitted since it could have been employed to transmit information from the agent to E_3. The presence of E_1, E_2, and E_5 was not sufficient to stop E_3, E_4, and the agent influencing the experiment if they so desired.

Complete isolation of the subject, except for a buzzer to awaken him after his dream, until after the targets had been judged against the dreams would have been preferable, since the postdream interviews seemed to serve no useful purpose and omission of any discussion between the experimenter and subject was desirable.

An excellent feature of the replication experiment was that each of the precautions taken was later checked as part of the procedure. There is no mention of this being done in the original experiment.

Approach II: If ESP Exists, What Were the Changes in the Second Experiment That Led to the Lack of Results?

This is the second approach suggested by Foulkes and Ullman. It should be noted that the failure to replicate is typical of other ESP experiments reported in the past. When an experiment is carried out to check an initial experiment, it may be expected that improvements, extra safeguards, or improved care in conducting the experiment will be introduced. This is particularly likely if an outside person who is not a parapsychologist is included among the testing personnel.

Two features of any experiment are of particular importance:

1. The method or design employed
2. The procedure adopted during the conduct of the experiment

If a replication experiment is conducted using an identical *method* to the first experiment, it is still possible for changes in procedure to bring about a different result. The replication experiment of Foulkes and Belvedere had features incorporated in the design to ensure that an exact procedure was followed. (See italicized passages in the description of the procedure.)

The presence of a new and critical experimenter, not part of an established team, is likely to ensure that careful attention is paid to exact procedure. An experiment is likely to be conducted in a less informal atmosphere than has been customary, particularly if the stranger is taking some interest in the conduct of the experiment.

If the lack of evidence for ESP in the second experiment was due to tightening up of method and procedure, and if ESP only manifests itself in loosely designed and conducted tests, it becomes impossible to provide experimental evidence for its existence. Perhaps the most important feature of the second experiment was the presence of a new member of the team who was not strongly committed to establishing a case for ESP.

The two "lines of inquiry" suggested by Foulkes and Belvedere would be better rephrased so as to reflect on the observations rather than on inferences made from them:

1. If the experimental conditions do not permit information that could affect the subject's dreams to reach him, why did the first experiment indicate a gain of information by the subject in relation to the target?
2. What were the differences between the two experiments that were responsible for the different results?

The main differences were, first, that extra precautions were taken in the second experiment to ensure that the identity of the target card could be known only to the agent until the matching procedure was completed; second, that a new investigator was present; and third, checks were incorporated into the experimental design to ensure that each part of the procedure was fully adhered to.

FURTHER STUDIES

Other studies at the Dream Laboratory employed experimental conditions less rigorous than those in the experiment described above. Thus, in an early study, the agent sometimes monitored the polygraph for a short period of time to relieve the experimenter. In another experiment, called the second Erwin study, where Dr. William Erwin acted as subject, it was decided that, in addition to the target picture, the agent would be provided with "props" that were supposed to reinforce the impact of the painting on the agent. The props consisted of objects such as toy soldiers and a boxing glove (used with a picture of a boxing match). The objects were placed in a box which was available to the subject together with the target picture.

Ullman and Krippner report that they set their staff in search of "multisensory" materials to accompany the pool of ten art prints. Thus, it was likely that a number of people, including the investigators, had some idea of the types of pictures in the target pool.

In an experiment reported by Krippner, Honorton, and Ullman, together with R. E. L. Masters and Jean Houston of the Foundation for Mind Research in New York,[7] the agent viewed audiovisual programs in a "sensory bombardment" chamber and attempted to influence the subject's dreams. The agent was situated in Masters and Houston's laboratory, fourteen miles from the subject, who was situated in the Maimonides Laboratory. Eight subjects were each tested for one night.

The dreams for each night were ranked against a list of six possible "audiovisual programs." Ranks 1, 2, and 3 were then considered to be hits and ranks 4, 5, and 6 as misses. Using this procedure 8 hits and 0 misses were obtained, a result having odds of 256 to 1 against arising by chance. (Each set of dreams had a probability of ½ of being judged a hit. The probability of obtaining 8 hits was thus [½] = 1/256.)

ATTEMPTED REPLICATION

An attempt to replicate this experiment using the original subject was made by Foulkes and Belvedere,[8] in conjunction with the original investigators. Again there was failure to confirm the result obtained in the original experiment.

The main differences in the replication experiment were, first, that the subject was situated 2,000 miles from the agent in Wyoming, rather than 14 miles away; second, the experimental procedure was tightened up.

SUMMARY

Looking at the dream research as a whole, it is clear that over a period of twelve years, some twelve investigations have been carried out in which experimental conditions have varied considerably and gradually become more rigorous, but positive results have not been obtained under rigorous experimental conditions. It was, moreover, possible on two occasions for a successful subject to be retested with a further outside investigator present. In one case, the original investigators were also present, but in neither case was the result of the earlier experiment confirmed.

The dream studies have features in common with other ESP research. It was claimed that the subject's dreams were affected by telepathy, but this did not manifest itself in any definite fashion. A number of dreams were checked against a number of targets. There might have been no apparent connection between any of the dreams and any of the targets, but the judge was required to rank them in order of similarity. The judge was acting like the percipient in a card-guessing experiment. It was as necessary to isolate him from any possible sources of information as it was to isolate the percipient and agent in a card-guessing experiment.

Precautions were taken to exclude the possibility of information being transmitted by normal means, but the original precautions did not appear to be adequate. When additional precautions were taken, above-chance scores were no longer obtained.

According to Belvedere and Foulkes, the extra precautions in the replication experiment inhibited the ESP powers of their subject;[9] but it is more logical to assume that these precautions removed a source of experimental error that was responsible for the result of the first experiment.

NOTES

1. M. Ullman, S. Krippner, and A. Vaughan, *Dream Telepathy* (New York: Macmillan, 1973). Foreword by Gardner Murphy.

2. B. E. Schwarz, Appendix to *Dream Telepathy* by M. Ullman, S. Krippner, and A. Vaughan (New York: Macmillan, 1973), p. 252.

3. M. Ullman and S. Krippner, *Dream Studies and Telepathy—An Experimental Approach,* Parapsychology Monograph, no. 12 (New York: Parapsychology Foundation, 1970), p. 99.

4. Ullman and Krippner, *Dream Studies and Telepathy,* p. 99.

5. Ibid., pp. 99–100.

6. E. Belvedere and D. Foulkes, "Telepathy and Dreams: A Failure to Replicate," *Perceptual and Motor Skills* 33 (1971): 783–89.

7. S. Krippner, C. Honorton, M. Ullman, R. Masters, and J. Houston, "A Long-Distance 'Sensory Bombardment' Study of ESP in Dreams," *Journal of the American Society for Psychical Research* 65 (1971): 468–75.

8. D. Foulkes, E. Belvedere, R. Masters, J. Houston, S. Krippner, C. Honorton, and M. Ullman, "Long-Distance 'Sensory Bombardment' ESP in Dreams: A Failure to Replicate," *Perceptual and Motor Skills* 35 (1972): 731–34.

9. Belvedere and Foulkes, "Telepathy and Dreams," pp. 787–89.

12

The Ganzfeld Experiments

THE FIRST GANZFELD EXPERIMENT

The first Ganzfeld experiment was reported by Honorton and Harper in 1974.[1] The aim was to control the normal sensory inputs during an ESP experiment by providing homogeneous stimulation to the eyes and ears. In the Ganzfeld situation subjects are fitted with diffusers in the form of halved Ping-Pong balls over the eyes to provide an even field of illumination over the retina. In these experiments white noise or a similar type of homogeneous auditory stimulation is also applied to the ears. Honorton had previously conducted experiments in the Dream Research Laboratory, and the methods adopted in the new research were similar in many respects to those employed in that laboratory.

In the experiment carried out by Honorton and Harper, thirty volunteers acted as subjects. During the experiment the subject was seated in a comfortable chair. The Ping-Pong balls were placed over his eyes. He was then instructed by the first experimenter to "think out loud" and "report all of the images, thoughts and feelings which pass through your mind."[2] He was then given further instructions regarding the procedure after which earphones were fitted over his ears and the sound of the seashore used as a means of providing a homogeneous auditory input.

The subject's utterances were recorded over a 25-minute interval. The idea was that this could be split into five 5-minute intervals in one of which—decided by a randomizing process—the agent in another room would be viewing a target.

The target material consisted of stereoscopic View-Master reels, each of which contained seven "thematically-related stereoscopic images."[3] The reels were stored in packs of four, the top one of which was to be used as the target. Thirty-one packs of four reels were available for the experiment.

A second experimenter determined which pack of reels was to be used by the agent by shuffling and cutting a pack of thirty-one numbered cards and "selecting the appropriate set of reels, and inserting the uppermost reel (without looking at its identifying label) into the viewer."[4] The second experimenter had no further contact with any of the participants in the experiment until after the subject had completed his blind judging of the target.

The agent was informed when the 5-minute viewing interval was to start and that he would be informed when the 5 minutes was up. He was further instructed, "At that point you will return the reel to the envelope and shuffle it with the other reels, without looking at them. Then wait in the other room until the subject makes his selection."[5]

Experimenter 1 monitored the subject's utterances via an intercom. She also indicated to the agent the start and finish of the "sending period." "She did not initiate verbal communication with S during the session unless there was a lengthy break in his continuous report."[6]

At the end of 35 minutes, as signaled on an auditory tape, the experimenter entered the subject's room and removed the Ping-Pong balls and earphones "without divulging the sending period."[7] The subject was then given the viewer and each of the four reels from the set. He had to decide which of the reels "corresponded most closely to his imagery, second best, etc."[8] When the subject had finished, the experimenter called in the agent who then revealed the identity of the target reel.

It is not clear where the "other room" was situated or how the subject was to be provided with the set of reels used by the agent. It is also not clear from the report how the main experimenter learned which set of reels was being used. The second experimenter, after giving the set of reels to the agent, was stated to have had no further contact with any of the participants in the experiment. The agent was only summoned to the room in which the experiment took place after the subject had completed his task, for which the subject would have had to have the set of four possible targets.

The thirty subjects each contributed one session. They secured 13 direct hits as against the chance expectation of 7.5, giving antichance odds of about 58 to 1.

ATTEMPTS TO REPEAT THE EXPERIMENT

According to Rao and Palmer[9] in their survey of the experimental evidence the results of the experiment were subsequently replicated by Terry and Honorton (1976), Braud, Wood, and Braud (1975), and Sargent (1980).

In the two experiments reported by Terry and Honorton eighteen undergraduate students were divided into groups of three, forming six experimental teams.[10] Each team consisting of a sender, a receiver, and a monitor completed ten experimental sessions. The monitor acted as the main experimenter supervising the subject. When the agent was given the packet of four reels from which he was to take his target, he had to take the uppermost reel in the pack. At the end of the experiment this reel was placed at the bottom of the pack so that it would not be selected again until the other three reels had been used as targets.

At the end of the "sending period" the agent placed the target reel in the packet together with the other three reels and shuffled them to mix their order before delivering the packet to the subject so that he could check them and decide which of the four agreed best with his experiences. This extremely precarious part of the procedure was improved to some extent as the two experimenters also further shuffled the set of four reels at "most of the sessions."[11]

In the first repeat experiment the combined result from five teams was selected and gave 21 hits in 27 sessions. This was claimed to give antichance odds of 338 to 1. In the second experiment one of the six teams obtained 7 hits in 10 attempts with antichance odds of 286 to 1. Allowing for the fact that this team was selected from the six teams involved, the odds would be near 48 to 1.

These experiments were complicated by the fact that they included much more than the direct selection by the subject of the target that best fitted his experiences in the Ganzfeld situation. As a result the subject was not isolated until he had made his decision owing to the system of recording utterances and monitoring the subject during each session.

The complex arrangements to isolate the target from the subject arose through the fact that the subject was not isolated but in conversation with the main experimenter during the experiment. The procedure that was optimistically supposed to remove the possibility of sensory leakage was similar to that adopted in the Dream Research Laboratory experiments. In those experiments similar results were obtained until in the repeat experiments extra safeguards were taken against sensory leakage and precautions were taken to see that each step in the experimental procedure was in fact carried out.

The experiment of Braud, Wood, and Braud used twenty subjects.[12] Ten of the subjects were tested individually and acted as an experimental group. The other ten formed a control group and merely rested in chairs while the agent was viewing his target. They used six pictures from which the subject had to make his choice. The subjects ranked these in order of similarity to their impressions. Ranks 1 to 3 were then called a hit and ranks 4 to 6 a miss, thus making the probability of success 0.5. Why this was done is difficult to understand, but it resulted in the experimental group achieving 10 hits in 10 attempts—with odds of about 1000 to 1 against chance. The control group achieved 5 hits as expected by chance.

THE CAMBRIDGE EXPERIMENTS

Dr. Carl Sargent completed six experiments in the psychology department at Cambridge University using similar types of procedure. One of these, conducted in conjunction with Hugh T. Ashton, Peter R. Dear, and Trevor

A. Harley,[13] has been claimed as being one of the best experiments using the Ganzfeld situation.

The experiment is remarkable in that there were four experimenters, but each of these acted as a subject in 8 of the 32 sessions. At each session a single target was attempted. Three of the investigators also acted as agent at some sittings. The precise duties of each investigator are not stated in the report, and it is possible that at some sessions a single experimenter tested a subject—one of his co-experimenters—with an agent who was also responsible for covering the duties of second experimenter. The dates on which the 32 sessions were conducted or the order in which they were carried out are not revealed in the report. The targets used in the experiment consisted of art reproductions on postcards. They included such diverse paintings as Manet's *A Bar at the Folies-Bergère* and what is popularly know as "*Whistler's Mother.*" Altogether, twenty-four sets of four pictures were used during the experiment.

The subject was located in a sound-attenuated studio, adjoining a control room used by the main experimenter. The pool of targets and other material used in the experiments were kept in another room "down the corridor" that will be referred to as the office.

The twenty-four sets of four pictures were available in duplicate form contained in A4 envelopes numbered 1 to 24. One of these sets consisted of four pictures labeled A, B, C, D contained in a nonsealed A4 envelope. The duplicate set contained the same pictures individually sealed in envelopes labeled with the set number and letter, i.e., 1–24 A, B, C, D. This set was used by the agent who selected his target from it. The other set was to be made available to the subject for him to match against his descriptions and imagery at the end of the session.

After the subject had been fitted with Ping-Pong balls and had had white noise applied by headphones to his ears, the experimenter and agent retired to the control room where the experimenter remained, viewing the subject through a one-way mirror. The agent then went to the office down the corridor where he selected one of the envelopes from the twenty-four envelopes containing targets. The actual procedure is not clear but the agent is stated to have used Rand Corporation (1955) tables with a "non-repetition provision."[14] Thus it is possible that the 4 sessions for each subject were completed before another subject was tested so that the pool of target sets would gradually reduce owing to sets not being replaced. Otherwise a record must have been maintained showing which target pool each subject had already used.

The agent also selected a small envelope from a pack of twenty sealed envelopes each containing one of the letters A, B, C, or D. There were five envelopes each containing one of these four letters. The agent cut the pack of small envelopes and randomly selected one of them using the Rand Corporation tables. If the report is complete, it would appear that the pack was at no time shuffled.

The agent then left the unsealed A4 envelope containing one set of the four pictures in the office and departed with the other A4 envelope and the small envelope containing the key letter to an adjacent building where he took up a position close to a corridor telephone.

When the subject was ready to start, the experimenter telephoned the agent and said "Go." The agent then retired to a soundproof agent's room. He then opened the small envelope, extracted the slip of paper bearing the key letter (A–D), and opened the appropriate envelope containing the target picture. He viewed it for 20 minutes.

The subject meantime was allowed his own time to produce his report. The experimenter noted his utterances, which were transmitted by a microphone in the studio and which also for some sessions (unspecified) were recorded on tape. When the subject had finished, he indicated this to the experimenter. The experimenter then turned on the background lights, relieved the subject of his Ping-Pong balls and earphones, and gave him a questionnaire to fill in. While the subject was occupied with his questionnaire, the experimenter went down the corridor to the office and collected the A4 envelope containing the duplicate set of four pictures that had been left there by the agent.

When the subject had completed his questionnaire, the experimenter brought to him the four pictures together with the "session transcript" that he had written down. The subject then had to judge each of the four possible targets against the transcripts and allot an independent rating between 0 and 99 in respect of each of the four pictures. The experimenter appears to have been present to assist the subject during this part of the procedure. This is not definitely stated in the report, but in a further paper published in the *Journal of the Society for Psychical Research* in which a group of visitors had been tested it is stated that: "The subject and E1 went through the record of the subject's verbal utterances during the session and examined each response in relation to the four pictures, using an arbitrary but consistent scoring scheme to score points for each picture for each response."[15]

When judging of the four pictures was completed the agent was summoned from the room to which he had retired. He came to the experimental studio and revealed which of the four pictures had been used as the target.

The method of judging the degree of success achieved was to allot ranks 1 to 4 to the marks allotted by the subject. The target then had a 1 in 4 chance of being allocated rank 1. The total of 32 attempts—8 from each of four subjects—achieved 14 ranks 1, against the expected number of 8. This result has odds of 80 to 1 against arising by chance. By regarding ranks 1 and 2 as a success and ranks 3 and 4 as a failure, in the manner used in the dream research, the scores achieved by the four subjects out of a possible 8 were 6, 5, 5, 5, compared with the chance expectation of 4.

WEAKNESSES IN THE EXPERIMENT

There are five main weaknesses in the experiment besides the fact that the experimenters also acted as subject and agent.

First, the experimental report is inadequate and inaccurate.

Second, an essential feature of the design was the use of a key letter in the small envelope that decided which of the four pictures was viewed by the agent. The agent selected one of these small envelopes from a closed pack of twenty envelopes containing five of each of the letters A, B, C, or D marked on a slip of paper. Inspection of the nineteen small envelopes left behind in the office by the agent would reveal to any person entering the office the identity of the target. Having located the key letter used he had merely to inspect the contents of the unsealed A4 envelope containing the four pictures. These were labeled A, B, C, and D. Anyone could have gained this information including the main investigator who subsequently assisted the subject in allotting marks to the four pictures. He had left the subject to complete a questionnaire while he went to the office to collect the unsealed A4 envelope containing the duplicate set of four pictures. The experimenter may not have wished to cheat, but he might have been interested in knowing what was the target for tonight.

Third, the fundamental weakness lies in the manner in which the activities of the agent were controlled. There were twenty-four sets of four pictures. These must have become fairly familiar to each of the investigators since they each used eight of these sets when acting as experimenter, and a further eight when acting as subject. They would also have seen at least one of the contents of a further eight sets and become fully familiar with it while gazing at it for 20 minutes when acting as agent. The agent might have been interested to have a look inside the unsealed A4 envelope when he went to the office to see which pictures were present in his target pool, and he might have felt tempted to take a fresh batch if they looked an unexciting bunch. It would no doubt have been more interesting to gaze for 20 minutes at Manet's *A Bar at the Folies-Bergère* than at *Whistler's Mother*.

Fourth, if we consider a particular set of four pictures, it is likely that they will have different chances of scoring marks when assessed by the subject according to the amounts and variety of things depicted in them—even without the assistance of the experimenter.

Finally, to have an experimenter assisting in the assessment of the subject's report and in the selection of the target presents every opportunity for experimental error.

Carl Sargent and H. J. Eysenck have pointed out that twenty experimenters have reported fifty-five Ganzfeld experiments of which twenty-seven "have given evidence of significant positive ESP scoring and only two have gone the wrong way significantly below chance."[16] What they are saying is that twenty-eight of the experiments fail to give above-chance scores. Since they adopt odds of 20 to 1 as indicating "significance," it is not unexpected that two experiments should provide significantly below-chance scores.

Further they write, "once again, this massive majority in favor of positive ESP effects suggests that we are dealing with a lawful phenomenon."[17] Thus what appears to be a minority of experiments that confirm ESP becomes a "massive majority" of experiments confirming ESP over experiments that fail to do so, provided the majority of experiments that fail to confirm ESP are omitted.

NOTES

1. Charles Honorton and Sharon Harper, "Psi-Mediated Imagery and Ideation in an Experimental Procedure for Regulating Perceptual Input," *Journal of the American Society for Psychical Research* 68 (1974): 156–68.

2. Ibid., p. 161.

3. Ibid.

4. Ibid.

5. Ibid., p. 162.

6. Ibid.

7. Ibid.

8. Ibid.

9. K. Ramakrishna Rao and John Palmer, "The Anomaly Called Psi," *Behavioral and Brain Sciences* (1988): 1–35.

10. James C. Terry and Charles Honorton, "Psi Information Retrieval in the Ganzfeld: Two Confirmatory Studies," *Journal of the American Society for Psychical Research* 70 (1976): 207–17.

11. Ibid., p. 209.

12. William G. Braud, Robert Wood, and Lendell W. Braud, "Free-response GESP Performance During an Experimental State Induced by Visual and Acoustic Ganzfeld Techniques: A Replication and Extension," *Journal of the American Society for Psychical Research* 69 (1975): 105–14.

13. Hugh T. Ashton, Peter R. Dear, Trevor A. Harvey, and Carl L. Sargent, "A Four-Subject Study of Psi in the Ganzfeld," *Journal of the Society for Psychical Research* 51 (1981): 12–21.

14. Ibid., p. 11.

15. Carl L. Sargent, "A Ganzfeld GESP Experiment with Visiting Subjects," *Journal of the Society for Psychical Research* 51 (1982): 222–32.

16. H. J. Eysenck and Carl Sargent, *Explaining the Unexplained* (London: Weidenfeld and Nicholson, 1982).

17. Ibid.

13

Remote Viewing

TARG AND PUTHOFF

Experiments having some similarity in the methods employed to those used in the dream research were reported in 1976 by Targ and Puthoff.[1] Further details were published in a book *Mind Reach* published in 1977.[2] The experiments were on "remote viewing," which implied the ability of some people to perceive, and to be able to describe, what they would see if they were at some distant location. In some cases this ability appeared to be of the telepathic variety, with people visiting and viewing the site; in other cases the agent was dispensed with and the subject was supposed to describe what he would see at some specified location, thus demonstrating clairvoyance.

In *Mind Reach* Targ and Puthoff described tests they had carried out with Pat Price, an ex-police commissioner who had, it appears, used his remote-viewing ability to track down suspects. When Price first phoned to offer his services, Puthoff gave him the coordinates on the map of the area on the East Coast that Targ was visiting. Three days later, he claims to have received from Price five pages of description that included such features as descriptions of buildings, details of equipment in the buildings, names from desks, and a list of labels on file folders locked in a secret cabinet. According to Targ and Puthoff the descriptions were essentially correct.

Price also sent them data concerning various situations that he gathered in during his nightly "scans." Much of this, it seems, related to political or military issues. After confirmations started to come in, Price was invited to participate in a "rigorous investigation" of his abilities. He then agreed to take part in experiments at Stanford Research Institute (SRI).

At SRI, Price took part in remote-viewing experiments in which he had to describe target locations situated a few miles from the SRI laboratories. These experiments were described as follows.

The subject was supervised by one experimenter (call him E₁). The second experimenter (call him E₂) was in charge of a team of two to four co-experimenters, who were called the "Target Demarcation Team." A division director at SRI who was not otherwise associated with the experiment had "chosen" a set of twelve target locations clearly differentiated from each other and within 30 minutes driving time of SRI. *Sets of traveling orders* were then prepared and kept in his safe.

During each experiment, E₂ left E₁ with the subject and then obtained a set of traveling orders from the division director, who picked one of these at random from the safe for each experiment. E₂ then set off with the demarcation team, which started viewing the target area 30 minutes after leaving the subject and E₁. Fifteen minutes was then allowed, during which time the subject described what he thought the target area looked like into a tape recorder and made drawings. The experimenter E₁ was with the subject while he did this and encouraged him to "clarify" his descriptions where he thought it necessary. After the demarcation team had returned, an "informal comparison" was made of the subject's descriptions and the target site. The subject was then taken to see the target site.

When nine experiments, each with a single target, had been conducted in this manner over a period of days, the descriptions and drawings made by Price together with a list of the target locations were given to independent judges. The judges visited the target locations, and each judge chose what he considered to be the best-fitting description for each target. A description that matched best with the target constituted a hit. A ranking procedure was also employed using another judge in which each description was ranked against each target.

Under these conditions, Price scored at well above the chance level. The five judges gave a total of 24 hits against a total of 45 (5×9), which was the maximum possible. In an article published in *Nature,* it is stated that the probability of this result arising by chance is 8×10^{-10}. This constitutes an elementary statistical error, since each judge matched the same set of drawings and descriptions against the nine targets. Given a set of targets and descriptions that happen to match in a particular way, any number of judges is likely to place them in approximately the same matchings. The probability is not changed by getting more and more judges to make more or less the same judgments.

FEATURES OF THE EXPERIMENTAL DESIGN

With this general design, it is important to know precisely how the targets were chosen and what instructions were given to the person making the selection. Were the targets to be well-known places in the vicinity which the subject might have seen? Were they to have easily recognizable features differentiating the one from the other, i.e., not to include more than one church, one tower, one lake, one radio telescope, etc.? Why were twelve targets selected and only nine used? Was the number of experiments decided beforehand?

The fact that Price saw the target location at the end of each experiment must have raised some difficulties. For example, anyone acting as a subject in a similar experiment carried out in Paris (France), seeing the Eiffel Tower after the first test, would omit it as a possibility for subsequent tests. Given, say, twenty differentiating features, the mere omission of some of these for a particular target would increase the possibility of achieving a hit in a mass of descriptive material that could apply in part to almost any target.

A vulnerable feature of the design lies in the fact that experimenter E_1 was with the subject, urging him on. How was this done? Did he interrupt Price when in full flow and ask him to elaborate a point, or did he ask him to add detail to a feature in a drawing? While E_1 did not know the target locations, he knew a good deal about the likely targets in the vicinity. The fact that he was with the subject and in a position to affect his responses increased the experimental safeguards required.

In fact, it transpires that there were more obvious reasons for the result achieved by Price. In a letter in *Nature,* August 17, 1978,[3] David Marks and Richard Kammann from the Department of Psychology, Otago University, New Zealand, revealed that Marks had visited SRI and attempted to rank the original descriptions given by Price against the target locations. Only five of the transcripts and locations were treated in this manner, since details of the remaining four had already been published and would have been seen by Marks.

Marks and Kammann reported:

Although not stated in the original reports the judges were provided with a listing of targets in the correct (original) sequence. In addition, careful examination of the transcripts indicated that a large number of cues were available indicating the position of a transcript in the series; for example: (1) Price expresses apprehension and an inability to do this kind of experiment (Target 1); (2) a reference is made to the fact that this experiment is the "second place of the day" (Target 2); (3) a reference is made to "yesterday's two targets"; (4) Targ says encouragingly, "Nothing like having three successes behind you" and mentions the nature reserve visited the day before (Target 4); (5) Price refers to the Marina which was the fourth target (Target 7). Using these, and other, cues I was able to match the five transcripts correctly with a rank of one giving a sum of ranks of five ($p < .0005$) (ref. 4). In this procedure it should be noted that I had never visited any of the five locations but completed the task solely on the basis of cues contained in the transcripts.[4]

Marks and Kammann concluded:

Until remote viewing can be confirmed in conditions which prevent sensory cueing the conclusions of Targ and Puthoff remain an unsubstantiated hypothesis. Our own experiments on remote viewing under cue-free conditions have consistently failed to replicate the effect.[5]

PRECOGNITIVE REMOTE VIEWING

Experiments similar to those of Targ and Puthoff on remote viewing have been reported by J. B. Bisaha and B. J. Dunne of Mundelein College, Chicago.[6] Their experiment was in many ways similar to that of Targ and Puthoff, but they were testing for *precognitive* remote viewing. Their subject described scenes that were not chosen or viewed until after his descriptions had been completed.

Seven subjects took part, a pair of them being selected each day for use with a particular target. In all, seven tests were made using seven different targets. In four tests the subjects were in the same building, but in different rooms and supervised by an observer. In the remaining three tests the subjects were at different locations approximately 10 miles apart and, it would appear, unsupervised.

When the subjects started generating their descriptions, the experimenter left the area. He had with him ten envelopes that had been randomly selected from a target pool of over a hundred targets consisting of locations in the city and suburbs of Chicago. It is not clear whether the target pool consisted of over a hundred sealed *envelopes* containing targets or whether it was a *list* from which ten targets were randomly selected. In addition, the method of obtaining a random choice is not stated. The experimenter departed at the time that the subjects started their descriptions. He then drove around for twenty minutes, at the end of which time he chose a number 1 to 10 by blindly selecting one of the ten sheets bearing numbers 1-10 from a container. He then counted down through the envelopes until he came to the target location for that day. He arranged that he would arrive at the location 15 minutes later and stayed there for 15 minutes taking photographs and making notes. The choice of target was thus made 5 minutes after the subjects had completed their descriptions, and the experimenter arrived at the target location 20 minutes after the subjects had completed their descriptions.

The descriptions given by the subjects were split into two batches A and B, each containing a description made by one of the subjects in relation to each target. Six independent judges were employed. Two of them ranked descriptions in batch A against the photos and descriptions of the targets given by the experimenter. Two more judges ranked the descriptions in batch B. The remaining two judges ranked the subjects' descriptions in batch A against those in batch B. Results indicating precognitive remote viewing were obtained with antichance odds of around 200 to 1. In terms of straight hits, i.e., where a description made on a particular day was ranked first against the target for that same day, the results were Judge 1, 2 hits; Judge 2, 5 hits; Judge 3, 3 hits; Judge 4, 1 hit. Thus there was considerable disagreement between the two judges on what constituted the best hit among the descriptions.

Bisaha and Dunne give examples to indicate the accuracy of the subjects' descriptions. Thus, where the target was a railway station, one subject's description included a railway station, railway lines, and other features; but whereas one judge placed this description first, the other judge only gave it a second ranking. Other descriptions probably contained references to stations and railway lines. It is thus likely that the example given was a fragment of a much longer description describing many different features, so that each description would be likely to have something in common with each target. But there is little point picking out the accurate details to impress the reader unless the amount of inaccurate detail is also mentioned.

The description of their experiment given by Bisaha and Dunne makes no mention of essential experimental controls and a large number of questions arise about the procedure adopted.

1. Why were ten targets randomly selected and only seven of them used?
2. Why were subjects numbered S_4 to S_7? What happened to Subjects S_1, S_2, and S_3?
3. How were the ten targets randomly selected from the pool of over one hundred targets? What form did the pool take?
4. When the sheet bearing a number from 1 to 10 was drawn from the container to decide the target, was it replaced in the container? What check was made to see that the experimenter went to the target that had been selected in this manner?
5. When the experimenter arrived back from viewing the target, did he keep details of the targets secret until all the judging had been completed? Did the experimenter reveal the identity of the target to anyone else, or talk to others involved in the experiment? What did he do with the photographs and notes he had made? Who developed the photographs?
6. What precautions were taken to ensure that the whole of the subjects' descriptions and drawings were included for judging? Were the descriptions edited in any way? Were descriptions made on a different tape each day? How were these tape recordings kept until judging was completed? Was the *date* recorded on each tape so that no mix-up could arise? When judges ranked the descriptions "blind," it would appear essential that the dates on which the targets were viewed and the dates on which descriptions were made should be unknown to them until rankings were completed. Was this control exercised? It may be observed that in Targ and Puthoff's experiment the order in which targets were viewed was available to the judges.
7. What were the duties of each experimenter? Was more than one experimenter involved? Who were the observers who were sometimes present with the subjects? What were the names of the subjects?
8. Where a great deal of descriptive material is written down that could apply in part to a large number of different targets, part of the material may be influenced by contemporary events, i.e., events in the news that day or television programs. The same may apply to descriptions made by the experimenter (agent) of the target area. Was any account

taken of this possibility? If the experimenter had been in conversation with a subject, a common element may similarly be established that could have been reflected in the descriptions made on the following day. Were subjects kept isolated from each other and from others taking part in the experiments?

These experiments were both inadequately reported and too loosely controlled to serve any useful function. They indicate the importance of giving complete details of every control feature. Lessons could have been learned by the investigators from studying the later dream research experiments. An important feature in any experimental report is that the names of both experimenters and subjects should be stated, since the subjects themselves may exercise control of the experiment by reading the experimental report and reporting any divergences from the stated procedure.

OTHER FINDINGS REPORTED IN *MIND REACH*

Targ and Puthoff in *Mind Reach* report a number of other tests conducted under various experimental conditions. In some of these tests, subjects were able, according to Targ and Puthoff, to identify places, objects, and drawings without any other person viewing them. Why, then, did they complicate their main experiment on remote viewing by having not only an agent, but also a team of viewers as part of the experiment? Uri Geller had identified the face uppermost on a die inside a steel box to their complete satisfaction. No other person had seen the die. Pat Price had already demonstrated his remarkable powers when identifying remote geographical locations and labels on files in a secret cabinet when, presumably, there was no one gazing at them.

In general, subjects tested by Targ and Puthoff displayed exceptional abilities in some tests but these were not maintained under strict conditions. Their subjects behaved as did the high-scoring subjects in the early days of card guessing. Their psychic powers were inhibited by more rigorous test conditions. Just as it would have been a simple matter to establish whether any one of Rhine's high-scoring subjects was genuine or bogus, so it should be a simple matter to determine whether a subject can identify the positions of dice in a steel box, describe remote locations in detail, or identify labels on file covers in a secret cabinet.

NOTES

1. H. E. Puthoff and R. Targ, "A Perceptual Channel for Information Transfer over Kilometer Distances: Historical Perspective and Recent Research," *Proceedings of the IEEE* 64, no. 3 (March, 1976); R. Targ, H. E. Puthoff, and E. C. May, *State of the Art in Remote Viewing Studies at SRI* (Stanford Research Institute).

2. R. Targ and H. E. Puthoff, *Mind Reach: Scientists Look at Psychic Ability* (New York: Delacorte/Eleanor Fried, 1977).

3. D. Marks and R. Kamman, "Information Transmission in Remote Viewing Experiments," *Nature* 274 (August 17, 1978), p. 681.

4. Ibid.

5. Ibid.

6. J. P. Bisaha and B. J. Dunne, *Multiple Subjects and Long Distance Precognitive Remote Viewing* (Chicago: Mundelein College).

Part Four

Psychokinesis

14

Early Research on Psychokinesis

EARLY INVESTIGATIONS

The first attempt to test whether a person's thoughts could influence the movement of a physical object was made by the great English scientist Michael Faraday (1791–1867) in 1853. At that time, the American mediums had arrived in Britain and a cult of table turning was sweeping the country. Faraday, who had become involved in a controversy over spiritualism at the Royal Society, thought it likely that the tables were moved through the application of a force transmitted by the hands of those touching them rather than by any psychic influence. This, he decided, could be established experimentally.

Faraday found that there was no need to have a group of people sitting round the table; a single person could cause the table to move. Also, he observed that the table's motion was not necessarily circular but might be in a straight line. He then glued together four or five pieces of cardboard, one over. the other, with pellets of a soft cement consisting of wax and turpentine. The bottom piece was attached to a sheet of sandpaper that was resting on the table. The edges of the cardboard overlapped one another slightly and a pencil line was drawn on their undersurface to indicate the positions of the cards before the test. The upper piece of cardboard was larger than the rest, so that it covered the remaining sheets. The cement was strong enough to offer considerable resistance to mechanical motion and also to hold the cards in any new position they acquired. However, it was weak enough to give way slowly to a continued force. The table turner placed his hands on the upper card and results were awaited. Faraday found that when the table, hands, and cards all moved to the left together, the displacement of the cardboard sheets, as compared to the line showing their original position, showed that the hands of the table turner moved farther than the table. His hands had pushed the upper card to the left, and the under cards and the table had followed and had been dragged by it.

Faraday's subjects were all successful table turners who believed in their own abilities. Thinking that they moved the table as a result of a "quasi-involuntary" motion, Faraday next carried out tests in which the turner could become aware, by watching an indicator, when he was exerting any pressure. Under these conditions the table did not move. Faraday wrote:

> No form of experiment or mode of observation that I could devise gave me the slightest indication of any peculiar natural force. No attraction or repulsions, or signs of tangential power—nor anything which could be referred to other than the mere mechanical pressure exerted inadvertently by the turner.[1]

Faraday had been investigating what is today called psychokinesis. A later investigation to determine the effects of thought on a physical system was carried out by Sir William Crookes using a delicate chemical balance, which, if there were powers of psychokinesis, might, he thought, be caused to move. He was, however, unsuccessful in moving the balance, and it is a remarkable fact that this rather obvious way of testing for psychokinesis has been ignored by later investigators.

At the turn of the century, a physical medium named Eusapia Palladino (see pp. 235–41) claimed to be able to move a balance, or at least to get her spirit guide, "John King," to move it for her. She was tested by a committee in Paris that included the French physicist and co-discoverer of radium, Marie Curie (1867–1934), but it appears that on this occasion Eusapia was assisting "John King" by the use of a fine thread held between her hands. When suitable precautions were taken to screen the balance, it no longer moved.

THE EXPERIMENTS AT DUKE UNIVERSITY

The topic of psychokinesis was almost forgotten until Rhine began his investigations of it in 1934. He was interested in finding out whether subjects could influence the fall of dice by wishing for a particular outcome. The early tests carried out at Duke University were conducted under informal experimental conditions. Subjects were often tested in private homes or in dormitories. Some investigators used themselves as subjects, and the experiments were hardly more than exploratory.

The results of some nineteen investigations carried out between 1934 and 1942 do not appear to have been very convincing at the time, since no mention was made of them in published reports of Rhine's work until after 1942. He has said that it was the discovery, in 1942, of a secondary effect in the old score sheets that convinced him of the reality of psychokinesis. Looking back at the records of the early experiments, he found that subjects tended to score higher in the first runs of a session than in the later ones and higher in early trials than in the later trials. He said: "The significance of these hit distribution data, found long after the tests had been made, was so great that we were at last fully convinced that the PK [psychokinesis] effect was a real one."[2]

In *Reach of the Mind,* published in 1949, Rhine reported the discovery of several new characteristics of psychokinesis. Subjects were more successful if they tried to influence many dice at the same time—the more the better; the distance of the subject from the dice did not affect the scores; metal dice produced above-chance scores whereas wooden ones did not; dice made of lead gave higher scores than those made of aluminum; rounding the corners of the dice so that they would roll more easily did not affect the scores. It is significant that techniques had developed to such an extent by 1949 that these detailed characteristics of psychokinesis could be determined, whereas in the first eight years of research (1934–1942) the scores had been insufficient even to provide a convincing case for its existence.

J. Fraser Nicol, at a symposium held by the Ciba Foundation in 1955, criticized these claims:

On the strength of dice throwing said to have been performed at Duke University, it is recorded elsewhere that the psychokinetic force is more effective on heavy metal dice than on wooded ones; and also, from the same source, that the shape of the dice—sharp corners, rounded corners, or extremely rounded corners—makes no difference to the power of the human psychic force. Neither of these strange claims can be validated in any of the published reports on psychokinesis. It is mainly on the basis of these and similar unverifiable assertions that the author concludes that "the finding that *mass, number, and form* [of dice] *are not determining conditions of PK tests,* takes its place, then, alongside the discovery that time and space were not limiting factors in ESP."

Only a few of these rash pronouncements have been quoted in the above paragraphs. Many others could be cited. One wonders what the more objective but friendly type of scientist must think when he is confronted with such highly adorned claims. He might, one surmises, rather easily turn away from psychical research, moved by the uncomfortable realization that a subject in which scientific method and the need for careful reporting are so casually pushed out of the way, is not a field of study in which he would care to indulge.[3]

The experiments on psychokinesis carried out up to 1962 have been assessed in an extensive review made by the American psychologist Edward Girden of Brooklyn College. He divided the investigations into four categories:

1. The early dice tests carried out between 1934 and 1937 and mostly published in the *Journal of Parapsychology* between 1943 and 1946.
2. Later dice tests in which more care was paid to experimental design.
3. Tests in which objects other than dice were used.
4. Tests in which subjects attempted to produce lateral displacement of an object.[4]

EARLY DICE TESTS

The main objections raised by Girden to the early dice tests were:

1. They were "largely free-wheeling and off the cuff." Variations of test conditions were a common occurrence.
2. When subjects attempted to obtain a particular face upper-most, they tended to attempt to throw a 6, and the dice were not tested for bias.
3. Little or no attention was paid to accuracy of recording.
4. Adequate control tests were lacking. Thus, if the proportion of, say, 6s arising in 960 trials when the subject had attempted to obtain them had been compared with the number of 6s arising in an equal number of trials when the subject had made no effort to obtain them, any bias on the dice could have been allowed for. Trials of the two types could have been alternated or targets could have been decided by a series of random numbers (1-6).

Only one of the early experiments employed a control series. This was carried out by Frick, a graduate student at the Parapsychology Laboratory in 1937. He tested himself when throwing dice from a cup under two conditions: (a) when wishing to throw 6s; (b) when wishing part of the time to throw 1s and part of the time *not* to throw 6s. When condition *a* operated, he obtained a positive deviation of 582 hits for the 6 face out of 52,128 trials, and under condition *b*, 576 hits for the 6 face out of 52,128 trials. Thus, the experiment provided no evidence for psychokinesis but clear evidence for bias of the dice, since the dice tended to fall with the 6 face uppermost whether it was being wished for or not. If the control series had been omitted, it could have been claimed that the experiment provided evidence for psychokinesis comparable to that provided by similar experiments reported at that time.

Frick's negative results indicated, according to Rhine and psychologist Betty Humphrey, then a research fellow in the Parapsychology Laboratory, that there was "no place in Frick's personal philosophy to accommodate the PK hypothesis. . . . It appears that Frick must have, as it were, completely deceived himself in the conduct of series B. He was not well unified in his motivational elements."[5]

Girden remarked:

On a number of interesting considerations, it is self evident that the most elementary requirement necessitated the equal representation of all six dice faces as targets in some randomized order and the tabulation of all dice faces in all trials. There is no need to make use of higher mathematics to conclude that biased dice could account for the obtained results.[6]

He also commented in his review that nineteen early reports from the Duke Laboratory were characterized by the presence of only one negative result, whereas two other experiments carried out at that time in other laboratories each gave negative results.

The first of these experiments in England, reported by Nicol and W. Carington, a well-known English parapsychologist, was far better in design than any of the American tests. All throws of the dice were recorded and all faces were used as targets in systematic fashion. No evidence was obtained for psychokinesis, and detailed examination showed that decline effects were not present.[7] The second study, carried out by C. B. Nash of the biophysics department at St. Joseph's College, Philadelphia, in 1944, in which all 6 die faces were used as targets equal numbers of times, also provided no evidence for psychokinesis.[8]

Since the majority of the early Duke experiments were conducted in the investigators' homes or in dormitories by students, business people, and interested amateurs without professional supervision, the observed decline effects might well have arisen because of the way in which the tests were carried out. As such effects had not been envisaged at the time of the experiments, it is unlikely that any precautions were taken to guard against them. Similar decline effects were reported in the early experiments on clairvoyance carried out by Miss Jephson (see pp. 31–32). When her experiment was repeated, the result indicated that her original result was not due to extrasensory perception but to the fact that the subjects were not supervised. Whatever brought about high scores in her experiment also, presumably, produced the decline effect.

If a number of reports are collected together from people who have been left much to their own devices, such decline effects may be expected. Thus, for example, if an investigator tests a number of persons before finding one who gives high scores, and then goes on testing him, we should expect, in the absence of psychokinesis, the subject's record to show a decline effect across the record sheet. His scores would be high at the start—that being the reason he had been selected as a subject—but they would be unlikely to remain high. Also, if the number of runs in a test is not specified at the start, similar effects may be expected to arise. The initially successful subject may become discouraged and terminate the tests after a run in which he has made a low score, but if he has made a number of hits in the last few trials of the run, he may feel encouraged to attempt a further run.

It is remarkable that the decline effects, when they were first noted, did not throw doubt on the experiments but were interpreted as providing convincing evidence for psychokinesis.

LATER DICE TESTS

These include investigations carried out after the development of the decline hypothesis. Following criticism of the earlier work, more attention was paid to experimental design and to effects such as bias on the dice. In some cases, all throws were recorded rather than only successes.

Among thirty of these later investigations listed by Girden, thirteen supported the psychokinesis hypothesis. The remainder did not produce a significant above-chance score, and in only one case was there a decline effect.

The conditions for a conclusive test for psychokinesis as stated by Rhine and Pratt in their book *Parapsychology* are: (1) a two-experimenter plan; (2) randomization of targets or systematic variation of the targets with all faces of the dice acting as target equal numbers of times; (3) independent recording of targets, hits, and misses.[9]

On these criteria, none of the thirteen tests giving positive evidence for psychokinesis can be regarded as conclusive, whereas several of the remaining seventeen investigations that failed to provide such evidence do satisfy the requirements.

EXPERIMENTS USING OBJECTS OTHER THAN DICE

Experiments using disks, coins, and other objects have been reported by four investigators. The first of the tests, reported by Elizabeth McMahon, a zoologist working at the Parapsychology Laboratory, was on children and college students; plastic disks were used, and the subjects wished for a particular face to fall uppermost. A decline effect was present, but the score in both cases was now significantly above chance.[10]

Dr. R. H. Thouless, who made the second of these investigations, used coins thrown ten at a time off a ruler and came to the conclusion, "It is obvious that the result is not of any value as independent evidence for PK."[11]

A third investigation, in which a subject tested himself by throwing a penny onto a rug for 100 trials per session over 10 sessions and also by throwing a die 216 times, was reported by Dorothy Pope, managing editor of the *Journal of Parapsychology*, with the comment that these attempts "offer suggestive data on the comparative success of dice and discs in PK experiments."[12] The odds against the combined score arising by chance were about 90 to 1.

The fourth and most extensive of these investigations was made by S. R. Binski, a government official, while working for his Ph.D. degree.[13] In one series, 117 subjects threw 100 coins at a time until altogether 153,000 coins had been thrown. In a second series, 123 subjects attempted to guess the winning number of roulette wheel spins. Neither series yielded evidence for PK.

Further tests were made by Binski with another subject whose scores, it was claimed, were highly significant. However, Girden has pointed out that these tests had no pre-experimental plan and involved no set number of runs. Gardner Murphy, when criticizing Girden's report in the *International Journal of Parapsychology*, pointed out that Binski's subject, using a coin, obtained 548 successes out of 1,000 attempts.[14] Such a result is not very unusual—the odds are about 3 to 1—if one takes into account the fact that Binski had tested 240 subjects. It should also be noted that the 1,000 attempts represented only 10 throws of 100 coins. In such tests, where a large number of dice, for example, are thrown together, the greatest care must be taken with the randomization of the targets, otherwise the observations cannot be said to apply to independent events, and the statistical analysis may yield a misleading result.

LATERAL DISPLACEMENT

The best known of the experiments in which subjects attempted to produce the lateral displacement of objects by wishing it has been carried out by H. Forwald.[15] He not only claims that subjects have been able to obtain lateral displacement of objects, but also that he has been able to measure the psychokinetic force by observing the distance a cube slides sideways along a surface when dropped on to it from a height. His calculations are based on the erroneous assumption that if the object moved laterally a greater distance than the height from which it was dropped, then a psychokinetic force was present. For his work he was given the $1,000 McDougall Award, which is presented each year by the Duke Parapsychology Laboratory for outstanding research. Two objections have been raised concerning Forwald's research. The late C. C. L. Gregory, formerly professor of astronomy at London University, criticized the assumptions underlying Forwald's calculation of a psychic force in *Psychic News,* after having attempted without success to air his criticism in the *Journal of Parapsychology.* Gregory pointed out:

If anyone cares to perform the experiment of successively pushing wooden blocks from a child's building set over the edge of a low table on to a linoleum floor, he can easily satisfy himself that the cubes will scatter in a random manner equally in any direction up to a distance even greater than the height of the fall. *The reason for this scatter is not a sideways force, psychic or otherwise,* it is determined by the horizontal distance between the cube's center of mass and the point of contact on striking the floor.

Unless this distance happens to be zero, an impulsive couple will be imparted to the wooden block causing it to leap in a contrary direction to that of the point of contact with respect to the point below the center of the cube. The sideways distance of the jump, roll or slide, will also depend on the friction, as Mr. Forwald found.[16]

The second objection was raised by J. Fraser Nicol. Forwald acted mainly as his own subject, and Nicol remarks: "At what state in the difficult history of psychical research it became permissible for sensitives to report their own results and expect them to be accepted as serious evidence in psychical research, I do not know."[17]

As Girden pointed out, Forwald's 1954 work began some nine years after publication of *Extrasensory Perception after Sixty Years,* and yet by the standards of that book, all his data would be unacceptable.[18]

NOTES

1. Michael Faraday, "Experimental Investigation of Table-Moving," *The Athenaeum* (July, 1853): 801–803.

2. J. B. Rhine, *New World of the Mind* (London: Faber and Faber, 1954), p. 37.

3. J. F. Nicol, "Some Difficulties in the Way of Scientific Recognition of Extra-sensory Perception," in G. D. Wolstenholme and E. Millar (eds.) *Ciba Foundation Symposium on Extra-sensory Perception* (Boston: Little Brown, 1936), p. 36.

4. E. Girden, "A Review of Psychokinesis," *Psychological Bulletin* 59 (1962): 353–88. Also published with comments in *International Journal of Parapsychology* 6 (1964): 26–77. Page numbers are taken from the latter publication.

5. J. B. Rhine and Betty M. Humphrey, "The PK Effect with Sixty Dice per Throw," *Journal of Parapsychology* 9 (1945): 215.

6. Girden, "Review of Psychokinesis," p. 33.

7. J. F. Nicol and W. Carington, "Some Experiments in Willed Die-Throwing," *Proceedings of the Society for Psychical Research* 48 (1946): 164–75.

8. C. B. Nash, "PK Tests of a Large Population," *Journal of Parapsychology* 4 (1944): 304–10.

9. J. B. Rhine and J. G. Pratt, *Parapsychology* (Oxford: Blackwell, 1954), pp. 164–68.

10. Elizabeth McMahon, "A PK Experiment Under Light and Dark Conditions," *Journal of Parapsychology* 9 (1945): 249–63.

11. R. H. Thouless, "Some Experiments on PK Effects in Coin Spinning," *Journal of Parapsychology* 9 (1945): 169–75.

12. Dorothy Pope, "Bailey's Comparison of a Coin and a Die in PK Tests," *Journal of Parapsychology* 10 (1946): 213–15.

13. S. R. Binski, "Report on Two Exploratory PK Tests," *Journal of Parapsychology* 21 (1957): 284–95.

14. Gardner Murphy, "Report of a Paper by Edward Girden on Psychokinesis," *International Journal of Parapsychology* 6 (1964): 77–89.

15. H. Forwald, "A Continuation of the Experiments on Placement PK," *Journal of Parapsychology* 16 (1952): 273–83.

16. C. C. L. Gregory, letter in *Psychic News* (May 9, 1959).

17. J. F. Nicol, "The Design of Experiments in Psychokinesis," *Journal of the Society for Psychical Research* 37 (1954): 355.

18. E. Girden, "Review of Psychokinesis," pp. 58–62.

15

The New Approach to Psychokinesis

The experimental work on psychokinesis received new impetus with the use of electronic machines. The machine could create a randomized series of outcomes that would operate a system such as, for example, lights showing which of two outputs, +1 or -1, had been generated by the machine. The subject could attempt to influence the machine by "willing" the light to produce a particular output. There were certain similarities between the developments in PK research and those that had arisen in the investigation of ESP. In the ESP research, cards that could be shuffled and counted were replaced with the outputs of the machine. In psychokinesis research, solid objects such as coins and dice and other paraphernalia were replaced with outputs of an electronic randomizer. There were great advantages in the use of a machine since it was found that results were obtained as easily using substitutes for objects as they had been with real objects.

HELMUT SCHMIDT'S EXPERIMENTS ON PSYCHOKINESIS

In 1969, at the start of his research in parapsychology, Helmut Schmidt used a machine to investigate psychokinesis.[1] It consisted of a random-number generator (referred to as an RNG) that provided a random binary series of outputs +1 and -1. In a variety of situations the subject tried to influence the machine or some appartus operated by the machine so that it would produce a surplus of +1 (or -1) outputs.

PSYCHOKINESIS IN A CAT

Schmidt's early experiments with the machine were in the area of animal behavior.[2] One cold winter's night he placed his cat in a garden shed that was heated only by a 200-watt lamp. The temperature was around zero in the shed, and the cat tended to "settle down" immediately next to the lamp. Schmidt thought that perhaps the cat's "feeling of pleasure" when the lamp was lighted might be utilized to affect the binary random-number generator. He connected the lamp so that each time the generator produced a +1 output the lamp went on and each time it produced a -1 it went off. The purpose of the experiment was to see whether the cat's "feeling of pleasure" when the lamp was lighted might cause the lamp to light more than the expected 50 percent of the time. This would, in turn, require the machine to generate more +1s than -1s. The machine, in fact, operated a lamp from each output, but one of the lamps was always outside the shed in a box. The lamps were interchanged each day so that any bias of the machine, whereby it might be producing a surplus of +1s, was cancelled out.

According to Schmidt, when the cat was in the shed, the lamp tended to be on at above-chance level, and the cat had affected the random-number generator to keep itself warm in some way unknown to physics. When the cat was not in the shed, the lamp was only on 50 percent of the time, showing that the random number generator was operating normally when the cat was not influencing it. The experiment was discontinued because it was said that the outside temperature had risen. If Schmidt's theory about the cat's "feeling of pleasure" was correct, the lamp would, presumably, stay off more than 50 percent of the time in warm weather when the cat wanted to keep cool.

COCKROACH EXPERIMENTS

These experiments were followed by others employing cockroaches as subjects. The animals received a shock or not according to the state of the randomizer. In this case the cockroaches, it seems, were unsuccessful in affecting the randomizer so as to avoid shock, but they caused it to produce 109 more shocks in 6,400 generated numbers than would be expected to arise by chance. Schmidt commented: "The magnitude of this deviation suggested that it might be a real effect, even though it raised the question of why a possible PK ability in cockroaches should work to their disadvantage."[4] He did not consider the possibility that there might be any fault in his randomizer or method of data collection, or even that the result might have arisen by chance.

In a further experiment with cockroaches, Schmidt, after generating 25,600 randomized outputs giving shock or no shock, found that the number giving shock was 13,109, which was 309 fewer than chance expectation. This result has odds greater than 10,000 to 1 against arising by chance. Here again, the important question is whether these values, in toto, were obtained from unresettable counters on the machine without necessitating the recording and addition of separate batches of results from the machine. In addition, a means of canceling out machine bias as described earlier would have been preferable rather than relying on tests made on the machine at some other time.

OTHER ANIMAL STUDIES EMPLOYING MACHINES

Schmidt's experiments with animals have been supplemented with several other studies where targets are generated by a machine and where scoring of the responses made by the animals is also automatic. Until recently, the animal studies were claimed to provide the first repeatable demonstrations of ESP.

The basis for the investigations was an experiment reported by Duval and Montredon on precognition in mice.[5] In their experiment a mouse was placed in a testing cage that was divided into two compartments by a partition. The mouse could remain in one compartment or jump to the other compartment in order to avoid a shock that was administered at random to one of the two compartments.

Duval and Montredon reported three experiments in each of which the animals moved about in such a manner that they occupied the side receiving shock less often than the other side of the cage. Results in two experiments were stated to be significant at less than the .001 level, i.e., had odds of less than 1 in 1,000. It will be noted that the mice expended much energy jumping from one side of the cage to the other. Schmidt's cat would, presumably, have remained still and affected the randomizer.

In 1971, at the Parapsychology Laboratory, a group of investigators headed by W. L. Levy, director of the Institute for Parapsychology, repeated these experiments and confirmed the findings.[6] In three successive experiments, they reported a statistically significant result. Further experiments followed.

In 1974, John Randall discussing the animal research was able to list twelve experiments of this type, constituting all those he knew to have been carried out, each of which produced a significant positive result.[7]

In July 1974 I wrote:

John Randall lists all experiments of this type known to have been performed. Each of these has produced a positive significant result. But of the 12 experiments he lists, three were reported by two "eminent" but anonymous French biologists: the remaining nine were conducted in the United States by Walter J. Levy and three co-workers. Levy has also found that fertilized chicken's eggs affect the randomizer so as to keep themselves warm in the same manner as Schmidt's cat.[8]

In August 1974, it was revealed that Levy had been caught cheating in an experiment, had admitted to having done so, and had been sacked from his post as director of the Institute of Parapsychology.

PSYCHOKINESIS EXPERIMENTS WITH HUMAN SUBJECTS

In 1970 Schmidt reported experiments using his machine on human subjects.[9] The subject sat in a cubicle viewing a panel containing nine lights arranged in a circle, one of which was lit at any time. Schmidt was in another room 20 feet away where the random-number generator and a paper-punch print-out were located. The panel of lights was connected to the random-number generator via a 30-foot cable.

In a test run the light started at the top of the circle. Each output then changed the position of the light so that it appeared to move to the adjoining position clockwise or counterclockwise. The random-number generator was set to produce a sequence of 128 numbers, at a rate of one every two seconds. Each +1 output from the machine caused it to move one position in a counter-clockwise direction.

The subject was instructed to try to force the light to move in a clockwise direction. This task was considered equivalent to making the generator produce more +1 outputs than -1 outputs.

Preliminary tests with eighteen subjects showed a generally below-chance scoring rate. Three of the eighteen subjects obtained above-chance results, fifteen of them failed to do so—although the actual number giving a below-chance score rather than a chance score is not stated.

Schmidt then stated that he was mainly interested in testing whether there was an effect rather than whether it was in a particular direction. For the main experiment he used a team consisting of nine subjects who had scored below chance, together with another six recruited later. With this team a total of 256 runs of 128 trials each was made.

The result was that jumps of the light occurred significantly more often in the nondesired direction (50.9 percent of trials) than in the desired direction (49.1 percent of trials). In a total of 32,768 trials, clockwise movements gave a negative deviation of 129 hits. This result had odds of 1,000 to 1 against arising by chance. When the machine was left unattended, it was found that no systematic bias was present.

It should be noted that it was not the movements of the light but the +1 and -1 outputs that were counted. It was assumed that the counter readings and the print-out readings would accurately register the +1 and -1 outputs.

THE FIRST CONCLUSIVE EXPERIMENT

A further experiment of this nature was reported in the *New Scientist* in 1971.[10] Here two subjects scored—the one high, the other low—over a period of 10 days, giving antichance odds of 10 million to 1.

The result constituted the first experiment on psychokinesis that might have been called "conclusive" in the sense earlier used by Rhine. For that reason it merits special attention since something must almost certainly have been responsible for the result.

For the experiment two subjects were selected, one of whom (K.G.) had consistently scored high and other (R.R.) who had scored low in earlier experiments. Each subject then had to complete 50 runs each of 128 trials over a 10-day period. Subject K.G. now had to aim for a high score and subject R.R. a low score. The sequence of +1 and -1 outputs was recorded on counters and on paper-punch tape. The results are shown in table 15-1.

TABLE 15-1

Hits Above-Chance Level and Odds against Result Arising by Chance for Two Subjects over 10-Day Period

Subject	Attempts	Aim	Hits	Hits above Chance	Successes
K.G.	6,400	High Scores	3,360	+160	160
R.R.	6,400	Low Scores	3,056	-144	144
Totals	12,800		6,416	+16	304

In the total of 12,800 trials, there were 6,416 +1 outputs and 6,384 -1 outputs. The difference was well within what may be expected to arise by chance and indicates that the RNG was not producing an excess of one output against the other. However, the 12,800 trials produced an excess of 160 in the high-score condition and of 144 in the low-score condition, giving a total number of successes of 304. This gives antichance odds of 10 million to 1.

The scores achieved were plotted against total trials as in table 15-1. This shows a consistent tendency for subject K.G.'s scores to be high and subject R.R.'s scores to be low.

A result of this nature clearly indicates that something extraordinary went on during or after the experiment to create the low and high scores recorded for the two subjects. Schmidt thought that the subjects in some way affected the emission of an electron from the radioactive source so that it would arrive at the Geiger counter at the right time (within a millionth of a second). This was supposed to stop a binary counter according to whether the subject was trying to "will" a light to go in a clockwise or counterclockwise direction on the display panel and also on whether the subject was a habitual high scorer or low scorer. The subject did this, it is claimed, by merely looking at the panel of lights and "willing" the light to move in a particular direction.

APPRAISAL OF THE EXPERIMENT

Criticisms raised in the case of Schmidt's experiments on precognition and clairvoyance also apply here.

1. Information Directly Provided by the Machine

Internal unresettable counters—if they were fitted internally in the RNG—would merely show the number of +1 outputs. Since the high-scoring subject would produce extra +1 hits if successful and the low-scoring subject a deficiency of +1 hits, it provided no check on the scores achieved by the subjects. It is remarkable, however, that any plus and minus scores of the high-scoring subject and low-scoring subject almost exactly balanced out.

2. Maintenance of Records

The result of the experiment was dependent on readings taken at the start and end of each run, together with the print-out. No precautions were taken to ensure the accurate maintenance and tabulation of the data so provided. The machine provided an efficient means of registering the numbers of outputs present during each run. Any bias present could have been checked by means of the print-out, which showed both the numbers of outputs and the order in which they arose.

The values in table 15-1 are dependent on precautions taken during the course of the experiment to ensure that there was no selection of data. The use of the print-out in conjunction with the experiment is in itself not an adequate safeguard against error unless it is used with a continuous roll of paper ensuring that all outputs of the machine during the experiment are accounted for together with the condition "High" or "Low" being used by the subject.

In the account of the experiment and also in preceding experiments of a similar type,[11] there is no mention of the print-out containing an indication of the high or low condition. In later discussion Schmidt has indicated that a special code was incorporated, but it is not clear how this was placed on the printer or used during the counting of results from the print-out. In the earlier report it is mentioned that "At the beginning of each run, the subject, having decided in which direction (clockwise or counterclockwise) he wanted to influence the light to go, set a switch on the panel accordingly."[12] This switch only changed the direction of the lights as they appeared to the subject, and could not have been used to enter a code on the print-out.

To control against error on the part of the experimenter when sorting out his data, similar precautions to those that were developed in the case of the card-guessing experiments would have been required. If at each session Schmidt had operated his machine in one room and a second experimenter had been with the two subjects and arranged an order in which they would use the machine, a record showing which subject had made each run could have been made independently of the record of the score compiled by the experimenter on each run. These records made on preregistered forms provided before the experiment started—as in the Pratt-Woodruff experiment—would have provided some check on the accuracy of tabulation of the data.

3. Safeguards against Trickery

If it be assumed that the print-out data provided an accurate record of the experiment and that the record of the counter readings was consistent with the print-out, it is still possible that the result was produced by trickery on the part of the subjects or of some outside person.[13] These possibilities have to be considered in the face of claims for such an unlikely process. It is considered much more likely that the president of the United States went along to the Parapsychology Laboratory in the dead of night and interfered with the data than that Schmidt's subjects were affecting the output of electrons from a radioactive source so as to produce the effects required to account for the experimental result.

The experimenter was in a position to affect the print-out, and he also was responsible for recording the values on the counters at the end of each run. A clear demonstration that the RNG and print-out could be rigged was provided when W. L. Levy was caught doing such rigging and admitted having done so. Levy was working in the same laboratory as Schmidt and in a report stated that he used Schmidt's RNG.[14]

The subject sat alone in a separate room. He was supposed merely to gaze at the display of nine lights arranged in a circle on the display panel. It might appear difficult for him to affect the RNG and print-out located in another room, but if the outputs on the cable to the panel of lights were not isolated from the outputs to the print-out, shorting the +1 or -1 input to the display panel to the common line could affect the print-out. It need only have been shorted for a few seconds in each run to result in an excess of +1 or -1 hits being recorded. Anyone conversant with the circuitry could possibly have brought about the same result by tapping the cable connecting the display panel to the RNG between the two rooms.

Full details of the circuits employed have not been published and it is possible, as claimed by Schmidt, that the outputs to the display panel, the print-out, and the counters were buffered against each other. Even if they were, the effects of switching on a 30-foot cable leading to the other units has to be considered since there was a switch on the display panel that changed the inputs to the display panel. This had the effect of changing the direction, clockwise or counterclockwise, in which the light moved. According to the report, subjects could, if they wished, change this switch frequently during a run.

4. The Effects of Bias in the Machine

In ESP tests where subjects are given knowledge of results after each trial the danger arises that, if the series of targets is not adequately randomized, above-chance scores may arise owing to the manner in which people make their guesses. In the PK experiments guessing habits of the subjects are not involved. Thus the relative frequencies with which the two outputs are present are the main concern. But given a method of randomization in which a bias may be present, it is possible to measure the extent of the bias and to offset its effects in the following manner. Given a coin being tossed for heads and tails, it may be suspected that there is a bias on the coin so that the probabilities of getting heads or tails are not equal to 1/2 each. In such case it would be expected that the numbers of heads and tails obtained over long runs would show a bias towards one output.

The effects of such bias and a measure of its extent may be obtained as follows. The two sides of the coin are labeled A and B. A series of outcomes is obtained in which A is converted to heads, B to tails on even-numbered throws, and A to tails, B to heads on odd-numbered throws. Any bias is now equally distributed among heads and tails, and the extent of the bias is obtained by comparing the numbers of outcomes A and B.

Such a method is efficient with an even-numbered number of outcomes, but a constant error is present that decreases in proportion to the length of the series if an odd number of outcomes is present.

Schmidt sought to remove the effects of bias by interchanging the +1 and -1 outputs from the counter in his RNG. If this had been done after each outcome bias would have been eliminated, but he reversed the outputs only after each run of 128 targets.

Assuming that this adjustment was correctly allowed for when calculating the result of the experiment, the possibility arises that if the two subjects in the PK experiment each made an equal and odd number of runs at each session, the one could have obtained a bias in one direction, the other in the reverse direction.

The experiment took place over a 10-day period in which each subject was subjected to 6,400 outcomes of the randomizer. If each subject was given 5 runs on each day, and if the one subject was tested before the other each day, any bias present in the generator would mainifest itself in reverse directions in the two subjects.

If adequate records had been presented in the report as might be expected in an experiment of this nature, each subject's "score" would be shown for each run under the two conditions (1+, -1 and -1, 1+). The extent of any bias could then have been determined and its effects made equal between the two subjects.

5. Inadequate Use of Control Series

In criticizing Schmidt's experiment, it was pointed out by the writer that the two subjects aiming for low and high scores, respectively, had operated the same machine and that the machine did not record any deviations from chance.[15] In addition a control series was not used in the experiment. It was however claimed by Schmidt in reply that the high- and low-scoring subjects operating on the same machine acted as a control series since bias in outputs would be allowed for. This, of course does not constitute a control series in the normal sense of the words. Runs of 128 outputs could have been used under two conditions in which (1) the subject would try to influence the lights (the experimental series); or (2) the subject would not try to influence the lights but would be given some other task (the control series).

Had runs been made at random with the one series or the other, with the type of series unknown to the experimenter maintaining the record of scores, an effective control could have been established. The method would then have been similar to that employed by Coover fifty years before with playing cards. The two records (1) showing the series to be experimental or control and, (2) showing the outputs from the randomizer would be brought together only after the experiment had been completed.

CONFIRMATION OF RESULTS

In their review, R. Rao and J. Palmer write:

A defense of the existence of probabilistically conclusive parapsychological studies requires a detailed review and discussion of any experiments that might qualify. Because such a treatment must be rather lengthy, we will limit ourselves to a single group of experiments as an example. Although they are somewhat dated we have chosen Helmut Schmidt's (1969a; 1969b) reports on random event generator (REG) experiments because (a) they represent one of the major experimental paradigms in contemporary parapsychology; (b) they are regarded by most parapsychologists as providing good evidence for psi; and (c) they have been subjected to detailed scrutiny by critics.[16]

POST-1969 REVIEW

Rao and Palmer also state that a review has been conducted of all binary two-choice experiments published since 1969 when Schmidt published his first REG experiment. Fifty-six reports were obtained from "approximately" thirty principal investigators describing a total of 332 individual experiments. They state that for 30 of the nonsignificant experiments, insufficient data were provided to allow the result to be expressed quantitatively, and a correction was made for this. Following these corrections, in the words of Rao and Palmer, "Seventy-one of the 332 experiments (21%) yielded results significant at or beyond the 5% level (2-tailed), and the combined binomial probability for all the studies was 5.4×10^{-43}."[17]

The outcome was still significant, although more modestly so. When the data from Schmidt and the Princeton group were removed the probability value dropped to 4.25×10^{-7}.

The main fact that emerges from this data is that 71 experiments gave a result supporting Schmidt's findings and 261 experiments failed to do so.

A further feature that emerges is that these 332 experiments were not presumably conducted by independent investigators, since Schmidt's experiments are included. The experiments were "uncovered" from fifty-six reports submitted by "approximately" thirty investigators including Schmidt. It is thus important to know what is meant by thirty investigators. Independent confirmations of Schmidt's experiment would need to be undertaken by thirty different investigators or thirty independent teams of investigators, each team containing no investigators who had taken part in any of the other experiments.

It is also apparent that few of the investigations could be considered as repeats of Schmidt's original experiment described above. They only constituted a set of experiments in which a random-number generator similar to Schmidt's was claimed to have been affected during an experiment.

The "most prominent of these replications" is stated to have come from the laboratory of Robert Jahn at Princeton University. Two reports are quoted, the first published by Jahn in 1982, the second by Nelson, Dunne, and Jahn in 1984. These will be examined in the next chapter.

NOTES

1. Helmut Schmidt, "A PK Test with Electronic Equipment," *Journal of Parapsychology* 34 (1970): 176-81.

2. Helmut Schmidt, "PK Experiments with Animals as Subjects," *Journal of Parapsychology* 34 (1970): 261.

3. Ibid., p. 258.

4. Ibid., p. 259.

5. P. Duval and E. Montredon, "ESP Experiments with Mice," *Journal of Parapsychology* 32 (1968): 153-66.

6. W. J. Levy, L. A. Mayo, E. Andre, and A. McRae, "Repetition of the French Precognition Experiments with Mice," *Journal of Parapsychology* 35 (1971): 1-17.

7. John Randall, "Biological Aspects of PSI," in *New Directions in Parapsychology,* edited by John Beloff, (London: Eleckserence, 1974), p. 86.

8. W. J. Levy, "Possible PK by Chicken Embryos to Obtain Warmth," *Journal of Parapsychology* 35 (1971): 321.

9. Helmut Schmidt, "A PK Test with Electronic Equipment."

10. Helmut Schmidt, "Mental Influence on Random Events," *New Scientist* (June 24, 1971).

11. Other experiments reported using the random number as in 9 above.

12. Helmut Schmidt, "A PK Test with Electronic Equipment," p. 179.

13. C. E. M. Hansel, "A Critical Analysis of H. Schmidt's Psychokinesis Experiments," *Skeptical Inquirer* 5 (1981): 26-33.

14. W. J. Levy and Andre McRae, "Precognition in Mice and Birds," *Journal of Parapsychology* 34 (1970): 220, note 2.

15. Ibid.

16. R. K. Rao and J. Palmer, "The Anomaly Called PSI," *Behavioral and Brain Sciences* 10 (1987): 542.

17. Ibid., p. 545.

16

Independent Repetitions of
Schmidt's PK Experiment

RESEARCH AT PRINCETON UNIVERSITY

In a section of their report entitled *Examples of Replicability in Parapsychology* Rao and Palmer give the experiments with random event generators (REG) as their first example where other experimenters can confirm the result obtained by Schmidt. They state: "Schmidt has carried out several other successful REG experiments, mostly involving PK. More to the point, a number of other experimenters have successfully used the same devices or similar ones to test for psi. The most prominent of these replications comes from the laboratory of Robert Jahn at Princeton University. (Jahn 1982: Nelson, Dunne and Jahn 1984).[1]

This replication appears to be derived from two experiments. The first of these was reported in 1982 by Robert G. Jahn, dean of the School of Engineering/Applied Science at Princeton University;[2] the second, reported in 1984 by Jahn with two collaborators.[3]

The first experiment—later referred to as Experiment A—was reported in an article in the *Proceedings of the Institute of Electrical and Electronics Engineers*. It consisted of an experiment using a random-number generator similar in many ways to that used by Schmidt. The second experiment— referred to here as Experiment B—was reported in a Technical Note PEAR 84003 of the School of Engineering/Applied Science, Princeton University.

From the description given by Rao and Palmer the two experiments were in general similar. In their article they presented the overall result for the two experiments. In 195,100 trials with 22 subjects, when they were trying for a high score they obtained a mean score of 100.043 (where the mean chance expectation is 100). In the same number of trials, where they were trying to score low they obtained a mean score of 99.965 (where the mean chance expectation is 100). The combined probability of the result was approximately 10^{-4}.

Since only the first report (for Experiment A) as published in the *Proceedings of the Institute of Electrical Engineers* is readily accessible this experiment will be examined.

BASIC FORM OF THE EXPERIMENT

The subject (or operator as he is referred to) was in the same room as the random event generator, print-out, and other parts of the apparatus. This supplied a series of random binary events in blocks of 200 at a time. This run of 200 events was referred to as a "trial." In each trial, the subject tried to obtain either a high score or a low score according to the requirements of the experiment. His score in each block of 200 events was displayed on a counter together with the mean score for trials completed. His aim was to obtain a high or low score on the counter.

The chance-expectation score from the 200 binary events contained in each trial is 100. Thus the subject had an indication of how well he was succeeding by seeing whether his count was above or below 100 at the end of the trial. In addition he saw a running mean showing him the mean score for trials so far completed.

METHOD EMPLOYED

1. A random binary series of outputs was obtained by using a commercial-noise source module based on a solid-state junction. The output from this was amplified and clipped to give a flat-topped profile going positive and negative. During each trial this profile was sampled by a regular train of 200 pulses (p) to provide +1 outputs on one line and -1 outputs on a second line according to the sign of the wave form provided by the noise at the time of sampling. Either the +1 or the -1 outputs were then counted according to the position of a switch, or the switch could be placed in an "Alt" position in which +1 or -1 outputs were counted on "successive samples." It was this final output—call this OP (whether it was dependent on the +1 or -1 outputs from the randomizer)—that the subject tried to influence. By chance it was expected that an average value of 100 outputs OP would arise on each trial.

2. Each "trial" in the sense used in the paper contained 200 events as decided by the train of pulses p. A switch was provided by means of which the number of events could be changed to 100 or to 1,000 events. The rate at which the pulses arose could be adjusted to 1, 10, 100, 1,000, or 10,000 per second. The 100 rate was normally used so that each trial containing 200 events took 2 seconds. Some of the results were, however, obtained at the 1,000 pulses per second rate, in which case each trial would presumably take 0.2 seconds.

3. The subject was provided with a remote "initiation switch" that he operated to start the sequence of operations. The initiation switch could start each trial or it could be operated in an automatic mode to start a sequence of trials.

4. The number of outputs OP was displayed on a light-emitting diode (LED) counter that was reset before each trial. The subject could see how he was affecting the outputs. Since each trial contained 200 events the subject could observe at the end of the trial whether he had scored above or below the chance value of 100. Details of the instructions given to the subject are not given, but he was presumably aware of the fact that by chance he was expected to score around 100 and that he was attempting to increase or decrease this count according to whether he was trying for a high or low score.

5. In order to record the number of trials, the number of pulses p were counted on a trial counter. Since 200 events were present in each trial this count was, presumably, divided by 200 and shown on an LED display. This count also operated the printer on which the outputs OP were recorded for that trial. It then recorded on the printer the trial number and closed a gate supplying pulses p, thus ending the trial. The subject saw the "running count of each trial and the concurrent mean relative to a preset origin."[4] These values were also recorded on the printer. Thus the number of events was determined by the number of outputs OP, and the number of trials by the number of runs of 200 pulses p generated.

RESULTS

It is stated that the major portion of the results given comprised three separate experimental series extending over fifteen months, labeled REG I, REG II, and REG III, respectively. "All other data acquired under slightly less formal conditions of protocol during this period, included for completeness, are grouped under two other series, labeled REG Ia and IIa."[5]

The results for the three main series are shown in table 16–1 as reproduced from the table given in the report. Successes in this table are obtained by combining the mean below-chance deviation for the low-scoring condition with the mean above chance for the high-scoring condition.

It will be seen that in each of the three sections the mean score per trial under the PK+ condition was above-chance expectation and the PK- value below chance. A similar effect was obtained in the two other series REG Ia and REG IIa although the results were less impressive than those in the three series REG I to III.

TABLE 16–1

Mean Hits per Trial of 200 Events under High- and Low-Scoring Conditions
Together with Baseline Readings for
Experiments REG I, REG II, and REG III.

Series	Condition	Trials	Mean	Odds v. Chance
REG I	Base Line	12,000	100.009	2:1
	High aim	4,500	100.264	166:1
	Low aim	3,850	99.509	10,000:1
	Successes	8,400		3 million:1
REG II	Base Line	2,500	100.003	2:1
	High aim	1,950	100.247	18:1
	Low aim	1,800	99.597	10,000:1
	Successes	3,750		500:1
REG III	Base Line	3,500	99.977	2:1
	High aim	2,400	100.227	3,300:1
	Low aim	2,600	99.600	36:1
	Successes	5,000		160:1

It will be seen that in each of the three sections the mean score per trial under the PK+ condition was above-chance expectation and the PK- value below chance. A similar effect was obtained in the two other series REG Ia and REG IIa although the results were less impressive than those in the three series REG I to III.

APPRAISAL OF THE EXPERIMENT

The main defects in this experiment are similar to those in Schmidt's experiments as discussed in the 1980 edition of this book. Jahn appears to have read that book since it is listed in his references. Rather than consider these defects, he appears to have supplemented them with further sources of error. Very little information is provided about the design of the experiment, the subjects, or the procedure adopted.

1. The Subjects

Details are not given about the subjects, the times they were tested, or the precise conditions under which they were tested. It is merely stated "The experiments reported here were performed by a single operator, seated in front of the device with the remote initiation switch in hand. . . ."[6]

It is possible that more than one person acted as operator, combining the roles of experimenter and subject. In the acknowledgments at the end of his report Jahn thanks his research colleague Ms. B. J. Dunne who "played a primary role in the generation and interpretation of much of the data reported herein," and Dr. R. D. Nelson "who contributed heavily to the experimental program."[7] It is possible that Dunne and Nelson also acted as experimenters or subjects or as both simultaneously; but if that were so it might be expected that any similarities or differences in their performance would have been mentioned in the report.

2. The Experimental Plan

The precise plan of the experiment does not appear to have been fixed in advance. Thus, the number of trials conducted under each condition is different in each of the five sections and varies between the sections.

An essential feature of the arrangements to ensure accuracy of the records was that details of trials and mean values or some measure of the "score" should be printed on tape or recorded together with the conditions under which the values were obtained. No mention is made of the manner in which the allocation into high-scoring or low-scoring groups was recorded on the print-out or computer used to analyze the results. Thus from the circuit diagram it appears that means were not provided whereby the condition, high- or low-scoring, was registered on the print-out or recorded at the start of a trial.

3. Procedure Adopted

The most remarkable feature of the experiment emerges when considering the procedure adopted by the subject or operator. Thus it is stated:

> This operator attempted, on instruction or volition, to distort the trial counts either toward higher or lower values. The several options of sampling number, sampling frequency, +/- polarity, and manual/automatic sequencing were variously determined by random instruction, operator preference, or experimental practicality, and recorded before the beginning of each trial. Clearly, the full matrix of such possibilities could not be explored, and for our first sequence of experiments only 200-sample trials were used, at 100 or 1000 counts/s, all counted in the +/- alternating mode. The automatic/manual and high/low options were more thoroughly tested, in both the volitional and instructed choice modes.[8]

This reads as if the experimenter was testing himself and deciding what to do as he went along.

4. Lack of Control Series

A further difficulty arises through the lack of an adequate control series. It will be remembered that an adequate control series is one in which the process being investigated does not operate but which is similar as far as possible in all other respects to the experimental series.

The measurement of base-line values for the counters did not help very much since any such readings should be taken under conditions as close as possible to those operating in the experimental series. A control series should also ensure that independent records are maintained of targets and hits—or in this case number of random events on chance basis and number actually recorded during the experiment. For that reason trials should best be at random in the experimental and control conditions, with information about the condition kept secret until all scores have been recorded and made public.

The other essential feature is that the investigator is kept blind in regard to which results apply to the control series and which to the experimental series until the results have been established in terms of the effect being investigated.

COMPARISON OF JAHN'S EXPERIMENT
WITH SCHMIDT'S EXPERIMENT

The main differences in Jahn's experimental arrangements compared with those used by Schmidt were:
1. Jahn combined 200 events into a "trial." Schmidt considered each binary output as constituting a trial.
2. Both Schmidt and Jahn tested under the high-scoring condition and the low-scoring condition. Jahn's subject tried to influence scores towards higher or lower values in different trials. Schmidt used a high-scoring subject and a low-scoring subject, each of whom was tested over a number of trials.
3. Jahn appears to have used one "operator" or subject—possibly himself—who had to attempt a high or a low score according to instructions. Schmidt had selected his subjects after initial testing in which they attempted to obtain high scores. For the experiment he used one who had obtained high scores and another who had scored low under these conditions.
4. Jahn's subject(s) appeared to get results less easily than Schmidt's. Thus in the REG I series that produced a result comparable to Schmidt's experiment with the panel of lights, a total of 8,350 trials under the high and low conditions required 1,670,000 events (i.e., 8350 × 200) compared with Schmidt's total of 12,800 trials.

5. In Jahn's experiment the apparatus confronting the subject was complex. Thus it had controls for adjusting: (a) the number of events in each trial; (b) the number of events per second; (c) the start control giving either manual start of a trial or automatic running of a sequence of 50 trials; (d) an event mode selector; (e) a print on/off control; (f) a reset for the event counters and one or two other controls for setting up the apparatus. Schmidt's subjects were situated in another room at a distance of 20 feet from the randomizer and merely saw the panel containing the nine lights.

6. Jahn used a number of units connected together to give a random series of events, to record the number of trials and "hits" in each trial, and to display the results to the subject. The number of events in each trial was assumed to be 200 owing to the fact that 200 pulses p were generated. The possibility has to be considered that a pulse p might have failed to provide an output owing to its coinciding with a transition point in the wave form. If this were so the number of events for the trial would have been better obtained from the actual number of outputs provided by the randomizer. The result of the experiment was mainly dependent on the manner in which during the final analysis observations were allocated to the high-scoring or low-scoring categories. The large number of values considered together with the small extent of any departures from chance-expectation values ensured that even small sources of error arising infrequently would assume importance.

DIFFERENTIAL SCORING

A feature common to the two experiments was the use of differential scoring. Taking high-scoring and low-scoring readings from the subject has obvious dangers and would appear to confer no advantage on the experiment since the subjects scored roughly equally under the high and low conditions. Data for the base-line trials conducted by Jahn would have been available from readings taken in a control series in which the subject would not look at or attempt to influence the indicators.

A remarkable feature of the results in both Jahn's and Schmidt's experiments is that positive and negative scoring always balances out. The end result in terms of events rather than "successes" in no case achieves any degree of statistical significance. In Schmidt's experiment his high-scoring subject performed as well as his low-scoring subject. In Jahn's experiments his subjects performed equally well—no better and no worse—when trying to obtain a high score than when trying to obtain a low score. This equality was apparent over millions of events reported under the two conditions.

EXPERIMENT OF NELSON, DUNNE, AND JAHN

This addition to the original experiment was published in a Technical Note PEAR 84003 of the School of Engineering/Applied Science, Princeton University, and has not been available to the writer. Details of it may be gleaned from the description of Jahn's two experiments given by Rao and Palmer. They describe the two experiments in common terms:

> Each trial in Jahn's experiments incorporated alternate positive and negative counting on successive samples to provide an on-line internal control against any systematic bias in the noise source (i.e., positive and negative noise pulses alternated as hits). Also baseline trials were recorded under a variety of conditions before, during, and after the active PK trials (Jahn 1982, p. 148) in a manner resembling that recommended by critics.[9]

In this second experiment—(B)—22 subjects took part, and from the title it would seem that the individual differences of the subjects were being considered. A total of 390,200 trials were conducted constituting more than 78 million events.

The scoring rate was much lower than in Jahn's first experiment (Experiment A). Table 16-2 gives the scoring rate for Experiment A, consisting of five sections (I, II, III, Ia, and IIa). The scoring rates for Experiment B are based on data given by Rao and Palmer.

TABLE 16-2

Scoring Rates, Total Deviations from Chance Expectation,
and Antichance Odds for PK+ and PK- Values Shown Separately for
Experiment A and Experiment B

Exp't	Type	Trials	Events	Deviation	Odds
A	PK+	13,050	2,610,000	2,910	6,250:1
A	PK-	12,160	2,432,000	-3,539	>10000:1
B	PK+	195,100	39,020,000	8,389	280:1
B	PK-	195,100	39,020,000	-6,828	68:1

It will be seen that with an increase of more than ten times in the number of trials in Experiment B, the antichance odds of the result fell markedly. In this experiment under the PK+ condition, one extra hit in each 4,650 events accounted for the result. It is then clear that the result of the first experiment was much reduced under the conditions prevailing in the second, where more subjects were tested and they mainly persons who were not conducting the experiment.

SUMMARY AND CONCLUSIONS

1. It would appear from the table of results that the experiment was not adequately preplanned. The number of trials varied with each series and with each section in each series. The numbers of trials vary in blocks of 50 as supplied by the automatic provision of 50 trials. The smallest number of trials for conditions PK+ or PK- was 1,750, the largest 8,900, or in terms of blocks of 50, varied between 35 and 178. Since the running average "from a preset origin" was available and seen by the operator, it would have been a simple matter to terminate trials at an appropriate point where either a positive or negative deviation was present.

2. A satisfactory control series was not employed. If the experiment had been confined to the one condition (PK+) and trials interspersed randomly in which the subject did not see the indicators or attempt to exert his PK efforts, the condition being employed could have been unknown to whoever was obtaining the data until it had been compiled and made public. Alternatively, information regarding the series being presented could have been signaled to the computer and print-out by the subject before the start of each run.

3. The procedure employed was unsatisfactory in the first experiment where a single operator was employed who was both experimenter and subject. Instructions (verbatim) as given to the subject are not stated. The subject was confronted with a complex assemblage of apparatus containing a number of dials and switches. He had to make at least one adjustment or make a record before starting each trial or block of trials to show the condition under which he was operating. No details are provided of how this was done or of the forms used to record large amounts of data.

NOTES

1. R. K. Rao and J. Palmer, "The Anomaly Called PSI—Recent Research and Criticism," *Behavioral and Brain Sciences* 10 (1987): 545.

2. R. G. Jahn, "The Persistent Paradox of Psychic Phenomena: An Engineering Perspective," *Proceedings of the IEEE* 70 (1982): 136-70.

3. R. D. Nelson, B. J. Dunne, and R. G. Jahn, "An Experiment with Large Data Base Capability, III: Operator Related Anomalies" (Technical Note PEAR 84003), School of Engineering/Applied Science, Princeton University.

4. R. G. Jahn, "The Persistent Paradox of Psychic Phenomena," p. 146.

5. Ibid., p. 147.

6. Ibid.

7. Ibid.

8. Ibid.

9. R. K. Rao and J. Palmer, op. cit.

17

The Schmidt-Morris-Rudolph Experiment

EXPERIMENTS WITH PRERECORDED TAPES

In Dr. Schmidt's experiments with human subjects he claimed that they had affected the outputs of a random-number generator by merely gazing at a panel of lights on which they directed their PK efforts. The random-number generator was not used in his next experiment. Instead, a random series of outputs was supplied that had been recorded on a magnetic tape before the experiment. An identical copy of the tape was made at the time of recording. This enabled a check to be made after the experiment, to see whether the subject's PK efforts had changed the tape used for the experiment.

Results when using prerecorded tapes were similar to those obtained using the random-number generator, although the tape had not changed when it was compared with its identical copy. But, it was argued, the tapes had been made using the random-number generator. Ipso facto, the subject's efforts must have stretched back in time so as to affect the random-number generator when it was being used to record the tapes.

An experiment reported by Schmidt, Morris, and Rudolph in 1986 appears to have arisen in consequence of Schmidt's findings with prerecorded tapes.[1] It is of particular interest because Schmidt worked together with two other experimenters and appeared to have taken some note of criticisms of his earlier work. An abstract to the published report reads: "We conducted a PK experiment under controlled conditions that were unusually tight. In particular, the experimenter was supervised by observers from another laboratory such that negligence and even fraud by the experimenter could be ruled out as an explanation of the observed effects."[2]

The experiment was conducted by Schmidt working at the Mind Science Foundation in San Antonio, in collaboration with Dr. R. L. Morris, who now holds the Arthur Koestler Chair of Parapsychology at Edinburgh University, and Professor L. Rudolph at Syracuse University.

196

In order to make clear the aim of the experiment the authors first describe the features of an earlier experiment carried out by Schmidt.[3] A binary, random-number generator (RNG) was used to record a series of 1s and 0s simultaneously on two cassette tapes. One of the tapes was then used in an experiment in which the subject attempted to increase the number of one output or the other. The other tape (the duplicate tape) was lodged with an independent observer.

The authors write, "Thus the independent observer can at the end, confirm the success of the PK effort firsthand, by playing his copy of the tape into a computer that counts the recorded 0's and 1's."[4] They also state: "Previously reported experiments (without independent observers) suggest that PK still operates under these conditions and that the two records will agree after the PK effort."[5]

The conclusion that might be drawn by a skeptic is that one of the prerecorded tapes acted as a control series. The result of the experiment would then indicate that there was no evidence that the subjects could affect the random-number generator as had been claimed previously. In addition, the result indicated that there was some form of error present in experiments where it was claimed that the subject had affected the outputs of a random-number generator, since a similar result was obtained with a tape recording that could be checked after the experiment.

Schmidt decided on the other hand that the PK mechanism may be "truly noncausal," and that the subject's effort may have reached back to the time when the random numbers were generated, thus explaining why the two copies of the tape agree.[6] The researchers write:

As an alternative, one might try to avoid such noncausality by the argument that perhaps, events are not physically real until there has been an observation. From this viewpoint the PK effort would not have to reach into the past because nature had not yet decided on the outcome before the PK subject, the first observer, saw the result. Then, the PK effort should no longer succeed if we have some other observer look at the prerecorded data previous to the PK subject's attempt. The only experiment to study this situation so far has, indeed, reported a blocking of the PK effect by a previous observation (Schmidt, 1985).[7]

This theoretical background may appear obscure and make the reader feel like Alice in Wonderland. But the essential aim appears to have been to conduct an experiment to see whether subjects could affect a random series of targets when those targets had been determined before the experiment began and had not been seen by the subject or experimenters.

BASIC STRUCTURE OF THE EXPERIMENT

The authors then describe an experimental method that was intended to illustrate the basic features of their main experiment.

Prerecorded tapes are dispensed with. They are replaced with prerecorded "seed numbers" that will later be used to generate a pseudo-random series when entered into a computer program. The pseudo-random series produced by a computer is dependent on the seed number placed in the computer and the particular algorithm incorporated in the program with which it is used. Given the seed number and the algorithm used to generate the pseudo-random series, the same series of digits can be produced on any computer. Thus the independent observer does not need to be given a tape containing the series of numbers to be used in an experiment. He needs merely to know the seed number and to have a computer program that will generate the pseudo-random series of numbers.

The subject is tested by entering the seed number into a computer. The computer then provides a series of, say, one hundred 1s and 0s individually displayed to the subject at the rate of one per second. The seed number entered completely determines the score in terms of the number of +1s in the series. The authors remark "if the seed number is chosen by a truly random process, then the score contains some truly random elements and might be subject to a PK effort."[8]

If independent observers have a record of the seed numbers to be used in an experiment they can check the result by placing the seed number into their computer, which will then calculate the score of hits obtained by the subject who may be several hundred miles away. They must be careful only to check the result after the subject has made his effort otherwise, according to Schmidt, PK will not operate.

The authors remark that this kind of experiment lends itself easily to tight supervision by an independent observer. They provide the following test procedure.

1. The experimenter generates a print-out of many truly random 6-digit seed numbers and sends this list to the independent observer.

2. The independent observer uses a random method to assign to each seed number the letter H or L.

3. The subject receives a copy of this list of seed numbers with the target assignment H or L.

4. Whenever the subject feels in the right mood, he does a test run. He enters the next seed number and aims at a high or low number of 1s, depending on the target assignment H or L.

At the end, if the PK effort has been successful, the seeds marked H show significantly higher scores than the seeds marked L. This, however, can be confirmed by the independent observer.

5. The independent observer simply uses the computer algorithm (which he has received at the start) to calculate the scores from the seeds.

"And if the subject has been successful, the independent observer finds the 'inexplicable' result that the seeds he happened to mark H led to higher scores than the seeds marked L. Without having to trust anybody else, the independent observer can detect, firsthand, an anomalous correlation between his random assignments and the actual scores."[9]

THE METHOD USED IN THE SCHMIDT-MORRIS-RUDOLPH EXPERIMENT

In the experiment the subject tried to influence the motion of a pendulum seen on a TV screen. The pendulum increased its amplitude of swing following a +1 output in a binary random series and decreased it following a -1 output. Two different arrangements for varying the motion of the pendulum were used, called SWING1 and SWING2. A third type of program called CLICK was also used at some sessions. Here the subject was given auditory feedback via earphones, rather than visual feedback. He heard a CLICK that could appear to be "coming from the center of the head" or "to originate outside the head."[10]

The experimental procedure and the final statistical evaluation to be carried out were decided in advance. It is stated: "The whole experiment was to consist of 10 sections of test runs. Each section was to be evaluated independently, and the total significance was to be calculated from the resulting 10 scores."[11] The various displays SWING1, SWING2, and CLICK were used in different sections. The number of test runs conducted in a section varies from 40 to 240. Each test run consisted of 128 binary events that had been determined by the randomizer. In the paper the word "trial" was used to denote a test run.

THE PROCEDURE ADOPTED

1. The experimenter used a computer to generate a supply of truly random 6-figure seed numbers sufficient for the whole experiment. At the start of each section he decided on the number of test runs to be made in that section and the test arrangement to be used (SWING1, SWING2, or CLICK). He then mailed a corresponding list of seed numbers to the home address of the first observer (L.R.) and informed the second observer (R.M.) by telephone of the number of trials to be made and the test arrangement to be used.

2. The second observer had no knowledge of the seed numbers. He had to prepare a list to show the order in which the assignments high and low were to be used by the subject in the successive 40 runs to be made during the test. It had been arranged that seed numbers should be used in successive pairs, the first member of each pair to be used in either the H=(high) or L=(low) scoring condition and the second member in the opposite condition. Observer 2 labeled the first member of each pair either H (high assignment) or L (low assignment) at random using an electronic random-number generator. He then allotted the second member of each pair the opposite assignment

(H or L). Thus, Observer 2 merely prepared a list of the letters L and H to indicate the manner in which the tests were to be carried out. He had no knowledge of the seed numbers at this point.

3. Subsequently the two observers met to exchange copies of the seed number lists and the assignment list. Copies of the two lists were deposited with an administrative secretary of the School of Computer and Information Science at Syracuse University.

4. When this had been done the experimenter (H.S.) phoned the administrative secretary and received the list of target assignments to enter into his copies of the seed numbers.

5. The testing could then start.

6. The subjects were sent a list of the seed numbers and the target assignments together with a small test computer. They could then work at home at their own convenience. The instructions given to them are not stated. The subject presumably placed the seed number into the computer program and observed the assignment (H or L) that told him whether to try to make the pendulum seen on the screen swing with greater or lesser amplitude.

After a section was completed the experimenter informed the two observers. They were then in a position to work out the result of the experiment for themselves by placing the appropriate seed numbers into a computer and reading off the scores.

Scores were to be calculated in the following manner. Taking each pair of seed numbers (an H and an L), the scores were first obtained by inserting the seed number for each run into a computer program. This program produces a list of 128 of the numbers 0–7 followed by the total value (or score for the run). Only the total value was used for assessing the score. The other values were presumably included only to produce the image of the pendulum on the TV screen.

The two scores, one of which should be high if PK is operating and the other low, are then converted into a "pair score" where

$$\text{Pair-score} = (\text{score of H-seed}) - (\text{score of L-seed})$$

EVALUATION OF RESULTS

Details of the program (SWING1, SWING2, or CLICK) used for each of the ten sections of the experiment together with the subjects involved and the number of runs are given in the first four columns of table 17-1, reproduced from the report. It should be noted that column four headed "Trials" indicates the number of seed numbers involved, where each seed number determines a run of 128 randomized events constituting trials in the usual sense of the word.

TABLE 17-1

Result of the Ten Sections of the Experiment

Section	Program	Subjects	Trials	z
1	SWING1	H.S.	40	1.66
2	SWING1	H.S., F.G.	40	0.39
3	SWING2	H.S., F.G.	40	0.49
4	SWING2	F.G., J.N.	40	0.20
5	SWING2	H.S., D.R.	120	1.71
6	CLICK	H.S.	120	1.13
7	SWING2	G.S.	120	1.17
8	SWING2	H.S.	120	0.89
9	SWING2	6 Ss.	240	-0.17
10	CLICK	H.S.	160	1.18
Total			1040	2.73

A note under the table reads:

The subjects were selected because of their promising scores in pilot tests. The experimenter (H.S.), in the role of a subject, contributed a considerable part of the results.

The programs SWING1 and SWING2 provided feedback in the form of a pendulum swinging with randomly varying amplitude. The CLICK program gave auditory feedback by two types of clicks.

The z values measure the deviation of the scores from chance in the desired direction in units of one standard deviation.[12]

It is also stated that "From the run scores, the observers could derive a significance measure for the whole section. The corresponding calculations were also carried out independently by the experimenter."[13] The z values (or critical ratios) in the fifth column of the table provide this significance measure when converted into probability values.

Information about the subjects other than that in table 17-1 is not provided nor are the observed values from which the z values in column five are obtained. The method of assessing the results and obtaining these z values is given as follows in the report:

Let us explain the details of the evaluation taking the third section as an example. This section comprised 40 trials. The corresponding 6-digit seed numbers that had been generated and recorded by the the experimenters at the start were the following:

735563 808629 330749 606721 761655 740931 657043 829872
268771 920672 585294 048780 171792 427853 093289 621908
758408 720250 265557 560370 152185 481572 904786 515511
604665 690171 137490 300651 229029 236569 553928 813059
212347 200200 679407 964502 317076 002361 538852 039613

These seed numbers were sent to the first observer. The second observer generated with his own random number generator the following target assignments:

H L H L H L H L H L L H L H H L L H L H H L
L H L H H L L H H L L H H L H L H L H L L H

These assignments refer to the first member in successive pairs of seed numbers, the second member having the opposite assignment.

The observers had been informed at the start that this section was to use the SWING2 arrangement, and they had received a copy of the experimenter's computer to calculate the scores for the 40 seeds. The reader may make the corresponding calculation with the help of the BASIC listing in Appendix 1. The first two scores, for example, are Score (735563) = 580, and Score (808629) = 332. From these scores we can derive for each trial pair a pair-score:

Pair-score = (score of H-seed) – (score of L-seed)

The resulting 20 pair-scores are:

248 80   72 –236 201 368   90 335   5 –64
–113 15 –188 173   41 –39 –278 –193 140 –217[14]

It is pointed out that: "Under the chance-hypothesis, positive and negative values in this sequence are equally likely. The subject's PK effort, however, was directed toward biasing these numbers toward positive values. To check for such a bias, a t test might seem appropriate. To avoid any assumptions about the distribution, however, we used a nonparametric rank order test (Hoel 1962)."[15]

Details of the test are then given together with the probability value for obtaining a result as obtained in section 3. By chance, this value (p) is equal to 0.31, which gives the z value of 0.49 as shown in table 17–1.

The overall result of the experiment is then obtained by combining the z scores in table 17–1 to give z where

$$z = (z(1) + z(2) + \ldots + z(10)) / 10 = 2.71$$

giving against chance odds of 300 to 1 as shown in table 17–1.

The report then states: "At this level of significance, the independent observers could confirm the existence of an anomalous correlation between their target assignments and the actual scores."[16]

In a discussion the authors state:

> The reported study represents our first attempt to confirm previously reported PK results under full supervision by independent observers. We had decided in advance to submit the results for publication no matter what the outcome would be.
>
> From the view of the independent observers the result appeared as an "anomalous correlation," not understandable in terms of current physics. By labeling the effect as psychokinesis (PK), we do not want to imply any particular underlying mechanism. The term should only characterize the experimental set-up with a test subject who tried to mentally affect some form of display.
>
> We make no claims about the validity of the theoretical speculations that led to the design of the experiment. One might even wonder whether the PK effect did not enter through the second observer, subconsciously forcing his random number generator into producing favorable target assignments.[17]

The report also states that copies of the original seed number lists with their target assignments are on record with the *Journal of Parapsychology* and available to readers who want to perform any further analysis of the data.

APPRAISAL OF THE EXPERIMENT

In order to assess the result of an experiment of this nature the scores attributed to PK must be compared with those that would be expected to arise by chance in the absence of any such process. We assume that PK is impossible to see whether the result can be accounted for in terms of established processes. In the case of the experiment the odds of 300 to 1 claimed for the result hardly eliminate the likelihood of chance occurrence, but past experience of experiments in parapsychology makes it likely that some form of error is present.

There are two main areas that must be questioned: first, the procedure adopted, and second, the statistical treatment of the data.

The general basis for the experiment is simple and ingenious. It provides the basis for a foolproof experiment. In it the relationship is examined between two sets of random data: the one relating to the seed numbers that are determined by a pseudorandom series that anyone can know before the experiment and that can be made public or communicated to observers before the experiment is made; the second, a randomized list of letter pairs (H and L or L and H) that is prepared by an observer who has no information regarding the list of seed numbers. Thus the result is dependent on the number of correspondences between two binary lists:

1. A list of the letter pairs HL or LH in random order.

2. A list of values that are positive or negative produced by taking two seeds and subtracting a value produced by one from the value produced by the other. These difference values have equal probabilities of arising by chance.

Forty seed numbers produced twenty such pairs, thus the situation is similar to that where an individual has twenty guesses at heads or tails following the spin of a coin.

In order to avoid error, similar precautions have to be taken as in the early card-guessing experiments:

1. Independent recording of guesses and targets brought together by a third person after the test.

2. Planning the number of subjects and the number of trials to be made in advance.

3. Accurate maintenance of records.

4. Provision of randomness in the two lists representing targets and guesses and maintenance of independence between these lists.

1. Independent Recording

If the procedure adopted in the report was followed, and if checks were made that this was done, i.e., independent scoring by the experimenter, the observer 1, and observer 2, and if checks were also made with the lists held by the secretary, this might be sufficient; but no mention is made of any check between the records and calculations made by each person involved or with the list held by the secretary.

In the experiment the seed numbers were obtained in random order by the experimenter. The list was sent to observer 1 who could ensure that its order was not changed. Observer 2 prepared the list of HL values in random order. It is stated: "Subsequently R.M. and L.R. met to exchange copies of the seed number lists and the corresponding target assignment sequences. A copy of the seed number list and a copy of the generated target sequence were deposited with an administrative secretary of the School of Computer and Information Science at Syracuse University."[18]

The two lists should have been deposited with the administrative secretary before the two observers met, as it has been recognized since the days of card guessing that all contact betweeen experimenters in an experiment of this sort should be eliminated so that the result cannot be affected.

2. Planning in Advance

It might be expected that the plan of the experiment should be included in the report and that sufficient detail should be included to enable the results to be assessed by the reader.

There is little evidence of careful planning in advance. The experiment used three different methods for providing the display for the subject. If this was necessary and planned before the experiment began it might have been expected that a balanced design would have been used. Each program (SWING1, SWING2, and CLICK) would then have been employed for the same number of runs and with the same number of subjects.

The subjects consisted of four whose names are given and six unnamed whose results are lumped together in section 9. It is not, in fact, clear whether the six unnamed subjects included any of the named subjects who took part in other sections. The number of runs varies from 40 to 240 in the ten sections being largest in section 9 where the overall result was below chance level. Schmidt acted as both experimenter and subject in seven of the ten sections in the experiment. Four other subjects are named. Six subjects in section 9 are unnamed, possibly because in total they scored below the chance level.

3. Accurate Maintenance of Records

In a carefully preplanned experiment it might be expected that forms should be preregistered and collected again after each experiment so that it could be ensured that for any section of the experiment all runs planned before testing started were included; that none were omitted; that the predetermined number of runs was made with each subject; and that nothing was omitted from the final calculation.

No dates are given in the report. No mention is made of the result of any checks that were carried out between the results calculated by the three persons involved.

4. The Maintenance of Independence between Records

Control series were not incorporated in the design except insofar as the low-scoring and high-scoring series interposed randomly-controlled-against-bias values produced by the seed numbers. There were three sources of randomization in the experiment. The seed numbers were randomized by Schmidt using a truly random generator. The HL assignment values were randomized by Morris using a second randomizer providing a series dependent on electronic noise as a source of randomness. The seed values determined the 128 values arranged in pseudo-random order and the overall value.

The essential control feature in the experiment is the list of HL-LH values prepared by Morris. Only he knew the order of these values present in the one list that he had prepared before he had any knowledge of the seed numbers. The list of seed numbers in the order they were to be used had been sent to the first observer (L.R.) and deposited with the secretary before (although not quite) the HL list was made known to anyone other than L.R.

A possible source of error arises when considering the randomization of the seed numbers and the order in which they arose on the one list, and the randomization of HL values and the order in which they appeared on the other list.

The list of seed numbers gave successive pairs of values:

$$a1, a2 : a3, a4 : \ldots : a39, a40$$

This gave a list of difference values:

$$b1 = a1 - a2 : b2 = b4 - b3 \ldots b20 = b40 - b39$$

The list $b1$, $b2$, $b3$, $\ldots$ $b20$ provides + and – values in random order and could be substituted with a list of +1 and –1 values for the purpose of this example.

In the same manner the list prepared by observer 2 with his electronic random generator consists of a series of letters H and L arranged at random for positions 1, 3, 5 in his forming pairs of letters in the list of the form HL or LH. This list can be reduced to a list of twenty items in which the couple HL or LH arises at each position. This list can be reduced by making HL = +1 and LH = –1 into a sequence of twenty binary events.

If such lists always contained twenty items owing to the pairing of forty assignments, as is suggested although not made explicit in the text, there were twenty-six such lists compiled in pairs during the course of the experiment.

Any bias present in either of the two randomizers was effectively eliminated owing to the use of pairs of values, but an essential feature of the two lists is the order in which the items in them arise. Such a form of bias is most likely in the case of the first item in each series. Thus, if the list of forty seed numbers supplied by the experimenter tended to start with + (or –) value (due to a higher value for the first seed than the second) and the electronic random generator tended to start with a + (or a –) a correspondence would be established between the first item on the two lists. Thus while it is claimed that "negligence or even fraud even by the experimenter could be ruled out," this was not necessarily the case.[19]

The second observer was in no position to alter his list, but the experimenter decided on the seed numbers that were sent in a batch to the first observer. If these tended to have a high-value seed position 1 and a lower-value seed position 2 (or vice versa) this could account for higher values being obtained with H-seeds than with L-seeds. Since Schmidt was not supervised when he produced his batches of seed numbers, he was in a position to take advantage of any bias of this nature if it was present in the random series produced by the observer.

STATISTICAL EVALUATION OF THE RESULT

The method employed for assessing the results was different from that employed by Schmidt in his earlier work. Thus in the experiment with the light moving on a panel of lights, the number of +1 binary outputs that arose from the randomizer was compared with the total number of +1 and –1 outputs. Each event was treated as a trial. In the case of the present experiment what was called the "Trial" in table 17-1 was dependent on 128 binary outputs. The ten sections of the experiment thus consisted of 122,120 binary events— or trials as previously used. Each seed number produced a series of values that were used to change the position of the image of the pendulum. The pendulum could swing with eight different amplitudes ranging from 0 to 7. At each position along the series of 128 targets the value (0–7) was increased by one or decreased by one according to the output of the binary series. Values were, however, limited to the range 0–7.

Thus a random series of +1s and –1s increases or decreases the value representing the amplitude of swing in the image of the pendulum. The total value is meant to represent the mean amplitude of swing. The first value in the list, however, appears to be arbitrary, being any value from 0 to 7.

The mean value is dependent on the initial value and the order in which +1s and –1s arise in the series. Thus a seed number series starting with the value 7 followed by outputs –1 and +1 alternating will give a series of numbers 7, 6, 7, 6, followed by outputs +1 and –1 alternating will give a series 0, 1, 0, 1 with a total value 32. The two series are formed from the same numbers of +1 and –1 outputs but the resultant total or average amplitude is dependent on the initial value produced by the seed number. If the subject is exerting PK to influence his score and obtain a high average-amplitude value, his result is thus partly a matter of luck depending on the seed value he has been allotted.

The pair-score being the difference of two numbers taken at random from a range of 0 to 1792 gives a symmetrical distribution with its mean at zero. In the event of this deviating from normality so as to require a nonparametric test, a chi square or a sign test could have been used. It would also have enabled allowance to be made more accurately for the odds against chance for the whole experiment, taking into account the varying numbers of "trials" in the ten sections of the experiment. Thus it is stated:

Table 1 lists the obtained z values. Calculate a combined z value:

$$z = (z(1) + (z(2) + \ldots + z(10)) / 10 = 2.71$$

Under the null hypothesis, the probability for obtaining such a high or a higher z value (as the result of chance) is

$$p = .0032 \text{ (odds against chance of 300:1)}[20]$$

Since the largest number of subjects included in section 9 were responsible for the largest number of observations and scored negatively, their effort (or lack of effort) is minimized in the method employed for assessing the experiment. If one wishes to consider the fact that nine of the ten sections gave positive z values and the one a negative z value, odds of around 100:1 would have been achieved.

In the case of section 3, they were considering twenty values that had equal chances on the null hypothesis of being negative or positive, the observed values—twelve of which were positive and eight negative—could have been assessed using a simple nonparametric test based on the binomial distribution using the summation of the first eight terms of $(\frac{1}{2} + \frac{1}{2})$ *20* or by using the chi-square test. This would have given a value of p = 0.25 compared with the value 0.31 given in the report.

In Schmidt's experiment with the panel of lights, a random binary series of +1s and –1s changed the position of the light that the subject was attempting to cause to move around the circle of lights. The result was assessed in terms of the number of +1 and –1 outputs that arose in the random series of 128 targets. In the present experiment, rather than considering the +1 and –1 outputs, the effect of these on the amplitude of swing is considered that has little relationship to the efforts of the subject.

If the results with the pendulum are assessed in terms of the +1 and –1 elements in the random series, the values so obtained from each seed number will certainly conform to a binomial distribution and enable a t test to be employed on each run as well as on each set of 40 runs in the manner employed by Schmidt in the past.

The values for section 3 of the experiment can be obtained by placing the seed values for this section as given in the report into the computer program listing also provided. A modification of this program given in Appendix A (page 275) prints out the values and also a list of the +1 and –1 outputs that created those values.

To check whether the H-assignments give more + than – values, and the L-assignments more – than + values, the data may be entered into a contingency table as follows:

TABLE 17–2

Contingency Table Showing the Observed Values (0) for Section 3 of the Report in Terms of + and – Outputs in the Random Binary Series

	+ Values	– Values	Total
H-assignment	1,267	1,273	2,540
L-assignment	1,231	1,309	2,540
Totals	2,498	2,582	5,080

The values expected to arise by chance (E values), taking into account the numbers of + and – outputs that were present, are shown below.

TABLE 17-3

Expected Values in Respect of Data in Table 17-2

	+ Values	– Values	Total
H-assignment	1,249	1,291	2,540
L-assignment	1,249	1,291	2,540
Totals	2,498	2,582	5,080

This gives chi square = 1.02, n = 1, $0.25 < p > 0.50$.

It is thus seen that there is little to indicate a result greatly different from what might have been expected by chance. The probability value obtained also differs considerably from the value of 0.31 given in the report.

It may be noted that the numbers of + and – outputs in a total of 5,080 outputs are 2,498 and 2,582, respectively, compared with the chance-expectation values from the randomizer of 2,540 in each case. Chi square in this case = 1.39 gives a value for p of between 0.1 and 0.25.

CONCLUSIONS

The experiment showed a marked improvement compared with Schmidt's earlier experiments in that three investigators were involved, together with a secretary who registered the receipt of records. A method was employed that aimed at the elimination of any possibility of error.

The experiment showed little evidence of careful preplanning of the procedure to ensure that all results were included in the relevant sections of the experiment as planned. The procedure was unnecessarily complicated by the use of three different techniques for presenting the image and possibly for obtaining an average value. Insufficient detail was provided in the report of the method of randomization employed by the second observer. It is not clear that complete independence of values for the seed numbers and the assignments high and low was maintained since records were not sent to the secretary before the two observers met. The statistical method employed was unnecessary and of doubtful relevance. More direct means for obtaining z scores and the associated probabilities could have been employed.

The lodging of lists of seed numbers and HL assignments with an independent secretary was an important control feature. It meant that each of the investigators could independently calculate the result before communicating with each other and any disagreement could be noted and if necessary a check made.

In a preplanned experiment it would be preferable if the complete list of seed numbers to be used throughout all the tests, together with the section of the tests in which each block was to be used, was lodged in a sealed envelope with the secretary before the experiment started; that after each test the records of seed numbers employed in that test and the list of assignments were independently lodged with the secretary before the observers met to exchange lists; that the calculations of the result made by the three investigators were lodged with the secretary before the investigators checked their calculations; and that the records held by the secretary should then be made public. It would appear unnecessary for the investigators to have any communication until all tests were completed.

The experiment provides, however, a basis for the development of a repeatable demonstration in the event of the supposed processes being real. It would require further preliminary tests to establish the distribution of the ability to obtain above-chance scores in the population, and to make a decision on the number of tests to be carried out to ensure that the result could be repeated. On the other hand since Schmidt himself was the most successful of the subjects tested, further repetitions could be planned in which he would act as subject.

NOTES

1. Helmut Schmidt, R. L. Morris, and L. Rudolph, "Channeling Evidence for PK Effects to Independent Observers," *Journal of Parapsychology* 50 (1986): 1–16.
2. Ibid.
3. Helmut Schmidt, "PK Effect on Pre-recorded Targets," *Journal of the American Society for Psychical Research* 70, no. 3 (1976): 267–91.
4. Helmut Schmidt, R. L. Morris, and L. Rudolph, "Channeling Evidence for PK Effects to Independent Observers," p. 3.
5. Ibid.
6. Ibid.
7. Ibid.
8. Ibid., p. 4.
9. Ibid., pp. 4–5.
10. Ibid., p. 6.
11. Ibid.
12. Ibid., p. 10.
13. Ibid., p. 7.
14. Ibid., p. 8.
15. Ibid.
16. Ibid., p. 10.
17. Ibid., p. 12.
18. Ibid., p. 7.
19. Ibid., p. 1.
20. Ibid., p. 10.

18

Psychokinesis
Summary and Conclusions

ATTEMPTS TO OBTAIN A
REPEATABLE DEMONSTRATION

During the last twenty years, following the use of an electronic randomizer and the introduction of techniques developed by Helmut Schmidt, psychokinesis has emerged as a major area of research in parapsychology. Schmidt's experiment using the panel of lights gave a result having antichance odds of 10 million to 1 under conditions that were claimed to exclude the possibility of erorr. As such, it merits special attention since something or other is likely to have been responsible for the result. In the form put forward by Schmidt it provides the basis for a repeatable demonstration of PK and therefore should be of profound importance to those who have considered such a process as PK to be possible.

In order to provide a repeatable demonstration it may be expected that some teething problems will arise requiring modification to the original design. If the result is not confirmed under such conditions, the original demonstrations should be discarded. Its result may then be attributed to any weaknesses in the original design that have subsequently been removed. It might be expected that Schmidt himself would have provided further evidence by repeating his experiment, taking into account changes in procedure to take account of criticism. It is remarkable, however, that he appears to have made no attempt to do so. If he has, the results have not been reported.

The experiments discussed in the preceding two chapters do not constitute repetitions of Schmidt's original experiment, which was discussed in chapter 10. They merely include some common features and employ similar procedures. A common feature is that an electronic randomizer is employed to create a randomized series of events.

The use of a randomizer in PK experiments is of interest when considering the manner in which the early PK experiments developed alongside the card-guessing experiments at Duke University. In the card-guessing experiments it was necessary that the subject should have no information through sensory channels or other information that would enable him to predict the target. Using a fixed number of choices presented in random order gave the opportunity of making systematic tests that could be subjected to a straightforward statistical test enabling his performance to be assessed.

Early tests for PK using dice or cards utilized events whose outcome had fixed probability so that success could be analyzed statistically. It was suggested at the time that if a subject could influence a coin so that, when tossed by an experimenter, it turned up heads when on some occasions it would have turned up tails, he should then be able to influence an event whose outcome was fixed beforehand. Thus by using a coin-tossing device that would ensure that it fell heads up, the effects of PK would become immediately apparent following a single throw.

Schmidt's first experiments with his randomizer sought to demonstrate that PK could affect a random event, i.e., the time at which an electron was emitted from a radioactive source. This idea appears to have been superseded since the subject is now said to affect the outputs of a machine that are initially determined. Two questions may then be asked.

1. WHY IS A TRULY RANDOM SERIES OF EVENTS NECESSARY?

Card-guessing experiments initially used closed packs of cards in which there were 5 of each of the 5 different symbols. Provided that the subject had no knowledge of results until he had made all his guesses, his expectation of success with 25 cards was still $1/5 \times 25$ although the distribution of possible scores was changed.

In a PK test knowledge of results cannot affect the outcome. Thus by using a closed series of events in which there are equal numbers of the two outcomes speculation about nonrandomness or bias in the series does not arise. At the end of a run of, say, two hundred events, the expected score in the absence of PK is one hundred and the subject becomes aware of any effect he has had on the score.

2. WHY USE A RANDOM SERIES OF ANY SORT?

If a random series of events is generated, any arrangement of the outcomes is equally probable. Thus a series of two hundred +1s has exactly the same probability of arising as any other sequence. It is a simple matter to modify the modulo-2 counter system used by Schmidt so that it will generate a known sequence of events of a patterned nature so that the subject will see when he has achieved a hit. Subjects thus have knowledge of results after each event. This should be more encouraging for them than, for example, when the effects of their efforts are only expected to have an effect on the system once in every hundred or so attempts, and only then do they see whether a light moves in one direction or the other.

In the case of experiments with prerecorded targets or with targets determined completely by a pseudorandom number generator and a seed number, it is merely required to replace the algorithm used for the generation of the series with one that produces an ordered sequence or a regular sequence of a particular target. Failure to obtain results with such series and not with other series should, in any case, be of interest to the investigators in indicating the nature of those series of events that produce optimum effects in their experiments.

SUMMARY

Schmidt's result using the panel of lights required a large number of trials to be conducted in an experiment controlled by a single experimenter. It clearly did not provide a repeatable demonstration, but it provided the basis on which such a demonstration could have been developed.

Jahn's experiment at Princeton required a vast increase in the number of events that were to be influenced in order to achieve a result comparable to that of Schmidt. In addition, it was unsatisfactory in its method and procedure. In the case of the second experiment at Princeton, it appears to have been realized that it is necessary to include more than one investigator; but in the course of improving the experimental conditions the number of observations then had to be increased into the millions rather than the thousands in order to obtain a diminished effect.

The experiment conducted by Schmidt, Morris, and Rudolph should theoretically be repeatable. Those parapsychologists who can stomach the bizarre nature of the results and underlying logic have the opportunity of developing a demonstration of PK to silence all criticism.

Part Five

Nonexperimental Investigations

19

Anecdotal Evidence

Accounts of unusual experiences that appear to contradict accepted ideas of what human beings can or cannot do are continually being reported in the media. Such accounts were studied in the early days of psychical research in the attempt to provide proof of telepathy, clairvoyance, foreknowledge, and other processes. Any such story may be examined to decide how closely it checks with what is known about what actually happened and how far it has been elaborated and distorted. If it is decided that the event did take place, it is then necessary to decide how likely or unlikely its occurrence would be in the ordinary run of events. If the happening still appears unusual after such an examination, an explanation may then be sought to account for it.

Anecdotal data of this nature tend to be unreliable since what is reported is dependent on observations made at the time of the event, on their interpretation at the time, and on their memory of it when it is reported.

It is known from experimental work within psychology that different observers may give different accounts of what they see and hear in the same situation, and that changes may occur in memory before the event is recalled at a later date. With the passage of time accounts may show progressive changes and become increasingly less accurate when checked with the original events.

THE APPARITION SEEN BY SIR EDMUND HORNBY

An early case reported by Gurney and Myers was thought at the time to provide irrefutable evidence for the appearance of an apparition. It concerned Sir Edmund Hornby, formerly Chief Judge of the Supreme Consular Court of China and Japan at Shanghai. He had been in the habit of allowing reporters to come to his house in the evening to get his written judgments for the next day's papers. On January 19, 1875, he wrote out these judgments in his study an hour or two after dinner. His report concerning subsequent events, as taken down by Gurney and Myers, was as follows:

I rang for the butler, gave him the envelope, and told him to give it to the reporter who should call for it. I was in bed before twelve. . . . I had gone to sleep, when I was awakened by hearing a tap on the study door, but thinking it might be the butler—looking to see if the fires were safe and the gas turned off—I turned over . . . to sleep again. Before I did so, I heard a tap at my bedroom door. Still thinking it the butler . . . I said "Come in." The door opened, and, to my surprise, in walked Mr. ————. I sat up and said, "You have mistaken the door; but the butler has the judgments, so go and get it." Instead of leaving the room he came to the foot of the bed. I said, "Mr. ————, you forget yourself! Have the goodness to walk out directly. This is rather an abuse of my favor." He looked deadly pale, but was dressed as usual, and sober, and said, "I know I am guilty of an unwarrantable intrusion, but finding that you were not in your study, I have ventured to come here."

I was losing my temper, but something in the man's manner disinclined me to jump out of bed to eject him by force. So I said, simply, "This is too bad, really; pray leave the room at once." Instead of doing so he put his hand on the foot-rail and gently, and as if in pain, sat down on the foot of the bed. I glanced at the clock and saw that it was about twenty minutes past one. I said, "The butler has had the judgment since half-past eleven; go and get it!" He said, "Pray forgive me; if you knew all the circumstances you would. Time presses. Pray give me a précis of your judgment, and I will take a note in my book of it," drawing his reporter's book out of his breast pocket. I said, "I will do nothing of the kind. Go downstairs, find the butler, and don't disturb me—you will wake my wife; otherwise I shall have to put you out." He slightly moved his hand. I said, "Who let you in?" He answered, "No one." "Confound it," I said, "What the devil do you mean? Are you drunk?" He replied quickly, "No, and never shall be again; but I pray your lordship give me your decision, for my time is short." I said, "You don't seem to care about my time, and this is the last time I will ever allow a reporter in my house." He stopped me short, saying, "This is the last time I shall ever see you anywhere."

Well, fearful that this commotion might arouse and frighten my wife, I shortly gave him the gist of my judgment. . . . He seemed to be taking it down in shorthand; it might have taken two or three minutes. When I finished, he rose, thanked me for excusing his intrusion and for the consideration I had always shown him and his colleagues, opened the door, and went away. I looked at the clock; it was on the stroke of half-past one.

[Lady Hornby awoke, thinking she had heard talking; and her husband told her what had happened, and repeated the account when dressing the next morning.]

I went to court a little before ten. The usher came into my room to robe me, when he said, "A sad thing happened last night, sir. Poor ————

was found dead in his room." I said "Bless my soul! Dear me! What did he die of, and when?" "Well, sir, it appeared he went up to his room as usual at ten to work at his papers. His wife went up about twelve to ask him when he would be ready for bed. He said, 'I have only the Judge's judgment to get ready, and then I have finished.' As he did not come, she went up again, about a quarter to one, to his room and peeped in, and thought she saw him writing, but she did not disturb him. At half-past one she again went to him and spoke to him at the door. As he didn't answer she thought he had fallen asleep so she went up to rouse him. To her horror he was dead. On the floor was his notebook, which I have brought away. She sent for the doctor who arrived a little after two, and said he had been dead, he concluded, about an hour. I looked at the note-book. There was the usual heading: 'In the Supreme Court, before the Chief Judge: The Chief Judge gave judgment this morning in the case to the following effect'—and then followed a few lines of indecipherable shorthand."

I sent for the magistrate who would act as coroner, and desired him to examine Mr. ———'s wife and servants as to whether Mr. ——— had left his home or could possibly have left it without their knowledge, between eleven and one on the previous night. The result of the inquest showed he died of some form of heart disease, and had not and could not have left the house without the knowledge of at least his wife, if not of the servants. Not wishing to air my "spiritual experience" for the benefit of the press or the public, I kept the matter at the time to myself, only mentioning it to my Puisne Judge and to one or two friends; but when I got home to tiffin I asked my wife to tell me as nearly as she could remember what I had said to her during the night, and I made a brief note of her replies and of the facts.

[Lady Hornby has kindly confirmed the above facts to us, as far as she was cognizant of them.]

As I said then, so I say now—I was not asleep, but wide awake. After a lapse of nine years my memory is quite clear on the subject. I have not the least doubt I saw the man—have not the least doubt that the conversation took place between us.

I may add that I had examined the butler in the morning—who had given me back the MS. in the envelope when I went to the court after breakfast—as to whether he had locked the door as usual, and if anyone could have got in. He said that he had done everything as usual, adding that no one could have got in even if he had not locked the door, as there was no handle outside—which there is not. . . . The coolies said they opened the door as usual that morning—turned the key and undid the chains.[1]

The following November, the *Nineteenth Century* contained a letter from a Mr. Frederick H. Balfour pointing out certain discrepancies between the account and the facts:

1. Mr. ———— was the Rev. Hugh Lang Nivens, editor of the *Shanghai Courier*. He died not at *one* in the morning but between eight or nine A.M. after a good night's rest.

2. There was no Lady Hornby at that time. Sir Edmund's second wife had died two years previously, and he did not marry again till three months *after* the event.

3. No inquest was ever held.

4. The story turns upon the judgment of a certain case to be delivered the next day, January 20, 1875. There is no record of any such judgment.[2]

Before publishing Balfour's letter, the editors of the *Nineteenth Century* had sent it to Judge Hornby, who commented:

My vision must have followed the death (some three months) instead of synchronizing with it. At the same time this hypothesis is quite contrary to the recollection of the facts both in my own mind and in Lady Hornby's mind. . . . If I had not believed, as I still believe, that every word of it [the story] was accurate, and that my memory was to be relied on, I should not have ever told it as a personal experience.[3]

The late John E. Coover, one of the greatest critics of psychical research, in discussing this case wrote:

All these discrepancies are concordant with the results of psychological research on testimony, and are to be attributed to psychological law rather than to either dishonesty or culpable carelessness.

The readiness of metaphysics to rely upon observations of séance phenomena, their insistence that illusion can be avoided, and their quick condemnation of the competence of an observer who is tricked, clearly indicate that they do not understand that error is inevitable. Consequently the psychologist remains incredulous in the face of all the accumulating "evidence."[4]

Gurney and Myers stated when introducing their report that its evidential value depended on the high authority on which it came. But the story illustrates that an eminent judge is no less liable to errors of memory and recall than anyone else.

SOME OTHER STRANGE HAPPENINGS

In 1886, Gurney, Myers, and Podmore published *Phantasms of the Living*.[5] Its 2 large volumes contained accounts of more than 700 unusual happenings, many of a type to make the flesh creep. The accounts were based on reports received from members of the public about their own unusual experiences. Since that time, thousands more such cases have been collected together by various societies and groups interested in psychical research in the effort to provide conclusive proof of ghosts, apparitions, telepathy, clairvoyance, and precognition. None of the stories investigated has withstood critical examination.

The journals and files of the Society for Psychical Research must contain thousands of these accounts of spontaneous occurences. In his *The Personality of Man,* written in 1947, G. N. M. Tyrrell gave a few examples drawn from those investigations.[6] He was a firm believer in the supernatural, and it is reasonable to assume that the cases he reports are the best ones he could collect to demonstrate the reality of extrasensory phenomena. But it is necessary only to read them to see how trivial and unsatisfactory they are. Anyone who says, "That may be so but I know of a case far more difficult to explain," should remember that Tyrrell had at his fingertips all the data that could survive any sort of investigation. He reported the first case as

A certain Canon Bourne and his two daughters were out hunting, and the daughters decided to return home with the coachman while their father went on. "As we were turning to go home," say the two Misses Bourne in a joint account, "we distinctly saw my father waving his hat to us and signing us to follow him. He was on the side of a small hill, and there was a dip between him and us. My sister, the coachman, and myself all recognized my father and also the horse. The horse looked so dirty and shaken that the coachman remarked he thought there had been a nasty accident. As my father waved his hat I clearly saw the Lincoln and Bennett mark inside, though from the distance we were apart it ought to have been utterly impossible for me to have seen it. . . . Fearing an accident, we hurried down the hill. From the nature of the ground we had to lose sight of my father, but it took us very few seconds to reach the place where we had seen him. When we got there, there was no sign of him anywhere, nor could we see anyone in sight at all. We rode about for some time looking for him but could not see or hear anything of him. We all reached home within a quarter of an hour of each other. My father then told us he had never been in the field, nor near the field in which we thought we saw him, the whole of the day. He had never waved to us and had met with no accident. My father was riding the only white horse that was out that day.[7]

Tyrrell comments on this story:

The cause which set the telepathic machinery in motion in this case is obscure. No accident had happened to Canon Bourne. It more often happens that the vision coincides with some accident or peculiar event happening to the agent. . . . Canon Bourne unconsciously imposed the pattern or theme of his presence in that particular field, with details of horse, etc., on the minds of his two daughters and the coachman.[8]

If the definition of telepathy is to be extended so that it includes cases where the percipient has information that does not accord with any actual happening, it would appear that normal means of verification do not apply. In this case, certain people thought they had had a telepathic communication but on checking found that in fact they had not had one. If, on the other hand, an accident had occurred it would no longer have been a case of telepathy but of normal observation. The feature of the story that appears to require an explanation is why three people simultaneously saw— or thought they saw—a figure on a horse in a distant field. Thus, the explanation is likely to be psychological rather than parapsychological.

To investigate the story fully, it would have been necessary to question the three witnesses independently, but as they had had the opportunity of discussing the matter among themselves, their statements could not be independent. It would appear likely that the witnesses saw something they thought was Canon Bourne although, in fact, it was not Canon Bourne—that is, if his statements about where he had been that day were truthful or if he had had no lapse of memory. They reported that the horse looked dirty, but at a distance they would not recognize dirt as such; they would only infer its presence from the appearance of the horse. They apparently saw a horse that was similar, but not identical, in appearance to Canon Bourne's; they assumed it to be the Canon's and that its changed appearance was due to dirt.

That one of them should see the Lincoln and Bennett mark inside the hat is not unusual. Any psychology student who has worked with a *tachistoscope* encounters many instances of this sort of thing. In the tachistoscope, a drawing is exposed very briefly to a subject so that he sees it for, say, 1/50 of a second. He is then asked to draw exactly what he has viewed. Under these conditions, most subjects tend to introduce changes and add details in their reproductions that were lacking in the original. They draw what they think they should have seen based on their identification of the drawing with some known object. In a real life situation, much more striking effects of this nature would appear than in the laboratory.

If the statements of the witnesses and of Canon Bourne are reliable, it would appear possible that some other person was present in the field that day whom the sisters mistook for their father. Identification of the father is supported only by the mark inside the hat, which the witness states was too far away for such recognition.

If these people made a false recognition of this nature, particularly if they were emotionally disturbed—as they could have been in this case because of the coachman's remark about an accident—and if they were able to converse together so that each could influence the others by suggestion, it is quite possible that they would feel convinced they had seen Canon Bourne, regardless of the fact that he later told them he was not in the field that day. There is no reason why the witnesses should have been greatly affected by the incident, but no one else in reading about it should suffer any perplexity.

An announcement by the Society for Psychical Research discussed

Phantasms of the Living in these words: "The conclusion drawn is that the coincidences of the type in question are far too numerous to be accounted for as accidents; and the establishment of some cause for them, beyond chance, is the proof of Telepathy."[9] However, stories of this nature, however numerous, cannot provide evidence for ghosts or extrasensory perception unless they are backed by corroborating evidence. Without such evidence, they merely indicate the generality of well-known psychological phenomena. The more of them that are gathered together, the better the chance of finding a really extraordinary coincidence.

The accounts constitute a selected sample from millions of experiences that have arisen; they are selected because they are unusual and, therefore, one would think, experiences that people would write or talk about. Members of the various societies who have reported these experiences in journals must be aware of the importance of supplying supporting evidence, but so far, these surveys have failed to provide a single story that is conclusively supported by ample confirmatory data.

Stories purporting to demonstrate supernatural processes are liable to be distorted by the personal characteristics of the witnesses. The following extract from the 1911 confession by Douglas Blackburn, which was discussed in pages 20–23, summarizes his impressions after acting as an investigator.

I am convinced that this propensity to deceive is more general among "persons of character" than is supposed. I have known the wife of a bishop, when faced with a discrepancy in time in a story of death in India and the appearance of the wraith in England, to deliberately amend her circumstantial story by many hours to fit the altered circumstances. This touching-up process in the telepathic stories I have met again and again, and I say, with full regard to the weight of words, that among the hundreds of stories I have investigated I have not met one that had not a weak link which should prevent its being accepted as scientifically established. Coincidences that at first sight appear good cases of telepathic rapport occur to many of us. I have experienced several, but I should hesitate to present them as perfect evidence.

At the risk of giving offense to some, I feel bound to say that in the vast majority of cases that I have investigated the principals are either biased in favor of belief in the supernatural, or not persons whom I should regard as accurate observers and capable of estimating the rigid mathematical form of evidence. What one desires to believe requires little corroboration. I shall doubtless raise a storm of protest when I assert that the principal cause of belief in psychical phenomena is the inability of the average man to observe accurately and estimate the value of evidence, plus a bias in favor of the phenomena being real. It is an amazing fact that I have never yet, after hundreds of tests, found a man who could accurately describe ten minutes afterwards a series of simple acts which I performed in his presence. The reports of those trained and conscientious observers, Messrs. Myers and Gurney, contain many absolute inaccuracies. For example, in describing one of my "experiments," they say emphatically, "In no case did B. touch S., even in the slightest manner." I touched him eight times, that being the only way in which our code was then worked.[10]

CAUSES OF "INEXPLICABLE HAPPENINGS"

It is likely that many people have personal experiences that puzzle them and appear inexplicable. In daily life certain types of events may appear strange if a cause cannot be ascribed to them. This inability may arise in a number of ways, some of which are described below.

A common link in two casual sequences. I was once walking along a country road and a tune was running through my head, but I was not whistling or humming it. A boy approached on a bicycle, and as he passed, I heard that he was whistling the tune precisely in time with me. As I walked on puzzling over this occurrence I passed a house and through the open window heard the radio playing the same tune. I therefore assumed that the boy and I had both started thinking of the tune through having heard it on different radios in houses we had passed. If I had not reached another house after passing the boy, I might have been very puzzled and, if there had been a series of similar experiences, might have started believing in ESP.

Seeming coincidences may often arise in this manner. A common stimulus in the pasts of two persons may set similar trains of thought going. The cause is no longer apparent when, some time later, one of the persons concerned says something about which the other is thinking.

Even if only pure coincidence could be involved, its possibility should not be dismissed. In a world of more than 3 billion people, each person having hundreds of experiences each day, there must, every day, arise numerous coincidences having odds of the order of a million to one against chance expectation.

The elusiveness of memory. Most people are aware of visual illusions. When looking at figure 19-1, most people will say that line *a* looks longer than line *b*. If the lines are measured it will be found that, in fact, *b* is longer than line *a*.

A visual illusion of this nature is puzzling, but its existence cannot be denied, since lines can be measured with a ruler. Illusions of memory are, however, much more intangible, since there is seldom an opportunity to compare our memory of events with what actually happened. When events from the past are recalled, a single fleeting incident that occurred once and was gone is all that can be relied on. In addition, when something happens in everyday life, one is not usually expecting it to happen. It may be necessary to remember something that was quickly over, that no effort was made to remember at the time. The memory of an incident may be vague or startlingly clear, but in both cases there usually is no way of checking its accuracy.

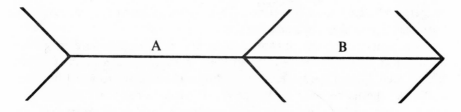

FIGURE 19–1

Which of the two lines A and B appears to be longer?
After deciding, place the edge of a piece of paper against that line
and mark off its length. Then compare the length marked off
with the length of the line that was judged to be the shorter.

The elusiveness of dreams. Remembering some event from one's wak-
ing life of a few years back is a relatively clear-cut process compared with
recalling a dream of last night. Many people recount dreams with the greatest
of confidence, but since a dream is a private experience there is no way of
checking its factual content. It is not surprising that a large number of so-
called psychic experiences involve them. The great danger in recalling the
content of a dream is not only the ease with which it may be changed or
embellished, but that the dating of a dream presents extreme difficulty. If
a person, after hearing about some event, remembers having dreamed some
days before that it would happen, no one can check this fact. He may be
remembering something that really happened, or the dream may have been
produced and placed at a suitable position in his past at the time he hears
the story.

Most memories of past events can be located at some point in time by
virtue of the fact that they arise in a context; there are events before and
after them. If this context is lacking, it will be difficult to place the memory
in time, and it will lack reality. A dream largely lacks this context, and when
it is recalled, there is little to guarantee that it happened last night, some
other night, or that it was not primarily generated at the time of recall. Just
as perception is affected by memory, recall is affected by contemporary conditions, and when the memory is vague, as when a dream is recalled, the
amount of material added to it may be large.

The effects of past experiences. Reactions to a situation are influenced
by expectations. If a superstitious man is roaming around in a house he believes to be haunted, he is likely to encounter a ghost at the slightest opportunity.
A man who does not believe in ghosts, but who has been told that the house
is infested with rats, is more likely to see rats. A relevant past experience
can be recent, or it can be in the remote past of a person. Early events of
childhood are particularly likely to affect a person's response in a "psychic"
situation. Most children encounter fairy stories, ghost stories, superstitious

beliefs, and religious ideas that are more compatible with the world as seen by parapsychology than by science. These ideas all embody principles that form the content of psychic belief.

The adult may have discarded them and no longer believe in ghosts, but the fact that he once believed in them is likely to affect him. He may still get a chill down the spine when reading a good ghost story. Early beliefs would be expected to manifest themselves at times of emotional arousal, stress, fatigue, sickness, and old age. Even the most hidebound skeptic of the paranormal is likely to find himself having what appears to him irrational thoughts at times.

But most people are not skeptics. They are only too eager to believe anything that will take them further from the world of reality toward the world of superstition and magic. It is not surprising that so many extraordinary experiences are reported, or that the accounts bear little critical examination.

MEDIA ACCOUNTS

Another explanation for the wide currency of stories of psychic phenomena lies in the fact that newspapers have to attract readers in order to maintain sales. For that reason, their accounts tend to be sensational. A simple account may be embroidered by both reporters and editors in order to liven it up. Such stories are often presented in a manner calculated to make the reader feel convinced of their authenticity. The distortions may not be intentional. The reporter is looking for news and will notice anything of value to him. He usually has little time to make a thorough investigation and has to rely on what he is told. Those he interviews will be no less eager to impress him than he is eager to impress his readers.

GERARD CROISET

An article "Crime Busting with ESP" by Jack Harrison Pollack appeared in *This Week* magazine on February 26, 1961.[11] It described the work of W. H. C. Tenhaeff, director of the Parapsychology Institute of the University of Utrecht, Holland, who claimed to assist the police in solving crimes with the aid of a group of people whom he called *paragnosts* who had clairvoyant powers. Pollack's report read, in part:

> An early success in this case I checked in the Parapsychology Institute and Dutch police files. On December 5, 1946, a pretty blonde 21-year-old girl was returning home at 5:45 P.M. along a quiet country road near Wierden, Holland. Suddenly, a man *leaped out from behind a stone storehouse,* and assaulted her, hitting her on the *neck and arms* with a hammer. Before he disappeared into the dark, she was able to wrench the hammer away from him.

Police *contacted Dr. Tenhaeff, who came to the station,* bringing Gerard Croiset, one of his team of paragnosts. Because *the girl was in the hospital,* Croiset did not see her. Instead he picked up the hammer, his large hand squeezing the handle as *police* watched skeptically. Croiset concentrated.

"He is tall and dark, about 30 years old, and has a somewhat deformed left ear," said the paragnost. "But this hammer doesn't belong to him. Its owner was a man of about 55 whom the criminal visits often at a small white cottage . . . near here. It is one of a group of three cottages, all the same."

The deformed left ear was a key clue. Several months later the police picked up a tall, dark 29-year-old man on another morals charge. *His badly scarred and swollen left ear* led to questioning about the first attack. Finally, he admitted assaulting the girl with the hammer. He said he had *borrowed it from a friend who, the police discovered, lived in a white cottage on the edge of town, with two others just like it on either side.*

Dr. Tenhaeff's files bulge with such cases. Each is documented with a recording or stenographic transcript of the prediction, and with statements confirming its accuracy from witnesses and police. [Italics added by C.E.M.H.]

I sent this account to the police at Wierden asking whether they could verify that the account agreed with data in their files. I received in reply the following letter from the burgomaster, E. D. Maaldrink.

Wierden, March 22, 1961.

Dear Sir,

With a great interest and even still greater astonishment, I read your letter of March 9th. How is it possible that a simple story can be mutilated in such a way! Maybe the answer is simple: when someone desires to see something special, after a certain time he will see it, even if it is not there.

Your letter was directed to me, as in Holland the burgomaster is normally also head of the local police, and so I'll try to answer it. My English grammar being rather poor, I do beg you to take the freedom of interrogating me about questions which are not described clear enough.

When the story began on December 5th, 1946, I was already burgomaster of the town of Wierden, Overijessel, Holland.

The whole community at whose head I have the honor and the pleasure to stand, has about 15,000 inhabitants, and contains two villages: Wierden with 6000 inhabitants, and Enter with 4000, the rest of the people living as farmers round about in the country.

So the young girl, indeed good-looking, lived with her family in a farm, about three kilometers from the village of Wierden.

In the evening of the fifth of December she returned home on her bicycle by a sand-road, with a big box of cardboard held in one hand, with a sugar-cake, as it was the evening of the national homely feast of Santa-Claus.

Being about 700 meters from her house she was indeed assaulted by a man. He did *not* leap from behind a stone storehouse. In the neighborhood there is not any building to be found.

The man hit her twice with a hammer on the head, *not* on the neck and arms.

Then he saw the light of another bicycle, which was nearing and fled away on his own cycle, leaving the wounded young girl and his hammer.

The girl was transported to her home and it was *not* necessary to bring her to an hospital.

The policemen of course did all their best to find the man, but without any result in the beginning.

After a few days there circulated the name of a certain young man, called K. Who called the name first, is not clear.

He was married since a year and a few months and his wife had a first baby.

It seems the name was mentioned because some people had noticed that he had committed or tried to commit exhibitional acts.

The truth hereabout we could not find out. As you know most people don't like to talk about such facts.

The only spur was the hammer. To find the owner it was showed behind the window of a grocer's shop in the midst of Wierden, but nobody seemed to recognize it.

Then after several weeks, perhaps even six, I received the visit of an elderly sort of landlord, who lives at a country place, not far from the spot where the assault was committed.

The family had as a girl-servant the sister of the attacked young girl and this girl did not dare to turn home when she was not guided by the landlord.

The last was of course rather annoyed about these trips every evening and asked me if I would allow him to take the hammer to Mr. Croiset and ask him information.

So happened. I don't know yet exactly who belonged to the party which visited Mr. Croiset, then living at Enschede.

And unhappily I don't neither know if the visit was beforehand announced to him. The last thing is in this kind of matter very important as later turned out.

About the hammer Croiset told that it had been behind a big window. In fact it had been behind the window of the grocer.

Further that the owner of the hammer or the owner of the window had a disease of the aerial ways. Indeed the grocer has bronchitis.

About the performer of the assault he told that he lived in a small house, rather similar to the houses of the two neighbors, with a stone well behind it.

When you believe in Telepathy, you can imagine that the policeman, who was present, thought at that moment about the rather likely house of Mr. K. and that Mr. Croiset felt this!

Further he told that it was a young person, but anybody will give young men greater chance to do such silly things than elder men. Mr. K. was born December 16th 1919.

And the man would have a deformed ear and a ring with a blue stone in it.

The police could do nothing with these communications. Mr. K. had two normal ears and when he might possess a ring with a blue stone, he seemed never to wear it.

So one month after another passed on without any result for the Wierden police.

Then in the early springtime 1947 Mr. K. was arrested near the town of Almelo (which lies only 5 Kilometers from Wierden) while committing the act of exhibitionism.

He was tried for several hours by our police and at the end he confessed.

We even yet don't know who was the owner of the hammer. This morning one of my policemen asked him, but Mr. K. refuses to tell us, so we suppose he has stolen it.[12]

Pollack said that he had checked the case in the Dutch police files. I wrote to *This Week* pointing out discrepancies in the account and asking that details of the police files consulted should be stated. My letter was not published, but from the reply received from Pollack, it would appear that the nearest he got to a police file was to see the burgomaster's original letter to Tenhaeff in the files at the Parapsychology Institute. Unless he read Dutch that would have meant little to him.

I received two further communications about this story, the first from a Dutch parapsychologist, P. B. Otterwanger, who for years had cast a critical eye on the activities of parapsychologists in Holland. He confirmed what the burgomaster had told me and stated that other cases reported by Pollack in his article were equally misleading.

Croiset lived at Enschede, less than 17 miles from Wierden and at one time worked as delivery boy for a grocer there. It is possible, therefore, that he knew of the grocer in whose window the hammer had been displayed and that he had heard about the crime. Thus, if all the information he gave had turned out to be true, it need have surprised no one.

It is of interest that the newspaper account introduced details that were lacking in Tenhaeff's account. Tenhaeff's report was accurate, but he did not mention that Mr. K. was suspected from the start by the police or that some of Croiset's remarks turned out to be wrong. He reported that the girl was hit on the head. He did not note the stone storehouse. He made no mention of the girl being in the hospital. Nor did he mention that Croiset could say nothing of value until after he had been told that the hammer had been used in a case of attempted murder.

The Wierden story appeared again in a 1961 article in *Maclean's* magazine, "First Report on Extra-Sensory Powers among Canadians," by Sidney Katz. It had by then undergone further changes.

One of Dr. Tenhaeff's most gifted psychics, it is said, described the unknown assailant of a pretty blonde as a tall, dark man of thirty with a deformed left ear. He went on to state that the weapon used was a hammer borrowed from a friend who lived in a small white cottage, which is one of a group of three white cottages. This information, according to one report, was enough for the police to make an arrest.[13]

Katz's account is typical of the type of story that emerges after a series of repetitions. At the present time, mediums or clairvoyants claim to assist the police in the detection of criminals, and in some countries the police have utilized their services and made decisions as a result of their advice.

Dr. F. Brink, who, as a Dutch police inspector, investigated the activities of parapsychologists in their attempts to assist the Dutch police in solving crimes, has sent me an article he published in the *International Criminal Police Review*. It is of great interest to see how a trained investigator reacted to the artfulness of the mediums and the tests he applied to check their claims. His conclusion was that while such persons were sporadically consulted, the police had, to his knowledge, never derived any help from their supposed powers of clairvoyance.

Brink described investigations he made of four clairvoyants, one of whom was very well known. These tests involved handing photographs to them of objects or people. Some were from police files and others were of persons or things with no connection with the police. Letters of an abusive nature, anonymous letters, and such things as weapons, knives, and keys were also handed to the clairvoyants. Such objects are referred to as "inductive material." Of them, Brink said:

> The several tests were marked by a diversity of procedure and circumstances. Those made during a period of over one year have not evinced anything that might be regarded as being of actual use to police investigation. Whether the relevations made by the clairvoyants had been inspired by any of the things, transmitted by way of inductive material, or by photos, of which as many as twenty-four had been occasionally given to them for the same purpose, the results invariably proved to be nil. . . .
>
> Another remarkable feature of the clairvoyant's manner of performance— which is bound to strike anyone who is listening in to the reproduction of their revelations, registered by a tape recorder—is that clairvoyants appear to favor the habit of expressing the greater majority of their remarks, communications, and conclusions in the interrogative form. Even though they should know, or at least presume, that they cannot expect a direct answer from the experimenter addressed in that manner, they persistently indulge in this habit.
>
> In this connection it is worth noting that in the event of any of their feelers, in the form of tentative questions, such as, "May it be possible that ————" being answered in the affirmative, they will instantly make the

experimenter feel that they have scored a hit, by saying "I told you so, didn't I?" thus creating the impression that their particular mode of speech should be regarded as an instance of knowing, really, and not of probing.

In those cases where the experimenter is not responsive to this form of enticement, it will nevertheless be hard to control involuntary reactions produced by the sensorimotor process, and showing emotional effects, such as mimic gestures, muscular contradiction, etc. It is practically impossible to restrain those unconscious reactions, especially in the case of a person who is confronted with a continuous flow of questions.[14]

Recently, a case was reported in the fortieth *Annual Report* of the American Civil Liberties Union (ACLU), in which a medium in the United States was responsible for the wrongful arrest of a man. This extract is taken from an article about the case by a psychiatrist, S. H. Posinsky:

The bizarre chain of events began when a local government hospital psychiatrist offered police the services of a . . . [European] telepathist to help clear up the unsolved murders of Mr. and Mrs. Carroll V. Jackson and their two young daughters early in 1959. Accompanied by state troopers, the savant went to the Virginia grave where the bodies had been found and advised police to search for a man whose business was "either junk or garbage." Police then arrested a trash collector, John Tarmon, and interrogated him extensively. Unable to obtain any evidence linking him with the crime, they induced his wife to sign a commitment petition, resulting in a hurried lunacy hearing being conducted at 3 A.M. with the psychiatrist sitting as one of the three members of the lunacy commission. As a result, Tarmon was found insane and whisked two hundred miles away to a mental institution for the criminally insane. He was released after a lawyer provided by the ACLU filed a habeas corpus petition which prompted the hospital to concede that he was not insane.

Later it appears another man was arrested by the F.B.I. for the crime after more conventional police work.

Posinsky concluded:

In a tragicomic time when superstition and psychiatry alike pass as science, while science itself is invoked like a primitive deity, the case of John Tarmon requires the satirical genius of a Jonathan Swift.

NOTES

1. E. Gurney and F. W. H. Myers, "Visible Apparitions," *Nineteenth Century* 16 (July, 1884): 89–91. Reprinted through permission of *The Twentieth Century*.

2. *Nineteenth Century* 16 (November, 1884): 451.

3. Judge Hornby, correspondence.

4. J. E. Coover, "Metaphysics and the Incredibility of Psychologists," in *The Case For and Against Psychic Belief,* edited by Carl Murchison (Worcester, Mass.: Clark University, 1927), p. 261.

5. Reprinted 1970 by Scholastic Facsimiles.

6. G. N. M. Tyrrell, *The Personality of Man* (London: Pelican Books, 1947), p. 63. Originally published in the *Journal of the Society for Psychical Research* 6, no. 103 (1893): 129.

7. Ibid., p. 219.

8. Ibid.

9. Notice inside back cover, *Proceedings of the Society for Psychical Research* 6, no. 17 (1888).

10. D. Blackburn, *London Daily News* (September 1, 1911).

11. J. H. Pollack, "Crime Busting with ESP," *This Week* magazine (February 26, 1961).

12. In a letter to the author. Printed by permission of E. D. Maaldrink.

13. S. Katz, "First Report on Extra Sensory Powers among Canadians," *Maclean's* (July 29, 1961): 44.

14. F. Brink, "Parapsychology and Criminal Investigation," *International Criminal Police Review* 134 (January, 1960): 8.

20

Spiritualism

THE FOX SISTERS

Spiritualism in its modern form apparently originated in 1847 because of the pranks of two girls, Margaret, aged 8, and Kate, aged 6, the daughters of John D. Fox, who lived with his wife in an isolated farmhouse in Hydesville, near Rochester, New York. For night after night, when the girls had been put to bed and were assumed to be fast asleep, raps were heard coming from the wall of their bedroom.

At this time, Mrs. Leah Fish, an elder sister of the girls, visited Hydesville. She promptly organized a Society of Spiritualists and encouraged people to come to the house to see the children. The affair received considerable newspaper publicity, and Mrs. Fish then took the children to Rochester and arranged meetings at which an audience paid to hear their questions answered from the "spirit world." The girls were later taken to New York and then toured many cities in the United States.

The remainder of their story is best told as it appeared forty years later in a statement by Margaret Fox in the *New York World* of October 21, 1888. Part of this story is reproduced below.

My sister Kate and I were very young children when this horrible deception began. I was only eight, just a year and a half older than she. We were mischievous children and sought merely to terrify our dear mother, who was a very good woman and easily frightened.

When we went up to bed at night we used to tie an apple on a string and move the string up and down, causing the apple to bump on the floor, or we would drop the apple on the floor, making a strange noise every time it would rebound. Mother listened for a time to this. She could not understand it and did not suspect us as being capable of a trick because we were so young.

At last she could stand it no longer and she called the neighbors in and told them about it. It was this that set us to discover a means of making the raps more effectually. I think, when I reflect about it, that it was a most wonderful discovery, a very wonderful thing that children should make such a discovery, and all through a desire to do mischief only.

Our eldest sister was 23 years of age when I was born. She was in Rochester when these tricks first began, but came to Hydesville, the little village in central New York where we were born and lived.

All the neighbors around, as I have said, were called in to witness the manifestations. There were so many people coming to the house that we were not able to make use of the apple trick except when we were in bed and the room was dark.

And this is the way we began. First as a mere trick to frighten mother, and then when so many people came to see us children, we were ourselves frightened and for self-preservation forced to keep it up. No one suspected us of any trick because we were such young children. We were led on by my sister purposely; and by my mother unintentionally. We often heard her say "Is this a disembodied spirit that has taken possession of my dear children?"

Mrs. Underhill [Mrs. Fish later remarried], my eldest sister, took Katie and me to Rochester. There it was that we discovered a new way to make raps. My sister Katie was the first to observe that by swishing her fingers she could produce certain noises with her knuckles and joints, and that the same effect could be made with her toes. Finding that we could make raps with our feet—first with one foot and then both—we practiced until we could do this easily when the room was dark.

In Rochester Mrs. Underhill gave exhibitions. We had crowds coming to see us and she made as much as $100 or $150 a night. She pocketed this. To all questions we answered by raps. We knew when to rap "yes" or "no" according to certain signs which Mrs. Underhill gave us during the seance.

Katie and I were led around like lambs. We drew immense crowds. We went to New York from Rochester and then all over the United States.[1]

There followed three more pages of confession, in which Margaret described her career as a spiritualist during the ensuing forty years.

During their long career, the Fox sisters had started a cult of spiritualism that swept the United States and rapidly spread to England and Europe. Margaret had appeared at séances for Queen Victoria, and Kate had performed before the Czar of Russia.

The story of the Fox sisters is important in showing how belief in the supernatural can outweigh all rational argument. The source of the raps was questioned almost from the start. E. P. Longworthy, a Rochester physician, investigated them and reported in the New York *Excelsior* on February 2, 1850, that the knockings always came from under the girls' feet or from objects such as doors or tables with which the girls' dresses were in contact. His conclusion was that Margaret and Kate themselves made the noises and that they voluntarily produced them.

John W. Hurn of Rochester, whose articles were published in the New York *Tribune* during January and February 1850, had come to a similar conclusion. In the same year, the Reverend John M. Austin of Auburn wrote to the *Tribune* to state that he had reliable information that the noise could be made by cracking the toe joints without any movement being visible. In December 1850, Reverend D. Potts demonstrated before an audience that he could produce raps in this manner.

By January 2, 1851, Reverend C. Chauncey Burr reported in the New York *Tribune* that he could produce the raps by cracking his toe joints and that he could produce sounds of such volume that they could be heard in every part of a hall large enough to contain a thousand people.

In February 1851, Austin Flint, Charles E. Lee, and C. B. Coventry of Buffalo University reported the results of an investigation they had made of the raps produced by Margaret Fox and her older sister Leah, who it seems was also by now participating in the act. Having studied Margaret's facial expression during the performance, they concluded that the raps were made by voluntary effort. They believed that the sounds were created by dislocation of the bones at the joints of the toes, knees, ankles, or hips; for they had observed that when the girls were placed on a couch with cushions beneath their feet the raps were no longer heard.

On April 17, 1851, Mrs. Culver, a relative by marriage of the sisters, admitted in a signed statement before witnesses that she had assisted Kate by touching her to indicate when the raps should be made. She declared that Kate had shown her how to make raps by snapping her toes and that Margaret had told her that she could produce raps with her knees and ankles when people insisted on seeing her feet and toes.

Professor Page of the Smithsonian Institute reported an investigation he had made in 1853. He concluded that the raps were produced by the girls and that every one was accompanied by a slight movement. He remarked that he was surprised to notice how the scrutinizing powers of the most astute fail as soon as they entertain the remotest idea of the supernatural.

In June 1857, the Boston *Courier* offered a prize of $500 to any medium who could pass an investigating committee. The Fox sisters were the first to try for the prize. Three Harvard professors were on the committee, whose report was unfavorable to Margaret and Kate; it suggested that the raps were produced by movements of the bones of the feet.

In spite of the criticisms and explanations that had been advanced, and even in spite of the statement by Mrs. Culver, belief in the Fox sisters grew. As the years went by, the sisters started introducing new tricks into their act, and they also took over many devised by other mediums.

The last official investigation of the raps took place in America under the auspices of the Seybert Commission. Henry Seybert (1801–1883), a mineralogist, philanthropist, and a keen believer in spiritualism, had donated a sum of money to the University of Pennsylvania to endow a chair of philosophy, and he had added the condition that the university was to appoint a commission to investigate "all systems of morals, religion, or philosophy which assume to represent the truth and particularly of Modern Spiritualism." The commission, established in 1884, consisted of members of the faculty of the university.

In a preliminary report published in 1887, it was stated that it had investigated a number of mediums, including Margaret Fox. It reported that raps were heard close to her that could easily have been produced by normal means. Moreover, while the raps were sounding, Professor Furness, the chairman of the commission, had placed his hand upon one of Margaret's feet and felt pulsations in her foot. It was also reported that Margaret knew when raps other than her own were produced, no matter how similar they were in sound to hers.

It was not only the uneducated that were impressed by the Fox sisters. The renowned William Crookes, who in 1871 held séances with Kate in London, was so impressed by her performance that he wrote:

> With a full knowledge of the numerous theories which have been started, chiefly in America, to explain these sounds, I have tested them in every way that I could devise, until there has been no escape from the conviction that they were true objective occurrences not produced by trickery or mechanical means.[2]

After their confession, the Fox sisters once more toured theaters together —this time to denounce spiritualism and demonstrate their tricks. They continued touring until 1889, when Kate's drunkenness caused cancellation of their bookings. Kate died in the street near her home in 1892, and Margaret, by this time also an alcoholic, died the following year. The Fox sisters' confession and numerous exposures of mediums at this time had little effect either on the public or on the zeal of the psychical researchers.

Remarkably, the Fox sisters are still discussed in the parapsychological literature without mention of their trickery. Thus, in 1961 Renée Haynes, a council member of the Society for Psychical Research, after relating how strange knocks were heard in a farmhouse in 1847, continues:

> A cumulative wave of interest in these happenings swept over America and into Europe, generating more phenomena in its course, some genuine, some the work of ingenious persons seizing the opportunity to make money and fame, some genuine at first but eked out by legerdemain as the unknown power to produce them waned.[3]

The account given in the *Encyclopedia Britannica* (1963 edition) is rather similar, and a striking feature of both reports is that the reader is given no reason to believe that the Fox sisters were anything but perfectly genuine.

EUSAPIA PALLADINO

The year that the Fox sisters made their confession marked the rise to prominence of the greatest medium of all time. Eusapia Palladino was born on January 21, 1854, in Minervino Murge, southern Italy. Uneducated and illiterate, she was employed as a servant at the age of 13 by a family who indulged in spiritualism. One day she was asked to make up a "circle" at a séance. Surprising manifestations of psychic activity were observed, and she declared herself to be a medium. In spite of her affiliations with the spirits, Eusapia remained very much a woman of this world. "An unlettered peasant, retaining," as one writer put it, "a most primitive morality and of such a decidedly erotic nature that it was said she thought of little else."[4]

After a long apprenticeship in the mediumistic circles of Naples, Eusapia came under the influence of Ercole Chiaja, a keen student of the occult. He was so impressed by her that in 1888 he published an open letter to Cesare Lombroso (1836–1909), the famous Italian criminologist and psychiatrist, inviting him to investigate the phenomena that arose in Eusapia's presence.

Eusapia was introduced to Lombroso in 1888, and by 1891, she had convinced him of her supernatural powers. This, it should be noted, need not have presented her with as much difficulty as might appear. Lombroso was no hidebound skeptic. In 1882, he had reported the case of a patient who, having lost the power of seeing with her eyes, saw as clearly as before with the aid of the tip of her nose and the lobe of her left ear.[5]

An idea of what went on during one of Eusapia's séances may be gleaned from the detailed report of an investigating committee. Two curtains were hung across the corner of the séance room to form a small triangular space, called the *cabinet*. A small table was placed inside the cabinet, and around and on it reposed a number of objects, including a tambourine, a guitar, a toy trumpet, a flageolet, a toy piano, and a tea bell. Eusapia sat at a light table, the *séance table,* with her back to the cabinet so that the curtains were just behind her chair. The investigators sat at the sides of the séance table.[6]

The scene during the séance, discreetly veiled by the dim light, must have been remarkable. The voluptuous Eusapia sat in the clutch of two very serious gentlemen: "One of us sat on either side of her, holding, or held by, her hand with his foot under her foot, his leg generally pressing against the whole of hers, often with his free hand across her knees, and very frequently with his two feet encircling her foot."[7]

In the dim light, the table in front of her rose from the floor, objects floated from the cabinet, the curtain bulged, sounds were heard from the musical instruments inside the cabinet, and spirit hands touched the investigators. Great thumps were heard. The curtains suddenly blew out over the séance table. Eusapia was in communion with her spirit guide, John King.

In 1892, sittings were held in Milan for the benefit of a committee containing many eminent scientists, including Lombroso and the French physiologist Charles Richet, then professor of physiology in the University of Paris. The conclusion, reached with some reserve owing to the unsatisfactory way in which Eusapia's hands were held—the one thing that really mattered—was that none of the phenomena produced in "good light" could have been due to trickery.

A further series of 14 sittings was held in Warsaw in 1893-1894. Among 23 investigators, 10 were convinced that trickery was not used, and 3 considered that the whole performance was fraudulent. One claimed to have detected, among other tricks, the substitution of hands and feet. He maintained that 2 persons who thought they were holding the left and right hands of Eusapia were, in fact, both holding one hand.

In the summer of 1895, Eusapia visited Cambridge, England, where she gave 21 sittings. Here, suspicions were again aroused, owing to the fact that the conditions imposed on the experimenters were such that fraud would have been difficult to detect had it been present. The investigators were not allowed to feel about in the darkness, and they were forbidden to grab at the hand that floated around, touched them, and played various tricks.

After the Cambridge sittings, Eusapia was classified as a fraudulent medium by the Society for Psychical Research. However, belief died hard. Although her repertoire was such as to invite suspicion, and though she had been detected indulging in trickery, she still had many supporters. During the next few years, many leading European scientists, including Sir Oliver Lodge, visited Eusapia and became convinced of her supernatural powers.

Several further investigations took place, including one series of 43 sittings under the auspices of the Institute General de Psychologie ("Psychological Institute") of Paris. These experiments extended over three years at a cost of 25,000 francs. They were attended by the great French scientists Pierre and Marie Curie; D'Arsonval, the physicist; the philosopher and psychologist, Henri Bergson; Richet, the physiologist; and numerous other scientists and savants. The French committee detected many signs of trickery on Eusapia's part, but they were clearly puzzled by some of the phenomena.

In 1908, 3 members of the Society for Psychical Research, the Hon. Everard Feilding, a barrister, W. W. Baggally, and Hereward Carrington, went to Naples to investigate Eusapia. They obtained the services of Albert Meeson, a stenographer of the American Express Company, and their 11 sittings were reported in considerable detail.[8]

The general arrangement of the curtain and tables at these sittings has already been described. Fielding, Baggally, and Carrington sat at the séance table. The stenographer sat at another table, some distance away and facing Eusapia, where he could witness the whole performance. His job was to record the remarks of the investigators and any visitors who were present.

During the séance there was considerable movement. Eusapia would twist and contort in her chair. The investigators, trying to maintain contact with her feet and hands, would follow her like marionettes. Extraordinary things happened. On one occasion, Baggally even managed to get himself kissed through the curtain, although he decided that there was an element of fraud as the head resembled a closed fist and the sound of the kiss resembled the clicking together of a thumb and finger. Psychic manifestations often followed one another at such a rate that the stenographer must have had difficulty compiling his record as the investigators called out anything they thought should be recorded. Mr. Meeson would write down the initial letter of the investigator's surname against each statement, for example:

R. (A visitor called Ryan). A white object came up by my right eye.
F. I saw it very well from where I am.
B. I saw it.
C. I also.
F. It looked to me like a boiled white cabbage.
R. It seemed to me like an ace of diamonds and about three inches from my right eye.[9]

The investigators were puzzled by what they saw and heard, but it will be seen that the conditions under which Eusapia worked were highly favorable to illusion.

1. The room was in semidarkness so that recognition of objects was difficult and easily affected by other factors, such as suggestion.
2. The investigators were voicing aloud what they saw or experienced, thus tending to influence each other by suggestion.
3. During the séance, the medium was continually moving and, for example, pinching the investigators' hands, thus distracting their attention.
4. The investigators were having to attend to more than one thing at the same time. They had to control the hands and feet of the medium and, concurrently, watch in the dim light for any "psychic manifestations."
5. The séances were held late at night or in the early morning, introducing the element of fatigue. Eusapia always slept until mid-day as she could not afford to be tired.
6. The investigators had a strong belief in the supernatural, hence they would be emotionally involved.
7. The investigators were men. The subject was a woman. Thus, control of her activities was hampered by the fact that they had to observe the proprieties.

The Naples investigators were convinced that Eusapia was genuine, and her prestige rose considerably. Since that time, many writers have claimed that the conditions of this investigation ruled out the possibility of deception. They have pointed out that Baggally and Carrington were amateur magicians and could have detected fraud had it been present. Looking back on Eusapia's subsequent career, it is only too clear, however, that the important point about an investigator is whether or not he believes in the reality of the phenomena he is investigating. The disbelieving skeptic will approach a study in quite a different frame of mind from the believer.

For example, in 1909 when Eusapia visited the United States, escorted by Carrington, who acted as her manager, the investigators were of quite a different nature.

In a fanfare of publicity, Eusapia started giving sittings. The early ones were mainly for the benefit of the press, but at one held on November 19, 1909, a number of scientists were invited to attend, including R. W. Wood, professor of physics at Johns Hopkins; Augustus Trowbridge, professor of physics at Princeton; and J. D. Quackenbos, a physician and novelist. Very little of a psychical nature happened at the sittings with scientific observers until, on the night of December 18, 1909, Eusapia was, at last, caught in the act. On this occasion, she was supervised by Hugo Münsterberg, the well-known Harvard psychologist, who showed himself to be a complete realist. His report, from which the following extract is taken, appeared in the *Metropolitan Magazine* for February 1910.

One week before Christmas, at the midnight hour, I sat again at Madame Palladino's favorite left side and a well-known scientist on her right. We had her under strictest supervision. Her left hand grasped my hand, her right hand was held by her right neighbor, her left foot rested on my foot while her right was pressing the foot of her other neighbor. For an hour the regulation performance had gone on. But now we sat in the darkened room in the highest expectancy while Mr. Carrington begged John to touch my arm and then to lift the table in the cabinet behind her and John really came. He touched me distinctly on my hip and then on my arm and at last he pulled my sleeve at the elbow. I plainly felt the thumb and the fingers. It was most uncanny. And, finally, John was to lift the table in the cabinet. We held both her hands, we felt both her feet, and yet the table three feet behind her began to scratch the floor and we expected it to be lifted. But instead, there suddenly came a wild, yelling scream. It was such a scream as I have never heard before in my life, not even in Sarah Bernhardt's most thrilling scenes. It was a scream as if a dagger had stabbed Eusapia right through the heart.

What had happened? Neither she not Mr. Carrington had the slightest idea that a man was lying flat on the floor and had succeeded in slipping noiselessly like a snail below the curtain into the cabinet. I had told him that I expected wires stretched out from her body and he looked out for them. What a surprise when he saw that she had simply freed her foot from her shoe and with an athletic backward movement of the leg was reaching out and fishing with her toes for the guitar and the table in the cabinet! And then lying on the floor he grasped her foot and caught her heel with firm hand, and she responded with the wild scream which indicated that she knew that at last she was trapped and her glory shattered.

Her achievement was splendid. She had lifted her unshod foot to the height of my arm when she touched me under cover of the curtain, without changing in the least the position of her body. When her foot played thumb and fingers the game was also neat throughout. To be sure, I remember before she was to reach out for the table behind her, she suddenly felt need of touching my left hand too, and for that purpose she leaned heavily over the table at which we were sitting. She said that she must do it because her spiritual fluid had become too strong and the touch would relieve her. As a matter of course in leaning forward with the upper half of her body she became able to push her foot further backward and thus to reach the light table, which probably stood a few inches too far. And then came the scream and the doom.[10]

But even that was not enough. Eusapia had clearly been indulging in trickery on this particular occasion, but what about all the things that had happened at other sittings? She was, according to her supporters, only 60 percent fraudulent; she would use a trick if the real thing was not at hand. Anybody could catch her using a trick; the task was to show that she could not produce any unusual phenomena when was stopped from using tricks. This presented some difficulty, as she and her manager, Hereward Carrington, laid down the conditions under which séances should be held.

In January 1910, a series of 6 sittings was held at Columbia University. A number of scientists attended, including R. W. Wood, C. L. Dana, a professor of psychology at Cornell, and E. B. Wilson, a professor of biology at Princeton. The sittings were organized by Dickinson Miller, a professor of philosophy at Columbia University.

The séances were held in the physics laboratory of Columbia University, and the committee managed to complete the case against her after enlisting the aid of 3 professional magicians, W. S. Davis, J. L. Kellogg, and J. W. Sargent, together with J. F. Rinn, an amateur magician who spent much of his time hounding mediums. The magicians, who attended the last 2 sittings, were introduced to Eusapia as professors so that she should suspect nothing. At a séance held on April 17, 1910, Davis and Kellogg sat on either side of Eusapia, controlling her hands and feet. Rinn and a Columbia student, Warren G. Pyne, had hidden themselves under the séance table where they could observe Eusapia's footwork at close range. During this séance, she was left free to do as she pleased, and the magicians showed appropriate surprise at the various phenomena.

At a sitting held a week later, on April 24, 1910, Kellogg and Davis again sat on either side of Eusapia controlling her arms, legs, and feet. On this occasion, it was arranged that conditions should be lax at the start so that Eusapia should have every opportunity to put up a good performance. Levitations and transportations were abundant under these conditions. Then, at a prearranged signal, Kellogg and Davis made their control expert and from then on nothing happened.

A full report was issued in the journal *Science*, with statements by the scientists who had attended. Miller stated that after her techniques had been observed and controlled there were no manifestations of psychic phenomena.[11]

Rinn, from his vantage point beneath the table, saw the medium free her left leg by maneuvering her right foot so that her heel rested on Davis's toe and her toe on Kellogg's toe. The following statement that Rinn made was published in *Collier's Weekly* in an article by Joseph Jastrow, professor of psychology at the University of Wisconsin, who was present at the séance held on April 24, 1910:

> In a few moments, after some ejaculations in Italian from the medium, the table began to wobble from side to side; and a foot came from underneath the dress of the medium and placed the toe underneath the leg of the table on the left side of the medium, and, pressing upward, gave it a little chuck into the air. . . . A short time after the lights were lowered she swung her left foot free from her dress at the back and kicked the curtain of the cabinet quickly, which caused it to bulge out toward the sitters. This was done several times so daringly that under the chairs where I lay it seemed almost impossible that the people above the table could not have observed it.
>
> Later the medium placed her left leg back into the cabinet and pulled out from behind the curtain a small table with certain articles upon it, which was dashed to the floor in front of the cabinet on the left-hand side. It remained there in varying positions and was kicked by the medium a number of times. At one time the medium juggled the table that had been kicked out from behind the curtain on the end of her left toe in a very clever manner, so that it gave the appearance as if the table was floating in the air.[12]

Eusapia had survived many investigative committees, and she might well have survived that at Columbia University, since few people who visit mediums read scientific periodicals such as *Science*, and for every newspaper account Carrington would produce a ready reply. But she now had to contend with magicians, who at that time were at loggerheads with the mediums. The magician earns an honest living entertaining people with tricks. He regards the medium as prostituting his art, for she uses tricks to convince people of her supernatural powers in order to make money. With much publicity, Eusapia was challenged by Rinn to a contest, and she was offered $1,000 if she could perform any trick that the magicians could not duplicate under similar control conditions. A great deal of haggling went on, with much newspaper publicity as to the conditions to be observed. Eusapia would not agree to being encased in a bag nor with being tied with thin thread. Eventually, the conditions appear to have been agreed upon, but Eusapia did not turn up for the contest and later returned to Italy.

One further investigation was reported. Feilding went to Naples in December 1910, and a series of 5 séances were held. This time, he observed only tricks. If there was any residual element of genuine phenomena present in Eusapia's performance, it made no appearance. Little further was heard of her, and she died on May 16, 1918.

It was at enormous expense of time and money—she was paid $125 per sitting while in the United States—that the secrets of Eusapia Palladino were finally revealed. Many parapsychologists are still convinced that not all of her act was fraudulent.

MARGERY CRANDON

The exposure of Eusapia Palladino by no means marked the end of scientific interest in séance-room phenomena. Numerous other mediums were headline news, and then in May 1923, Margery Crandon, the most famous of all American mediums, first came before the public eye. She was the wife of L. R. G. Crandon, a distinguished Boston surgeon who was present at all her séances and who, many of the investigators believed, was responsible for much of what went on.

Her performance was in some ways similar to that of Eusapia Palladino, but she had many new tricks in her repertoire. During a séance, she went into a trancelike state during which "Walter," purportedly her deceased brother and her master of ceremonies, manifested himself. Walter's voice emanated from Margery's mouth, and sometimes his hand would be seen. He had a great sense of humor, although some of his utterances were calculated to make any nice girl blush.

Margery operated under conditions very much in her favor compared with those enjoyed by Eusapia Palladino. Her séances usually took place in complete darkness relieved only by a flash of red light provided by an apparatus fixed up by Crandon and operated when Walter gave the signal. Also, investigators had to agree to rigid conditions laid down by the Crandons before they were allowed to take part in a séance.

Margery was also much better able to win the sympathy of her investigators than was Eusapia. She was young, witty, and attractive. Even in a photograph, in which a considerable quantity of what look like jellied eels have deposited themselves on her right ear, it is clear that her physical charms far surpassed those of the rather stout Eusapia.

Margery, like Eusapia, was studied by several groups of investigators. The first research was carried out by four Harvard psychologists, William McDougall, A. A. Roback, Gardner Murphy, and Harry Helson. They were not favorably impressed, but a report was not issued at the time.

The second investigation was made by a committee appointed by the *Scientific American,* which had offered $5,000 to anyone who could exhibit geniune psychic phenomena. The great American magician Harry Houdini was a member of the committee, but he was ignored until some eighty sittings had been held and Margery was about to get the prize. He was eventually asked to participate at a séance held on July 23, 1924. After he had detected trickery, the committee withheld the prize, although one of its members, J. M. Bird, an associate editor of *Scientific American,* appears to have been convinced that Margery was at least 40 percent genuine.

One of Margery's trick was described by Houdini as follows:

During the second intermission "Walter" asked for an illuminated plaque to be placed on the lid of the box which held the bell and Bird went to get it. This left the right hand and foot of the medium free. Bird had difficulty in finding the plaque and while he was searching "Walter" suddenly called for "control."

Mrs. Crandon placed her right hand in mine and gave me to understand that I had both her hands. Bird was requested to stand in the doorway, but without any warning, before he could obey, the cabinet was thrown over backwards violently. *The medium then gave me her right foot also, saying:*

"You have now both hands and both feet."

Then "Walter" called out:

"The megaphone is in the air. Have Houdini tell me where to throw it."

"Towards me," I replied, and in an instant it fell at my feet. The way she did these tricks is as follows: when Bird left the room it freed her right foot and hand. With her right hand she tilted the corner of the cabinet enough to get her free foot under it, then picking up the megaphone she placed it on her head, dunce-cap fashion. Then she threw the cabinet over with her right foot. As she did so I distinctly felt her body give and sway as though she had made a vigorous lunge. As soon as this was done "Walter" called for "Better control" and she gave me her right foot. Then she simply jerked her head, causing the megaphone to fall at my feet. Of course with the megaphone on her head it was easy and simple for her to ask me or anyone else to hold both of her feet and also her hands, and still she could snap the megaphone off her head in any direction requested. This was the *"slickest"* ruse I have ever detected, and it has converted all skeptics.[13]

Houdini's exposure did not convince those who believed in the supernatural. In 1925, Margery was investigated by E. J. Dingwall of the British Society for Psychical Research. His report is difficult to assess. He showed that most of the phenomena could have been produced by trickery on the part of Margery and her husband, but he seemed loath to come to any definite conclusion. Dingwall's underlying belief in the possibility of such things as ectoplasm almost certainly affected his actions and interpretations.

Toward the end of Dingwall's investigation, Hudson Hoagland, a young Harvard psychologist later to become well known in experimental psychology, became interested in the affair. Subsequently, a committee was formed consisting of Hoagland and four instructors from the university. A number of senior members of the university also attended some sittings and associated themselves with the findings.

In November 1925, Hoagland published an article in the *Atlantic Monthly* in which more than 20 separate items of evidence were produced to support the fact that Margery was a trickster. Although the Harvard committee had pronounced Margery fraudulent, the American Society for Psychical Research was not satisfied and wanted a further investigation.

Another committee was formed consisting of R. W. Wood, who had been on the committee investigating Eusapia Palladino; a skeptical psychologist, Knight Dunlap, of the Johns Hopkins faculty; and G. McComas, associate professor of psychology at Princeton. The Crandons terminated the proceedings after the fourth sitting with this committee when the following episode took place.

> Wood very cautiously *touched* and finally *pinched* the end of the "ectoplasm" that issued from Margery's mouth, without any sign of detection on her part. The significant point here is that a medium always insists that even *touching* the ectoplasm is sure to result in her illness or possible death. Wood states that it felt like a steel knitting needle covered with one or two layers of soft leather. As Wood, at the conclusion of the séance, solemnly dictated this stunt into the record, Margery shrieked and pretended to faint, and *that* was the end of the committee's séances with *her*. A full report of the committee's findings was sent to the American Society for Psychical Research, but the Society never saw fit to publish it.[14]

In 1929, Margery gave 3 séances in London in the rooms of the Society for Psychical Research. By this time, an important part of her act consisted of fingerprints that Walter impressed on a lump of wax. It was found that some of the fingerprints were Margery's, although her hands were supposed to have been controlled throughout the séances. Other fingerprints belonged to no one present—except perhaps Walter.

The main supporter of Margery, apart from her husband, had been J. M. Bird. He had been fired from the *Scientific American* after their investigation and had become research officer of the American Society for Psychical Research of New York. Another staunch supporter was a member of the Boston Society for Psychical Research, E. E. Dudley. It was Dudley who eventually made the discovery that gave the *coup de grace* to Margery.

In March 1932, Dudley found that fingerprints left behind by Walter were those of Margery's dentist, who had attended many of her séances prior to 1925. It was also found that prints left behind by Walter in London were those of the dentist. The New York Society for Psychical Research refused to publish Dudley's findings, but they were eventually published by its rival, the Boston Society for Psychical Research. Walter Franklin Prince, the principal research officer of the Boston society, declared that the Margery case would come to be considered the most ingenious, persistent, and fantastic complex of fraud in the history of psychic research, but that was 30 years ago.

She continued to give séances until 1938, when her husband died, after which she lost her powers. She died on November 1, 1941, at her home in Boston.

It may well be asked why it is necessary to explore in so much detail these ridiculous episodes in the history of psychical research. But it should be realized that, at the time, such things were taken very seriously by completely sane men. At great expense of time and energy, many eminent men provided evidence of the background of trickery that was responsible for the alleged psychic phenomena. Such efforts should not be required in a rational community but it is evident that, even in the twentieth century, superstition is far from dead.

Commenting on Professor Miller's report on the exposure of Eusapia Palladino, an editorial in the *New York Times* of May 10, 1910, concluded with the words: "But no one can read his trenchant analysis of her repeated and long continued conquests without feeling that the men of science have been her willing dupes and her abettors in a sort of conspiracy to mystify society."[15]

That sentence contained some truth. Both Eusapia Palladino and Margery Crandon were investigated by committee after committee, but it is significant that on all those occasions when professional magicians were present, the mediums were exposed. Neither Eusapia nor Margery could fool the magicians because they knew her tricks and how to combat them.

If another Eusapia or Margery were to arise tomorrow, how would she succeed? The answer is quite clear. If she could avoid the attention of investigating committees, she would find public credulity no less than it was in 1889 or 1924. The present spate of television programs dealing with the supernatural indicates how popular allegedly true accounts of supernatural happenings are and how strong must be people's underlying beliefs.

Today, there are Eusapias and Margerys by the thousand, but they are more concerned with making money than with convincing investigating committees of their abilities. Man will pay for what he needs. He pays heavily for quack medical remedies, since health is an invaluable commodity. He will also pay heavily a spiritualist who claims to be able to contact a departed relative, for this is a service that no one else claims to provide.

PHYSICAL MEDIUMS

The stock in trade of the mediums so far discussed was the production of physical phenomena in order to impress their clients. The phenomena produced by these mediums were reproducible by stage magicians. Claims about the cause of the various effects could be checked by seeing whether they still occurred after the possibility of trickery was removed. The medium's defense against detection lay in the imposition of rules and impositions to limit the scope of the investigator. One limitation was that the lighting was kept at a low level. With improvements in lighting and in means of observing and recording—for example, with the use of infrared photography—the task of the physical medium became more difficult.

MENTAL MEDIUMS

The mental mediums did not produce physical phenomena in the form of sounds, levitations, touches, materializations, and ectoplasm—they merely produced messages in some form or other. They had a far easier role to play than the physical mediums. The results, although not so entertaining for the customers, would get to the point in producing messages that the customer was keen to hear.

A number of extensive investigations have been carried out in psychical research on mental mediums, but these have been conducted in a manner that is unlikely to inspire much confidence in a critic. Thus disagreement may arise in assessing a medium's performance when the investigation merely involves taking part in a séance and deciding whether the medium has produced information that could not arise through normal means. Anyone who believes in the possibility of communication with a spirit world is likely to be impressed in circumstances where a nonbeliever would be unimpressed. Professional magicians are seldom impressed when they see techniques being employed with which they are fully familiar. The medium, in fact, has a relatively simple time compared with the conjuror since her audience is predisposed to believe in her and an occasional skeptic in the audience will not matter all that much. The conjuror does not usually claim to be psychic and is mainly interested in demonstrating his skill in deceiving his audience. Thus the reports on mediums given by skeptics such as J. F. Rinn[16] and Harry Houdini[17] are remarkably different from those published by parapsychologists.

It may be noted that many of the members of the Society for Psychical Research were expert conjurors and fully familiar with many tricks employed by fake mediums. Their faith in psychical phenomena was sufficient, however, for them to reason that mediums might be employing tricks part of the time but, on occasions when they did not detect trickery, that there was a residual element in the medium's performance that was not due to trickery.

The conditions in which séances were held were ill suited to exact observation. The observer had to note everything that was said by the medium and her audience and also any other responses made. This is clearly an impossible task. The observer will report on those utterances that attract his attention and his record may not agree with the original. He cannot record or even become aware of every sound and every change of expression or intonation of voice. Anyone reporting on a performer who finds hidden objects by using audience reactions would be at the same disadvantage. He is unlikely to detect cues utilized by the performer even though he may be aware of their possibility.

On the third of February 1960, the British Broadcasting Corporation televised a sitting between a professional medium, Douglas Johnson, and a complete stranger to him. The program was arranged by a psychiatrist, Dr. David Stafford Clark, whose wife acted as the sitter. Psychologist Professor H. J. Eysenck and psychiatrist Dr. Donald West acted as observers and gave their comments on the same program a fortnight later, from which it would have appeared that some quite impressive hits were obtained.

Dr. West, who was a former research officer of the Society of Psychical Research, in his book *Psychical Research Today* commented: "The medium scored some striking hits and many viewers, including the present writer, were impressed by his success."[18]

The program was recorded and broadcast again the following November with a critical commentary by Dr. Christopher Scott. West later commented that it then became apparent to him that almost everything the medium said could have been deduced from changes in facial expression and tone of voice induced in the sitter by the medium's leading questions. Statements had been attributed to the medium that seemed in remarkable accordance with the facts as revealed by the sitter at the end of the program, but when the sitting was seen for the second time, it was pointed out by Christopher Scott that these statements were at no time made by the medium during the program. Without the availability of a complete audiovisual recording, the medium's performance would have been greatly overrated both by the ordinary viewer and by experts like West.

A revealing account of the manner in which a present-day reputed psychic, Peter Hurkos, gains information and elicits responses from an unknown person is given by Ronald A. Schartz in an article "Sleight of Tongue." He concludes his article:

> The eagerness with which people latch on to the fanciful idea of extrasensory perception to explain the apparent accuracy of the utterance, rather than to the recognition of their own complicity, is the really intriguing aspect of the demonstration. Perhaps recognition of one's own contribution is just too lackluster an explanation to be given much credence. Our persistent delight with fanciful explanations suggests that skilled practitioners of sleight of tongue will enjoy a bright and prosperous future.[19]

NOTES

1. Margaret Fox, *New York World* (October 21, 1888).

2. William Crookes, *Researches in the Phenomena of Spiritualism* (London: Burns & Oates, 1874), p. 88.

3. Renee Haynes, *The Hidden Springs* (New York: Devlin-Adair, 1961), p. 223. First published in England by Hollis & Carter, 1961. Copyright 1961 by Renee Haynes.

4. E. J. Dingwall, *Very Peculiar People* (London: Rider, 1950), p. 190.

5. Herbert Thurston, *The Physical Phenomena of Spiritualism* (London: Burns & Oates, 1936), p. 336.

6. E. Feilding, W. W. Baggally, and H. Carrington, "Report of a Series of Sittings with Eusapia Palladino," *Proceedings of the Society for Psychical Research* 23 (1909).

7. Ibid., p. 328.

8. Ibid.

9. Ibid., p. 359.

10. H. Munsterberg, "Report on a Sitting with Eusapia Palladino," *Metropolitan Magazine* (February, 1910).

11. D. S. Miller, "Report of an Investigation of the Phenomena Connected with Eusapia Palladino," *Science* 77 (1910).

12. J. Jastrow, "Unmasking of Palladino," *Collier's Weekly* 45 (May 14, 1910): 21-22.

13. W. B. Gibson and Morris N. Young (eds.), *Houdini on Magic* (New York: Dover, 1953), pp. 141-42. Copyright 1953 by Dover Publications, Inc. Reprinted by permission of the publisher.

14. W. B. Seabrook, *Doctor Wood: Modern Wizard of the Laboratory* (New York: Harcourt Brace, 1941), p. 215.

15. Editorial, *New York Times* (May 10, 1910).

16. J. F. Rinn, *Searchlight on Psychical Research* (London: Rider, 1954).

17. Gibson and Young, *Houdini on Magic*.

18. D. J. West, *Psychical Research Today* (London: Penguin, 1962), p. 101.

19. Ronald A. Schwarz, "Sleight of Tongue," *The Skeptical Inquirer* 3, no. 1 (1978): 47-53.

21

Parapsychology and Magic

The relationship between spiritualism and stage magic is evident in the history of parapsychology. For example, the Fox sisters were originally claimed to be concerned with providing messages from the spirit world by means of rapping sounds. These sounds became the focus of interest rather than the messages that were transmitted. With the emergence of physical mediums in the nineteenth century, interest was not so much in the messages purporting to come from the spirit world but in the physical phenomena produced for the benefit of those present. The sitter might be more impressed with the cheesecloth emerging from the medium's mouth than in the message said to be arriving from a dead spouse. The physical phenomena had a resemblance to the effects produced by stage magicians in that objects appeared to materialize out of thin air, tables were levitated without any apparent reason for their doing so, and sounds were heard coming from musical instruments that were, it was supposed, untouched by human hand.

The mediums were not investigated experimentally. Like the early telepathists, they were tested by committees who watched and assessed their performance. The medium largely determined the conditions under which he was to perform. Any intervention by an observer was only allowed where it fitted in with the conditions required by the medium.

There were some exceptions. When the Fox sisters were tested at Buffalo University, the three medical men introduced a new condition by checking to see whether the raps were accompanied by any muscular activity that could account for them. They also tested the hypothesis that the raps were caused by dislocation of the bones in joints by placing the girls on a couch with cushions below their feet. Their supposition was correct since under this condition the sounds were no longer heard. Again, when Eusapia Palladino was investigated by Munsterberg at Harvard University, he broke the rules by having an observer present who, unknown to Eusapia, could see what was going on. The investigator was now able to test his own hypothesis concerning the cause of a series of events occurring behind Eusapia.

In an experiment the investigator decides on the procedure to be adopted. The subjects follow instructions given to them. In the early tests carried out by the Committee on Thought Transference, the subjects were engaged in conjuring tricks under conditions that were largely dictated by them. The investigators were, in fact, investigating conjuring tricks rather than thought transference. An experimental element might have appeared if the subjects had been asked to make some modification in their procedure. The important information that should then have been included in the report was a list of changes in procedure that had been asked for, those that the subjects had agreed to, and the effect of those changes.

Thus an essential requirement is that the effects of any change in the conditions of an experiment should be reported. It is immaterial whether the change increases the effectiveness of the subjects' efforts or makes them unable to operate successfully. In the early investigation of Smith and Blackburn, the investigators made some amendments to the procedure, but only when permitted to do so by the subjects. It is also clear that the investigators only reported what they considered to be of importance. Thus the failure of Smith to receive telepathic impressions of a drawing, after his blindfold was adjusted, was not considered important enough even to be mentioned in the experimental report.

BRUGMAN'S EXPERIMENT

An early investigation of a subject claiming special powers was conducted in 1919 by H. J. W. F. Brugman at the University of Groningen.[1] The subject, a young man called Van Damm, was an entertainer who located hidden objects, during live performances in front of an audience. Van Damm sat at a table with his head and shoulders inside a wooden framework that had been covered with black cloth. He had the back of his head toward the open side of this enclosure. His right arm extended through an opening so that he could touch any point on a board lying flat on the table in front of him. This board was divided into 48 squares with 8 columns labeled A to H and 6 rows numbered 1 to 6.

A hole had been cut in the ceiling directly above Van Damm. It was covered with two sheets of glass, placed so that there was an air cushion between them. The experimenters, sitting above the glass, looked down through it at the board in front of Van Damm and tried to "will" him to point to a particular square.

Before each trial, slips of paper were drawn from two bags. The first slip determined which column the square was to occupy, the second the row. The subject moved his hand over the board and gave a double tap on it with his forefinger to indicate his choice.

Van Damm obtained 60 successes in 187 trials compared with the expected value of 4. This result was clearly unlikely to have arisen by chance. Some trials were also made with the experimenters in the same room as the subject, but although he also succeeded under this condition, his scores were not as high as when the experimenters were in the room above him.

In a recent discussion, Christopher Scott[2] has indicated some highly undesirable characteristics of the manner in which the tests were conducted and reported. The investigator who recorded the square touched by Van Damm with his forefinger when viewing from a distance was also aware of the target. In addition, considering the fact that Van Damm was known to entertain by finding concealed objects when members of an audience knew their locations, the conditions under which he was operating are unlikely to have removed sensory information.

In view of the claims made by parapsychologists for this experiment, it is remarkable that no one appears to have made any attempt to carry out further tests of this nature. If they have done so the results have not been reported.

THE INVESTIGATION OF A MUSIC HALL ARTIST

The manner in which Van Damm's performance could have been investigated is provided in a report published in 1935 by Dr. S. G. Soal.[3] He carried out experiments on a vaudeville artist named Joseph Kraus, who performed under the name of "Marion." Soal, together with a small group of investigators, was allowed to carry out systematic tests in which the conditions were laid down by Soal with the aim of discovering the means whereby Marion obtained his results.

According to the account given by Soal, Joseph Kraus was born in Prague in 1902. While at school he claimed to have the ability to locate hidden objects. He left school in 1910 after which he spent two years perfecting his performance. Two years later, after achieving notoriety in the town when he found an object that had been hidden by a committee of journalists and policemen, he appeared (presumably at the age of twelve) in a concert hall in Prague. There he found hidden objects, identified numbers and colors thought of by members of the audience, and described events in persons' lives by studying their handwriting. He later appeared in theaters in Vienna, Budapest, Krakhov, Berlin, and Cologne. He fought in the First World War and was discharged because of ill health in 1918.

In 1934, Marion was investigated in London at the National Laboratory for Psychical Research. This was a private body set up by Harry Price, a leading psychical researcher at that time, who paid a substantial fee for Marion's services. The investigating committee consisted of Soal, Price, Goldney, and five others. The paper published by Soal was based on the work of this committee.

Marion's repertoire consisted of a number of conjuring tricks depending on the detection of sensory information rather than on manipulative skill. His main ability was in locating a hidden object, provided an audience (or a single individual) knew of its location. Soal investigated the effect of various possible sensory cues by successively removing them. For this purpose an observer, who knew the location of the object, was enclosed in a plywood frame that enclosed his arms, trunk, and legs down to the ankles. His head was enclosed in a cardboard hood that permitted him to see objects in the room through a stockinette screen but did not permit movements of his head to be seen by Marion. At each attempt, Marion knew that the object would be concealed at one of six locations as decided by throwing a die.

Marion failed at the first attempt when this contrivance was used, but after that, he was successful on the next six attempts. In further tests, the observer was placed in a plywood frame resembling a sentry box in which any part of his body could be revealed by removing a panel. His head was enclosed in a rigid cardboard cover, though he could see objects in the room through a stockinette screen that obscured from Marion's view his eye movements and changes in expression. He was wheeled around in this by someone who was unaware of the location of the object. Marion was now successful provided he could see the observer's stockinette-covered head.

By carrying out simple tests of this nature, Soal was able to determine the methods employed by Marion in a series of tricks locating hidden objects and identifying cards. In one of these tricks, Soal selected a card from a new pack and handed it to Marion. It was returned to Soal, after which Marion left the room. Soal then placed this card facedown on a table together with five other cards. Marion was recalled to the room and asked to identify the card Soal had handled. Marion tapped the back of each card in turn with his first and second fingers, sometimes pushing a card aside. He then turned up the correct card. The whole process took about a minute. It was found that Marion was detecting the card that he had handled rather than the value of the card. It was concluded that Marion used tactual discrimination to pick out the card he had handled. In fact, it would appear that he was using a trick familiar to many schoolchildren in which the card is bent when it is handled after being removed from the pack so that it can be distinguished when tapped while lying on the table.

Individuals like Marion, who claim some special psychic ability, appear at intervals in the media where they excite more public interest than the experimental work. Two such individuals have taken part in investigations conducted by parapsychologists that have later been considered important enough to be published in *Nature,* the leading British science periodical. These are considered below.

PAVEL STEPANEK

Stepanek was discovered in 1962 by Milan Ryzl, a biochemist at the Institute of Biology at the Czechoslovak Academy of Science in Prague. He displayed an ability not dissimilar to that formerly displayed by Marion (who also came from Prague) in discriminating a particular card from others. He was investigated extensively over a ten-year period although the conditions under which he was tested might have been greatly improved if account had been taken of the methods used by Soal when testing Marion.

An observer was given a pile of envelopes together with cards colored white on one side and green on the other. The observer placed each card into an envelope with either its green side or its white side uppermost. The envelopes were then given to Stepanek, who judged whether the card inside each envelope had its white side or its green side uppermost, separating the envelopes into two categories. A statistical analysis of the result then indicated that Stepanek was correctly separating the envelopes into the two categories at well above the chance level.

For session after session the same type of procedure was employed. Very little attempt was made to investigate Stepanek's supposedly clairvoyant ability rather than his performance under conditions reminiscent of a stage act.

The cards used with Stepanek might well have had a warp on them owing to the coloring of one side green. In 1966, I suggested that Stepanek obtained his results by detecting bending or warp on the card inside the envelope.[4] It was noted that when Stepanek had been tested by Dr. John Beloff, a psychologist from Edinburgh University, who had supplied his own cards, Stepanek's extrasensory abilities deserted him.[5]

In October 1968, a paper was published in *Nature*[6] in which further evidence for Stepanek's clairvoyant powers was revealed. The authors, seven in all, were from the Universities of Virginia, Amsterdam, Tasmania, Lund, and the Psychical Research Foundation, Durham, North Carolina. It appeared that, in 1965, Stepanek lost the ability to say which way up the cards were inside the envelopes. But around the same time, he developed a new ability. He now tended to call *white* to a particular *envelope,* irrespective of whether the card inside it was one way up or the other. It was decided that Stepanek was now using ESP to discriminate between the envelopes.

A series of eighteen experiments was then conducted in which the envelopes—now referred to as covers—were placed inside further envelopes—referred to as jackets. For some reason the green and white cards were still placed inside the covers, although they did not appear to contribute anything to what was going on.

In the first three experiments, the covers were exposed to Stepanek's view, in the remaining fifteen, they were placed inside the jackets. In the first five experiments, ten covers, each containing a card, were used. After the fifth experiment, the number of covers was reduced from ten to eight, and after the seventh experiment, it was further reduced to four. In each reduction covers were retained that had given the most positive results in earlier tests. One cover in particular (no. 15/16) appeared to give excellent results, and data for this cover was presented in the article in *Nature*.

The general procedure was as follows: The covers were randomized "outside the subject's sight," and the prepared stack of four to ten covers—normally inside their jackets—were placed in front of Stepanek. He then judged each in turn, placing it aside into a new stack as he did so. The experimenter recorded Stepanek's guesses and then recorded the targets from the order of the jackets in the pile at the end of the run.

Various changes were introduced as the series of experiments proceeded. After series 7 the targets were randomized by one experimenter using random number tables and another experimenter conducted the testing.

In series 1, where Pratt was the only experimenter, Stepanek responded to cover 13/16 by saying *white* eighty-six times and *green* fourteen times. According to the report "This consistency of choice showed that he somehow recognized this cover as an object regardless of which side was presented upward." It will be noted, however, that Stepanek was attempting to say whether a card inside the cover was white or green side up and this he appears to have been unable to do. Each time he came to cover 15/16 among the stack of ten covers, he tended to judge that the card inside it was *white* side up, without being correct at above the chance level.

In series 2, the contents of cover 15/16 were interchanged with those of another cover for which Stepanek had tended to call *green*. Stepanek seemed to be unaffected by this and continued to call *white* more often than *green* to cover 15/16.

After series 3, the covers were placed inside the further envelopes, referred to as jackets. These were made of two sheets of cardboard cut from manila file jackets stapled together on three sides. The open side of the jacket always pointed away from Stepanek. The tendency for cover 15/16 to produce the call *white* from Stepanek continued.

In series 6, the cards, covers, and jackets were interchanged randomly before each run. The effect was found to be dependent only on the covers.

In series 7, Stepanek was observed by two Czech citizens, a psychologist, and a government official. For the first time his performance deteriorated markedly, although he still scored at above the chance level on cover 15/16.

A number of other changes were introduced, the most important being:

1. Before series 9, in which the number of covers used was four, "the open ends of the four covers were closed up by taping onto them a folded piece of cardboard." High scores were obtained by Stepanek.
2. Before series 11, "several cotton balls were inserted between the two layers of the jackets." The investigators wished to ensure that any irregularities in the shapes of the covers, inside the jackets, could not be transmitted through the jackets. High scores were still observed.

3. After thirty runs of series 12, the covers were made equal in weight within a limit of variation of 0.1 gm. High scores continued.
4. In series 12, a third experimenter was present who watched Stepanek closely on each trial to see that he did not glimpse an edge or corner of the enclosed cover. This had no appreciable effect on Stepanek's performance.
5. In series 14, the *jacket* sides were stapled together throughout their entire length, including the fourth side. Stepanek's ability to say *white* to cover 15/16 now abruptly disappeared. But in series 15—where presumably the same precautions were taken—it made a brief reappearance. After that, in the remaining three series—16, 17, and 18—it was no longer in evidence. Now, however, according to the report, a new feature emerged. There was a shift in the pattern of response that yielded statistical significance (p. < 001). This was a consequence of the subject's tendency in that session to associate one color with one side of the cover and the other color with the other side.

Looking at the experiments in general, Stepanek not only touched, but handled, the covers or the jackets containing the covers throughout. The afore-named investigators did not report the fact that Stepanek was unsuccessful when objects he was attempting to identify were placed inside rigid boxes rather than cardboard covers, although such a result had been reported by another investigator.

Stepanek had full view of the jackets. Tests are not reported in which he was screened both from the object he was handling and from the experimenter. In many of the tests, he was merely required to identify a particular cover, but this fact appears to have escaped the attention of the investigators.

It is clear from other research, such as that of S. G. Soal on Marion, that it is necessary to take the same precautions with an experimenter who is present with a subject as it is with the subject to ensure that he will not have information about a target. It may appear strange that Stepanek's ability should desert him in series 14, when the fourth jacket side was stapled to exclude the possibility of his "glimpsing an edge or corner of the enclosed cover," because in the previous experiment, the fourth side was facing away from him. But, while it is difficult to see how the addition of a few extra staples should have affected Stepanek's extrasensory powers, they could have prevented the experimenter from seeing inside the jackets and voluntarily or involuntarily transmitting information to Stepanek.

It is not clear from the report whether a precaution once introduced into an experiment was thereafter retained for all later tests. Thus in experiment 6, the cards, covers, and jackets were changed before each run. This was a necessary precaution, since if a cover remained in the same jacket throughout, it would not be possible to say whether Stepanek was identifying the cover or the jacket. But, in experiment 14, when staples were placed for the first time into the fourth side of the jackets, the staples had, presumably, to be removed and reinserted after each four trials—i.e., a total of 100 times—in order to change the covers and cards. Stepanek was unsuccessful in this experiment, but were the precautions of changing the contents of the jackets and of stapling them retained for the four remaining experiments? If so, the staples would have had to be removed and replaced a further 300 times. If the precautions were not taken, the statistical evaluation of the results would have been affected, since Stepanek would have been discriminating between one of four jackets on each trial. If the precautions were not taken after experiment 14, it would appear that Stepanek was successful, provided it was possible for him or for some other person to glimpse "an edge or corner of the enclosed covers."

It is difficult to believe that the investigators did not ask themselves whether Stepanek's performance depended on his handling or seeing the materials But no tests are reported in which he was kept out of contact with the jackets. Discussing the article in *Nature,*[7] I asked whether such an experiment ever took place or whether Stepanek had refused to perform under such conditions. No reply was forthcoming.

The Stepanek investigations could hardly be called experimental. They were an attempt to obtain conditions under which Stepanek could provide an impressive performance that would convince a critic. It would have been far more convincing if tests had been repeated by teams of independent investigators and if all tests carried out had been fully reported whether they succeeded or failed. If a man can produce a performance that needs explaining, it is as important to know the conditions under which he cannot succeed as those in which he can do so.

A full and detailed account of Pavel Stepanek's long career in parapsychology together with indications of how he achieved his results has been published by Martin Gardner. This will doubtless provide essential reading in any study of parapsychology—or magic.[8]

URI GELLER

The best known of the professed psychics during the past twenty years is Uri Geller. He was by training a professional stage conjurer, who at one time toured the music halls in Israel. According to the *London Daily Mail,* in January, 1971, "a Beersheba magistrate ruled that Geller was guilty of a breach of contract in that he employed sleight of hand on stage, instead of telepathy which he had promised in his publicity material. The magistrate ordered him to pay costs and repay the price of the tickets to the member of the audience who had sued after seeing the show."[9]

On November 23, 1973, Geller appeared in "The Dimbleby Talk-in" on BBC Television. The program started with a test on a water diviner who tried to locate the position where water had been hidden under a stage. The result of the test was not given, presumably because the diviner had not indicated its correct location. Geller's performance was relatively simple compared to that of the average stage magician. A tray of objects including watches and spoons was provided. Geller started a watch, taken from the tray, that the audience was informed had not previously been operating. He also drew a picture corresponding to one that had been drawn by some other person before the program. As his crowning achievement, Geller bent a spoon until it broke into two pieces. Geller performed this feat by holding the spoon at one end with the fingers of one hand and placing the fingers of his other hand around the spoon at its center. He was then able to bend the spoon. Eventually, holding it only at its center with the one hand, he demonstrated that the spoon was either weakened at the center or already broken there by moving his hand up and down until he let the two halves drop onto the table in front of him.

The audience appeared to have been influenced by misleading statements Dimbleby made about Geller, including the fact that Geller had been investigated at a "think tank" at the Stanford Research Institute. They were not told that Geller had spent six months at the research institute during which time he had failed to provide any evidence that he could bend spoons. In addition, details were not given of his checkered career as a psychic in Israel.

In the discussion following Geller's performance, the one contribution from the audience that mattered was given short shrift. The questioner produced a small metal rod and asked if Geller would bend that. The request was refused.

The report from the Stanford Research Center was subsequently published in *Nature*.[10] Geller, it appears, was investigated by Targ and Puthoff, two physicists on the staff who were also keen parapsychologists and whose experiments on "Mind Reach" are a classic in the literature, both for the amount of work involved and the ineptitude with which it was carried out (see chapter 10, pp. 135–39). It was disclosed in the *Nature* article that, over some six months, Geller had failed to demonstrate any ability to bend spoons or any other objects. He had also failed to reproduce drawings when these were unknown to any other person present, or when an individual who went away and made his drawing did not return to the laboratory until Geller had completed his attempt at reproducing it.

Guessing the Uppermost Face on a Die

The seemingly most impressive of Geller's performances was in what is described as a simpler experiment designed to test Geller's ability to know which face was uppermost on a ¾-inch die contained in a 3 × 4 × 5 inch steel box.[11] The box was vigorously shaken by one of the experimenters and placed on the table, so that, presumably, no one present knew the face that was uppermost on the die inside the box. Geller then wrote down his guess. In ten attempts, Geller passed twice and was successful on the remaining eight occasions (three 2s, one 4, two 5s, and two 6s). He thus scored hits on eight occasions on which he made an attempt. The odds against this result arising by chance are greater than a million to one.

These experiments with the die, although called Series 3, were carried out in 1972 at the start of the investigations at SRI. The extremely impressive result was obtained under easily controlled conditions, and the whole experiment comprising eight attempts by Geller could have taken less than half an hour. What happened next? After eight attempts, why not a few more? Did Geller feel tired and want to go to bed? The experiments were conducted at the start of the eighteen-month period when Geller was at SRI. Is it conceivable that, having obtained such a remarkable result, the investigators should drop this form of experiment completely?

In their book *Mind Reach,* Targ and Puthoff state that "these ten trials were the only ten, and were not selected out of a longer run."[12] Since it is incomprehensible that, after this result, the experiment should be dropped completely it would appear likely that Geller refused to participate in any further tests.

The reaction of any normal person in such an experiment would surely be to wonder if a trick had been employed, particularly if he is dealing with a professional magician. He would then ask for further trials in which he would tighten up the experimental conditions, perhaps initially keeping Geller out of reach of the box. But there is no mention of this having been done.

If Geller's performance was genuine, it would be possible to produce overwhelming evidence for clairvoyance very rapidly and thus save large amounts of money—such as the $80,000 contributed by NASA. Two professional magicians—James Randi in the U.S. and David Berglas in the U.K.—have offered large rewards to Geller if he can give a genuine psychical performance. Why has he not spent half an hour convincing them?

Although professional magicians are loath to reveal the "modus operandi" of their profession, a number of accounts have been published to indicate possible methods employed by Geller in the various tricks in his repertoire. In particular James Randi,[13] the eminent American magician, has divulged details of various techniques, and Uriah Fuller[14]—a fictitious magician—has provided a most amusing and instructive account of how he went psychic and, with the aid of two assistants, Schlepi and Ms. ———, gave demonstrations similar to those of Geller.

NOTES

1. H. J. F. W. Brugman, "A Report on Telepathic Experiments Done in the Psychology Laboratory at Groningen," *Compe-Rendu du Premier Congres International des Recherches Psychiques,* Copenhagen, 1921.

2. Christopher Scott, "Why Parapsychology Demands a Skeptical Response," in *A Skeptic's Handbook of Parapsychology,* edited by Paul Kurtz (Buffalo, N.Y.: Prometheus Books, 1985), pp. 449–500.

3. S. G. Soal, *Preliminary Studies of a Vaudeville Telepathist,* bulletin 3 of the University of London Council for Psychical Investigations, London, 1937.

4. C. E. M. Hansel, *ESP: A Scientific Evaluation* (New York: Charles Scribner's, 1966), p. 173.

5. John Beloff, *New Scientist* 40 (1968): 76.

6. J. G. Pratt, I. Stevenson, W. G. Roll, J. G. Blom, G. L. Meising, H. H. J. Keil, and N. Jacobson, "Identification of Concealed Randomized Objects through Response Habits and Word Association," *Nature* 220 (October 5, 1968).

7. C. E. M. Hansel, "ESP Deficiencies of Experimental Method," *Nature* 221 (March 22, 1969): 1171-72.

8. Martin Gardner, *How Not to Test a Psychic* (Buffalo, N.Y.: Prometheus Books, 1989).

9. *London Daily Mail* (November 26, 1973).

10. Russell Targ and Harold Puthoff, "Information Transmission Under Conditions of Sensory Shielding," *Nature* 251, no. 5476 (October 18, 1974): 602-7.

11. Ibid., p. 604.

12. Russell Targ and Harold Puthoff, *Mind Reach* (New York: Delacorte, 1977).

13. James Randi (The Amazing Randi), *The Magic of Uri Geller* (New York: Ballantine, 1975).

14. Uriah Fuller, *Confessions of a Psychic,* Karl Fulves, Box 433, Teaneck, N.J. 07666.

Part Six

Conclusions

22

Conclusions

In 1966, I presented a review of findings in parapsychology in *ESP: A Scientific Evaluation*.[1] The main evidence considered then had changed little since 1940 when six "conclusive" experiments were selected by Rhine and his associates at Duke University.[2] These experiments were included in my 1966 review along with the Soal-Goldney experiment and further experiments carried out by Soal on two Welsh schoolboys. Group experiments and differential scoring were also included together with the VERITAC experiment. All these experiments used Rhine's card-guessing technique in which the subject makes a forced choice from one of a small number of targets. At that time experiments on psychokinesis had failed to provide anything like a conclusive experiment.

By 1980 when similar conclusions were reached,[3] the card-guessing experiments were being replaced. Helmut Schmidt's methods using an electronic randomizer to present random series of targets were replacing experiments with ESP cards, and at the Maimonides Dream Research Laboratory new techniques had been developed with which the forced-choice system was no longer used but in which complex pictures were used as targets.

At that time PK research had become active through the use of Schmidt's random-number generator, and for the first time results having high antichance odds were obtained. Experiments had been made that were claimed to provide evidence for PK in cats, cockroaches, and chickens' eggs. Experiments with mice were said to provide the first repeatable demonstration in parapsychology. The conclusions arrived at in 1966 and 1988 reviews will be repeated first since they do not require modification. Thus further conclusions formed after considering subsequent work will be provided.

IS ESP A FACT?

The basic problem of parapsychology is relatively simple when compared with problems in politics or esthetics. Either it is possible for at least some people to communicate by extrasensory perception, or else ESP does not and cannot exist because the underlying processes necessary for its occurrence do not exist. A great deal of experimental work has failed to produce a clear case for the existence of ESP, but at least two facts have been established: first, subjects when attempting to guess card symbols have obtained scores that cannot be attributed to chance; second, some of those taking part in ESP experiments have cheated in order to produce high scores.

The first fact cannot be disputed. Results such as those obtained by Hubert Pearce need no statistical analysis for the purpose of establishing that something was happening during the experiments other than pure guesswork. The second fact, that those taking part in experiments sometimes cheat, is know from admissions of trickery. The first two major experiments in Great Britain on the Creery sisters and on Smith and Blackburn in 1882 involved eight subjects, seven of whom admitted to cheating, and the other did also cheat according to his partner in the act. The last major investigation in Britain, on two Welsh schoolboys in 1955–1957, involved two subjects, both of whom admitted to cheating after being caught in the act. It would be remarkable if such attempts to assist the natural course of events ceased altogether in parapsychology between the years 1882 and 1955, and again between 1955 and 1989. In fact, close examination of the most spectacular findings in parapsychology invariably points to some form of trickery as an alternative to ESP. To the skeptic, psychical research seems to have been as much a history of the manner in which the artful can mislead the innocent as it is a reflection of any more esoteric form of activity.

secret, mysterious.

IS ESP A FRAUD?

Cheating in one form or another is one of the most common of human activities. If it never occurred, much of the expense and complication of modern life would be avoided. The paper work involved in accounting and auditing— tickets, bills, counterfoils, invoices—would no longer be necessary. Games, examinations, competitions, and numerous such activities would be simplified. On the other hand, it is unlikely that more than a small number of experiments on ESP are affected by cheating, since the investigator does his best to ensure that his subjects cannot cheat and, no doubt, usually succeeds. The majority of investigators are likely to have sufficient faith in the reality of ESP to believe that it will manifest itself without outside aid. It may then seem stranage to the reader that so much space has been given in this book to the matter of trickery. Why in the case of each of the so-called conclusive experiments should trickery invariably emerge as a likely alternative to ESP?

One reason is that an experiment is not classified as conclusive unless the known causes of experimental error have been eliminated in its design. If a trick is used in an experiment, it might be expected to produce an impressive result having high odds against arising by chance and, if the experiment is of the "conclusive" category, trickery would be the only alternative explanation to ESP. Thus the process by which conclusive experiments are weeded out will also bring to light experiments in which a trick has been used.

Parapsychologists are themselves to blame for the emphasis that has to be placed on cheating when considering their work. In science generally it is likely that, at times, investigators indulge in underhanded activities, but their experiments are shown up when other scientists fail to confirm their result. In such cases it may not be necessary to hold a long postmortem on the earlier experiment, it is just forgotten. However, parapsychologists—or at least some of the more vociferous of them—in denying the necessity to confirm experiments by repetition, make it essential to examine every experiment in detail in order to ensure that the result could not have been caused by cheating.

If a trick is used in an experiment, this fact might be expected to become apparent in the course of further research. But parapsychologists have erected a system that aids the trickster and at the same time preserves experimental findings.

SURVIVAL CHARACTERISTICS OF ESP

Scientists in general have been little influenced by philosophers who strive to inform them about the methodology and logic of their subject. Science has a basic methodological principle that is self-generating. It was not formulated by anybody, but it has the same basis and underlying logic as the principle of natural selection in evolution. Investigators are continually producing reports of their experimental findings that may be classified, for convenience, as good or as bad. The good ones survive because they are confirmed in further research. The bad ones are forgotten because they cannot be confirmed. Science advances through a process of natural selection. New findings become targets for criticism, and a finding must be confirmed by critics under their own experimental conditions. It then soon becomes clear when it is to be rejected.

If anyone invents a pseudoscience in which this principle ceases to operate, the result soon becomes apparent, for the new "science" fails to have predictive value and leads to more and more findings and theories that are incompatible with orthodox science. This is what has happened in parapsychology. When critics fail to confirm ESP, this is not accepted as a reason for dropping the subject. On the contrary, belief in the reality of ESP is so strong that the principle of repeatability has been rejected or rendered impotent by invoking new processes that are claimed to be subsidiary characteristics of the supposed phenomenon. Thus, given a high-scoring subject, it would in the normal course of events be only a matter of time before every critic could be silenced. But these subjects cease to score high when tested by critics. Extrasensory perception only manifests itself before uncritical investigators. As Rhine and Pratt have observed: "Most conspicious, perhaps, among failures is the fact that some experimenters have found themselves unable to conduct successful psi experiments; that is, when they have gone through the standard testing routines with their subjects they obtained only chance results."[4]

It further transpired that experimenters changed in their ability to obtain results as they pursued their investigations. Thus according to Rhine and Pratt, "Another major difficulty can be seen in the fact that some experimenters after a period of earlier success in obtaining extra-chance results in psi experiments have proved less effective in their later efforts. In such instances something apparently has been lost that was once a potent factor."[5] In other words, experimenters fail to confirm their own results. A further subsidiary characteristic emerges: ESP is affected by the mental state of the person investigating it.

If fresh characteristics are postulated in this manner, it is possible to survive almost any form of criticism. An experimental result cannot be confirmed or refuted since ESP does not operate in front of critics. After tightening up his experimental conditions, an investigator cannot disclaim the findings of his earlier work. Failure reveals that he has lost his enthusiasm.

Since the chief characteristic of the exploratory stage according to the statements of Rhine and Pratt is that the investigator carries out his work "without being burdened with too much precautionary concern,"[6] failure to confirm earlier work is likely to arise when the investigator graduates from the exploratory stage to one where he takes more care with his work. After an investigator becomes burdened with concern, his precautions will presumably be against error and trickery rather than against ESP. It may be assumed that any change in his experimental results is due to the effectiveness of his precautions.

A REVISED APPROACH

At the present time, there are signs that the arguments put forward to support the work on ESP may be changing. Rhine and Pratt writing in 1961 implied that the case for ESP does not, after all, depend on a small number of conclusive experiments, but on general features that emerge from the whole mass of studies, conclusive or inconclusive. It is as if quantity can make up for quality when the latter has been found lacking. They write:

> The body of fact in parapsychology is like a many-celled organism. Its strength is that of a growth-relationship, consisting not only of the compounding of one cell with another, but also of the many lawful inter-relations that emerge in the growing structure. Going back as Hansel has done, with a one-cell perspective, to fix attention on some incomplete stage of development within

a single experimental research is hard to understand in terms of healthy scientific motivation.[7]

What is the point of presenting conclusive experiments for the consideration of the scientific world if they cannot be criticized? How can an experiment be criticized unless it has first been isolated? If experiments are to be considered en masse, will not data be confused with results, such as those obtained with the Creery sisters and Smith and Blackburn? But as soon as criteria by means of which experiments are selected or rejected are set up, it becomes necessary to isolate each experiment to see whether it satisfies those criteria.

Moreover, what precisely are the "lawful interrelationships" within the body of fact in parapsychology to which Rhine refers? To date, not a single lawful interrelationship appears to have been established. How, for example, does distance affect extrasensory perception? The relationship between scoring rate and distance is completely chaotic, apparently dependent on the investigator, the subject, and experimental conditions. If it were possible to give a standardized test for ESP to different groups of subjects, systematically varying factors such as age, nationality, intelligence, previous practice, distance, and so on, some lawful interrelationships might eventually be expected to reveal themselves. But each reported investigation yields a result that has little relationship to any of the others.

Extrasensory perception is not a fact but a theory put forward to account for observations consisting of high scores obtained in experiments. Parapsychologists have made such observations under a diversity of research conditions from which a number of facts emerges. If these facts can be related to one another by a theory that enables any one to be deducible from knowledge of the others, that theory has some value and plausibility. By means of it predictions might be made of what will happen in further experiments so that it can be put to further test. However, a theory that fails to account for a variety of facts and that cannot predict what will happen in further tests is of no value.

If some facts gleaned from the literature of ESP are assembled, they might appear as follows:

1. Subjects, when attempting to guess card symbols, have obtained scores that cannot be attributed to chance.
2. Some of those taking part in ESP experiments have indulged in trickery.
3. Subjects who obtain high scores cannot do this on all occasions.
4. Subjects tend to lose their ability to obtain high scores. This often coincides with the termination of an experiment.
5. A successful subject is sometimes unable to obtain high scores when tested by a critical investigator.
6. Some investigators often observe high scores in the subjects they test; others invariably fail to observe such scores.

7. A subject may obtain high scores under one set of experimental conditions and fail to do so under other experimental conditions.
8. No subject has ever demonstrated the ability to obtain high scores when the test procedure is completely mechanized.

Fact 1 is directly applicable to a hypothesis of the existence of ESP. Fact 2 is not relevant to such a hypothesis. Fact 3 and 4 are not predictable but could be said to provide further information about ESP; that is, it appears to be spasmodic and temporary. The remaining facts (5–8) are not predictable and, in the case of any other supposed process investigated by psychologists, would throw doubt on its authenticity. These facts can only be explained by invoking subsidiary characteristics of ESP.

Again, fact 1 is directly applicable to a hypothesis predicting trickery. Fact 2 demonstrates that such a hypothesis is correct in the case of certain experiments. The remaining facts (3–8) are all predictable from what is well known about trickery.

Lawful relationships can readily be seen among the facts when they are interpreted in accordance with the hypothesis of trickery. Thus, for example, from fact 7 it might be predicted that those experimental conditions that eliminate the possibility of trickery will also be the ones in which high scores do not arise. This is confirmed by fact 8, and also by examining the experimental conditions under 7 in which high scores have and have not been observed.

Thus, the set of facts given above displays lawful interrelationships when interpreted in terms of the hypothesis of trickery, but they are difficult to reconcile with hypothesis based on the existence of ESP.

A number of other facts could be added to the above list in which neither a hypothesis of ESP nor one of trickery would be applicable. This is to be expected since a great deal of research both in parapsychology and elsewhere has revealed the manner in which results may be dependent on experimental error.

THE POSITION IN 1989

The case for parapsychology at the present time has been presented by Rao and Palmer in "The Anomaly Called PSI: Recent Research and Criticism." The abstract of their article begins:

Over the past hundred years, a number of scientific investigators claim to have adduced experimental evidence for "psi" phenomena, i.e., the apparent ability to receive information shielded from the senses (ESP) and to influence systems outside the sphere of motor activity (PK). A report of one series of highly significant psi experiments and the objections of critics are discussed in some depth. It is concluded that the possibility of sensory cues, machine bias, cheating by subjects, and experimenter error or incompetence, cannot reasonably account for the significant results.[8]

The "highly significant psi experiments" referred to above are Schmidt's REG experiments. Rao and Palmer examine in detail the various criticisms made of the experiments and provide their own answers to those criticisms. This is reminiscent of discussions in the past over the so-called "conclusive" experiments. As with those experiments, none of Schmidt's experiments has provided a repeatable demonstration. The most remarkable feature of his experiments is that in some cases the antichance odds are greater than 10 million to 1 making the experiment suitable as the basis for a repeatable demonstration. But it would seem that in no case has Schmidt himself made any attempt to repeat any one of his own experiments.

Another feature of Schmidt's experiments is that he has discarded the essential experimental conditions necessary to guard against experimental error. If he has made further experiments including such safeguards the results have not been reported, except in case of the experiment carried out in conjunction with Morris and Rudolph. This experiment, however, is not a repeat of any earlier experiment. It invokes new psychokinetic properties of such a bizarre nature that they are likely to puzzle some of the most fervent believers in psychokinesis.

REDEFINING THE REPEATABLE DEMONSTRATION

The necessity of providing a repeatable experiment has become apparent to many parapsychologists, but it is clear that they have failed to do so for any of their supposed phenomena. The result of this failure has been that some parapsychologists have rejected the principle of repetition as presently understood. They have substituted a revised version. Thus we read "In addition, less detailed reviews of the experimental results in several broad areas of psi research indicate that 'psi results are statistically replicable' and that significant patterns exist across a large body of experimental data."[9] They further state: "Replicability does not necessarily mean that a finding must be reproducible on demand. It is not strictly an 'either-or' situation, but a continuum. . . . In this sense of statistical replication, an experiment or an effect may be considered replicated if a series of replication attempts provides statistically significant evidence for the original effect when analyzed as a series."[10]

It will be seen that almost any hypothetical phenomenon could be established by this means. If any small percentage of results arises favoring the phenomenon among other results that do not favor it, in time what Rao and Palmer call "statistically significant evidence" must eventually be obtained.

Rao and Palmer indicate that each of the current forms of experiment gives their "statistically significant evidence." This must be expected if there is any selection of material that is published. Selection can arise (*a*) if experiments are not fully planned before they are started, including the number of observations to be made; (*b*) if all experiments so planned are not completed and reported; (*c*) if all experiments submitted for publication are not published.

As their main example of "replicability in Parapsychology" Rao and Palmer cite Schmidt's experiments using his Random Event Generator (REG). They first claim that Schmidt's experiments are repeatable because some investigators other than Schmidt have obtained positive results using his machine. They adduce as supporting evidence the fact that 71 experiments out of 332 reported by 30 investigators since 1962 yielded results having antichance odds greater than 20 to 1. Their claim in itself indicates the sorry plight of both experimentation and the understanding of scientific method within parapsychology.

These experiments, carried out between 1965 and 1984, are hardly repetitions of any particular experiment in any way other than that a binary (two-choice) Random Event Generator was used. If all experiments conducted since 1962 were included, they would include, no doubt, a hodge podge of experiments including those on cats, mice, cockroaches, and chickens' eggs.

It is, however, clear that the 71 experiments were not conducted by independent investigators, and that if 71 experiments yielded antichance odds greater than 20 to 1 then 261 experiments failed to do so.

Odds greater than 20 to 1 would be expected to arise by chance in about a sixth of all experiments considered. Thus the 71 experiments having antichance odds greater than 20 to 1 would be expected to arise by chance from a total of about 430 experiments. If 430 experiments were started and 98 of these were not completed, not reported, or not published, a "statistically replicable" result would of course be obtained. This would be so even if all the experiments were meticulous in design and free from any form of error—a state of affairs that is as unlikely as the phenomenon under investigation.

DEVELOPING THE REPEATABLE DEMONSTRATION

Consider again the statement of R. A. Fisher: "In order to assert that a natural phenomenon is experimentally demonstrable we need, not an isolated record, but a reliable method of procedure. In relation to the test of significance, we may say that a phenomenon is experimentally demonstrable when we know how to conduct an experiment which will rarely fail to give us a statistically significant result."[11]

For a demonstration of ESP or PK, an experimental plan is required in which the full experimental design, the method and procedure (including the number of observations to be made and the number of subjects to be tested), is stated. This should enable the experiment to be repeated as far as possible in its original form by other investigators.

If an experiment fails more often than "rarely," it is then necessary to change it in order to provide the repeatable demonstration. A first step may require increasing the number of observations to be specified in the plan of the experiment. If the experiment still fails with some investigators and not with others further research is required to find out why this is so. Only if an experiment gives the same result independently of the investigators in charge can it provide a repeatable demonstration.

A feature of contemporary research and discussion is that very little in the long history of parapsychology research has been discarded as unreliable. For, example the Pearce-Pratt experiment is still put forward as providing evidence for clairvoyance although it would be failed as a first-year college exercise in any other discipline. Experiments that have failed to repeat are still put forward as providing evidence for ESP, while other experiments that have failed to provide evidence for ESP, such as those of Coover and Jephson, Soal, and Besterman, have been dropped entirely as a basis for research. On the basis of Rhine's early experiments clairvoyance and telepathy are claimed to be equally effective despite the fact that reliable evidence has not be found for either of them.

The present position in psi research is summed up by James Alcock, professor of psychology at York University. In his reply to Rao and Palmer, he writes:

> It accordingly seems that parapsychologists who attack scientists and critics for their refusal to recognize the importance of psi and of psi research are attacking the messengers because they cannot face up to the message. Suppose that instead of psi, parapsychologists were promoting a cure for baldness, but the amount of hair produced by the treatment was tiny and was only detectable by some researchers, sometimes. If the effect is unreliable, unrepeatable, if it also contradicts all that is known about hair growth and alopecia, and there is no theoretical mechanism put forth for the putative effect, one would hardly expect the scientific community to cheer the end to baldness. Science will never take parapsychologists simply at their word; they must offer a clear, replicable demonstration of a basic phenomenon in order to gain acceptance in science.[12]

At the present time parapsychologists are no nearer finding such a demonstration than they were a hundred years ago. The most evident change during the past ten years is that more ambitious claims are now made for psychokinesis than for extrasensory perception. The Schmidt-Morris-Rudolph experiment is suitable, given minor modifications, of providing the basis for a repeatable demonstration of PK, but to date attempts to repeat it have not been reported.

PARAPSYCHOLOGY WITHIN THE SCIENCES

In view of its track record it may be asked why parapsychology should have infiltrated to such an increasing extent both science generally and university teaching and research in particular.

In the past the subject of psychology has been linked with a variety of pseudosciences. Mesmer's theory of animal magnetism—linking physics and psychology—was for many years entertained as an explanation for hypnotic trance states. Gall and Spurtzeim's phrenology—linking psychology and anatomy—was put forward within science and occupied public attention for some 100 years. Astrology—linking psychology and astronomy—is still more popular with the media than is either orthodox astronomy or psychology as they are taught in universities.

While animal magnetism, phrenology, and astrology failed to be accepted or to remain within science, the Parapsychological Association was admitted to affiliation with the American Association for the Advancement of Science in 1969. Higher degrees have been awarded in parapsychology and university departments have been set up in the subject. In the universities, parapsychology has become a splinter movement from psychology. With its own journals parapsychology enjoys a freedom of publication that is denied other debatable areas within psychology.

An encouraging feature in the past twenty years has been an increase in the amount of critical literature. In particular, it has seen the publication of the *Skeptical Inquirer*[13] by the Committee for the Scientific Investigation of Claims of the Paranormal. This serves to offset misleading claims made in the media about paranormal processes and pseudoscience.

SUMMARY

A great deal of time, effort, and money has been expended over a period of more than a hundred years, but an acceptable demonstration of the existence of extrasensory perception or psychokinesis has not been provided.

In 1966,[14] it was suggested that an acceptable model for future research had been made available at the United States Air Force Laboratories in the form of the VERITAC investigation. The plain fact is that the investigations carried out with VERITAC did not produce other than chance results. Repetitions of the experiment, if thought worthwhile, might provide a repeatable demonstration of the fact that, in the absence of sensory information, subjects are unable to identify symbols in the manner claimed by parapsychologists.

Since 1966, the attitude of the public and of the media has changed very little. The major experimental evidence at the time claimed to support the existence of ESP was far more impressive than anything presented since. The only comparable contemporary experimental data are those in the area of psychokinesis stemming from the work of Helmut Schmidt. Through the experiments of Jahn and his associates, Schmidt, Morris, and Rudolph, this had led to the design of experiments that, with little modification, should provide the basis for repeatable demonstrations. In the event that such demonstrations confirm the original result, it will then be necessary to determine in what way the underlying processes responsible for the result are related to ESP, PK, or any other hypothetical process.

It is, however, thought likely that in another ten years such experiments will have become matters of past history, being replaced by further so-called evidence for paranormal processes.

In any branch of science observations that are at variance with existing theory are of the utmost importance provided they can be confirmed. For a hundred years parapsychologists have sought to provide such observations. Their failure to do so indicates that prevailing ideas in psychology and sensory physiology are essentially correct.

NOTES

1. C. E. M. Hansel, *ESP: A Scientific Evaluation* (New York: Scribner's, 1966).

2. J. B. Rhine, J. G. Pratt, B. M. Smith, C. E. Stuart, and J. A. Greenwood, *Extrasensory Perception after Sixty Years* (New York: Henry Holt, 1940).

3. C. E. M. Hansel, *ESP and Parapsychology: A Critical Reevaluation* (Buffalo, N.Y.: Prometheus Books, 1980).

4. J. B. Rhine and J. G. Pratt, *Parapsychology: Frontier Science of the Mind* (Oxford: Blackwell, 1954), p. 131.

5. Ibid., p. 132.

6. Ibid., p. 19.

7. J. B. Rhine and J. G. Pratt, "A Reply to the Hansel Critique of the Pearce-Pratt Series," *Journal of Parapsychology* 25 (1961): 94.

8. R. K. Rao and J. Palmer, "The Anomaly Called PSI: Recent Research and Criticism," *Journal of Behavioral and Brain Sciences* 10 (1987): 539–55.

9. Ibid., p. 539.

10. Ibid., p. 543.

11. R. A. Fisher, *The Design of Experiments,* edited by Oliver and Boyd (Edinburgh: Oliver and Boyd, 1935), p. 16.

12. J. E. Alcock, "Parapsychology: Science of the Anomalous or Search for the Soul?" *Journal of Behavioral and Brain Sciences* 10 (1987): 24.

13. *The Skeptical Inquirer,* edited by Kendrick Frazier and published by the Committee for the Scientific Investigation of Claims of the Paranormal, P.O. Box 229, Buffalo, New York 14215-0229.

14. C. E. M. Hansel, op. cit. (1966), p. 241.

Appendices

Appendix A

Programme

(refer to chapter 17, page 208)

Programme in BASIC to generate pendulum movement data, total score and values based on + and - output. If a six-digit seed number is entered, a printout is given of the 256 amplitude values ranging from 0 to 7 together with the total value.

```
 20 DIM W(6), V(4), A(300)
 30 PRINT "enter seed number"
 40 INPUT A: REM transform to hex
 42 AL=A
 45 LPRINT "Seed Number "A:LPRINT
 47 LPRINT " Values based on Pendulum amplitude ":LPRINT
 50 FOR S= 1 TO 6: W(S)=A-10*INT (A/10)
 60 A=INT (A/10): NEXT S
 70 V(0)=85:FOR S=1 TO 3
 80 V(S)= W(7-2*S)+16*W(8-2*S): NEXT S
100 PRINT "wait"
110 FOR T=1 TO 256: GOSUB 220: NEXT T
120 SC=0:GOSUB 210: N=R AND 7
130 FOR T=1 TO 128
140 GOSUB 210: R0=R AND 1
150 N=N+2*R0+15: N=N-16*INT(N/16)
160 AMP=(15- ABS(2*N-15))/2
165 A(T)=AMP
170 SC=SC+AMP:LPRINT AMP;: NEXT T:LPRINT
190 LPRINT:LPRINT "          score= "; SC+52:LPRINT:GOTO 400
210 R=V(0) XOR V(1)XOR V(2) XOR V(3)
220 FOR S= 1 TO 3
```

277

```
230  V=8*(V(3) AND 1) +(V(3) AND 8)
240  FOR M=3 TO 1 STEP -1
250  V(M)= INT (V(M)/2) + 128*(V(M-1) AND 1)
260  NEXT M
270  V(0)= INT(V(0)/2) + 8*(V AND 8)
280  NEXT S:RETURN
300  LPRINT "Values based on + and - outputs ":LPRINT
390  LPRINT "First No. = "A(1)
400  LPRINT: LPRINT "Values based on +1 and -1 outputs ": LPRINT
402  LPRINT "            ";
405  FOR I =2 TO 128
410  IF A(I)>A(I-1) THEN AP=AP+1: LPRINT "+1 ";
420  IF A(I)>A(I-1) THEN AM=AM+1:LPRINT "-1 ";
430  IF A(I)= 0 AND A(I-1) =0 THEN AM = AM+1: LPRINT "-1 ";
440  IF A(I)= 7 AND A(I-1) =7 THEN AP=AP+1: LPRINT "+1 ";
450  NEXT
460  LPRINT:LPRINT
500  LPRINT " Total plus values =";AP;" Total minus values =";AM
505   AM = 0:AP = 0
506  LPRINT:LPRINT "_____";
510  GOTO 30
```

Appendix B

Replies to Critics

The present book is an updating of *ESP and Parapsychology* published in 1981. I replied to only two of the reviews at that time, both of which were published in Britain. The first of these replies was submitted to the *New Scientist* in reply to Brian Inglis. This reply was not published. The second was in reply to a lengthy review by Carl Sargent published in a magazine called *Alpha* that specialized in psychical affairs. In this case I was invited to make a reply by the editor. Copies of these two reviews and of the replies I submitted are presented below.

Several highly critical reviews were published in the United States to which replies were not submitted. Some of the more critical of these reviews are now produced below together with my replies to them.

FOR GULLIBLE SKEPTICS?*
(Review of *ESP and Parapsychology,* by Carl Sargent)

As the title indicates much of this book is a re-hash of Hansel's 1966 book written with a delightfully idiosyncratic disregard for almost all the criticisms made of that earlier effort. The Prometheus Press ought to be prosecuted under the Trades Description Act; this book, they claim, is 'comprehensive', 'dispassionate' and 'exhaustive'.

As for the other spiel, roughly one-third of the experimental papers in parapsychology's leading Journal (of the American Society for Psychical Research) in the 1970's were penned by one or more of the following: John Palmer, Rex Stanford, William Braud. Not one of them is ever mentioned in this book.

Since Hansel's grasp of the literature on mediumship is so frail that Alan

---

Alpha magazine (June 1980).

Gauld, a very sober and quiet man, was driven to comment that part of Hansel's writings about Mrs. Piper were 'nonsense' (this in the 1966 book, and the text is not much altered now), I shall restrict myself to comments on his experimental work.

First, I shall extol some virtues of the author and his book. Hansel is not a skeptic who indulges in scurrilous defamation of parapsychologists living or dead (apart from a disgraceful reference to Edmund Gurney's suicide, when Hansel knows perfectly well that the inquest verdict was accidental death; this will mislead readers). He has also exposed some weaknesses in the experimental literature, such as the Pearce-Pratt experiment's shortcomings, and this is all to the good. Problems arise firstly because Hansel's skepticism knows no limits and anything—even experimenter conspiracy—is a fair alternative to the psi hypothesis, and second because his grasp of the experimental literature is poor. Let me document some examples.

After the publication of his *ESP: A Scientific Evaluation* in 1966 Hansel got a tremendous amount of stick for his assertion that one should assume that psi was impossible when examining the evidence. In this book he claims that such an assumption should be made provisionally and would have to be given up if, for example, Geller was repeatedly successful in PK experiments run by skeptics.

But this won't do. Either something is impossible or it isn't. If one assumes that it is then logically it cannot happen and no evidence could prove that it does happen, and that's that. Geller's success would have to be put down to other factors than PK if one was being logical. What Hansel would have to say is that psi is *extremely unlikely,* highly improbable; but if that is the working assumption then his case largely falls to the ground.

Hansel shows hopeless philosophical muddlement, and in any case can we really trust a psychologist who states categorically that "ESP can only be possible if there are new and at present unknown *(tautology rules OK?),* processes and properties of matter that permit it to take place"? There are many physicists who would argue with that and certainly the issue is not settled. History is littered with examples of foolish people who asserted that certain things could not happen because they were not reconcilable with the physics of the time. And I would suggest that it's not for psychologists to start making assertions about the physics of matter.

When assessing experimental evidence, Hansel broadly divides psi studies into two classes: alleged 'definitive experiments', which are treated as one-offs, and other experiments which might be repeatable in nature (for example, group experiments studying relationships between ESP and some other factor, like extraversion). His priorities are truly bizarre here.

Nineteen pages are given over to the Jones Boys, who were never exactly feted by parapsychologists generally, and yet PK experiments (other than Geller and Schmidt's work) and the group experiments between them get a pitifully inadequate 14 pages. Since there are nearly 40 published reports on ESP and extraversion alone this is absurd.

Hansel's reporting of the work on the relationship between ESP and belief in it (the 'sheep-goat effect') is feeble; he plays his usual old trick of discussing the original work, (not mentioning Christopher Scott's wholly abortive attack on it), plus a couple of failures to replicate (one of which wasn't actually) and not one of the many successful replications.

He plays exactly the same trick when it comes to Betty Humphrey's work on expansiveness (a personality trait, a mixture of extraversion and low neuroticism, reflected in drawing style)—he references West's failure to replicate, but not the Kathamam and Rao experiment which gave results close to Humphrey's own. Now this is poor stuff; in the whole of this book only one successful replication study is mentioned at all. When one considers that there are over 30 successful replications of the extraversion/ESP effect and the sheep-goat effect alone—and not a single published study which significantly refutes either findings—Hansel's reporting is clearly not the legitimate writing with a slant but the much more dubious selection of evidence consistent with his ideas to the exclusion of all else.

Possibly the nadir of the book is the discussion of the experiments with Stepanek, and the reporting of Schmidt's work on electronic PK. Hansel's 1966 discussion of Stepanek was massacred by Pratt in 1973, who demonstrated nine gross errors in just 22 lines of Hansel's text; Hansel has never replied to Pratt and Pratt's paper is not referenced here either. Instead Hansel reiterates some criticisms refuted by Pratt and, even worse, he states that in the experiments he discusses Pratt was always present. He stresses the need for other experimenters to have been used instead—and he should know perfectly well that many other experimenters tested Stepanek with success (including Beloff, who obtained results significantly below chance with Stepanek—Hansel claims that this is a 'failure'). This is wickedly misleading.

On the Schmidt side Hansel lets fly; he states that he may just have been "a careless experimenter who had little idea of the precautions necessary in an ESP experiment". Unfortunately this rebounds on Hansel. In addition to getting his figures wrong in places, Hansel seems genuinely unaware of a key feature of some of Schmidt's work.

In some experiments Schmidt asked subjects either to aim low or to aim high in PK tests recorded in his absence. Hansel seems to believe—and the casual reader will surely believe—that subjects simply told Schmidt later which trials were run under which condition. In fact separate recording systems were used for the two-aim techniques so that subjects could not cheat here. Hansel also fails to mention that in the early work the subjects scored slightly higher in Schmidt's presence than in his absence, again not supporting any idea that they cheated. At a tangent, when discussing the Heymans' and others' experiment with the subject Van Dam, Hansel goes one better than this. He actually states that the subject scored better when the experimenters (who knew the targets and who could have given Van Dam sensory cues) were in the room with him, rather than outside it when exactly the reverse is the case! Typical.

This book is a minor irritant because one knows that ignorant, skeptically inclined people will be all too ready to read it, believe it all, and say 'Hear, Hear!' simply because it's what they want to read.

WICKEDLY MISLEADING?
(A Reply to Carl Sargent by C. E. M. Hansel)

I am grateful for the opportunity to reply to Dr. Carl Sargent's review of my book *ESP and Parapsychology: A Critical Re-evaluation,* particularly since my letter to the Editor of the *New Scientist* replying to a review by Brian Inglis, has not been published and has elicited no more from the journal than an acknowledgement slip.

Almost everything Carl Sargent writes in his review, that can be checked with the printed records, can be shown to be misleading and inaccurate. This is particularly evident in the latter part of the review where Sargent is presumably demonstrating that my "grasp of the experimental literature is poor". He deals there with what he calls the 'nadir' of my book—my "discussion of the experiments with Stepanek and the reporting of Schmidt's work on electronic PK".

In the case of the experiments on Stepanek, Sargent comments that my 1966 discussion was "massacred by Pratt . . . who demonstrated 9 gross errors in just 22 lines". In the account I saw Pratt did not list these errors; but three of them were presumably that I used the word *black* instead of *green* three times when describing the colour of the cards used in early tests. Since my new text includes that account in essentially its original form Sargent should have no difficulty "massacring" it. His criticisms will therefore be examined in some detail.

Sargent writes:

> . . . he (Hansel) states that in the experiments he discusses Pratt was always present. He stresses the need for other experimenters to have been used instead—and he should know perfectly well that many other experimenters tested Stepanek with success (including Beloff, who obtained results significantly below chance with Stepanek—Hansel claims that this is a 'failure'). This is wickedly misleading.

In my discussion, I distinguished between (1) experiments before 1966— as reported in my earlier book—in which Stepanek attempted to identify which way up cards (one side white and the other green) had been placed inside envelopes, and (2) experiments carried out after 1966, when following Stepanek's loss of the ability to perform successfully in the above manner, it was now claimed that he could identify particular envelopes, irrespective of which way up they happened to be, when they were concealed within further envelopes or 'covers'.

Concerning Beloff's experiment I wrote: "when tested by Dr. John Beloff Stepanek's extrasensory powers deserted him." This agrees with Beloff's own statement in the *New Scientist* (Vol. 40, 1968, p. 76) where he wrote "scoring in that experiment was at strictly chance level."

My statement that Pratt was present at each experiment was in a section of my book dealing with experiments carried out after 1966. Here I was discussing a paper published in *Nature* by Pratt and six other investigators, presenting the results of 18 experiments carried out between May 1967 and March 1968. (*Nature*, Vol. 220, Oct. 1968, pp. 89-91). In that article a table gives details of each of the eighteen experiments together with the initials of the investigators taking part. Pratt is listed as the sole investigator in the first 4 experiments and as taking part in each of the remaining 14 experiments.

Sargent states that I appear to be "genuinely unaware of a key feature of some of Schmidt's work", and he continues "In some experiments Schmidt asked subjects either to aim low or high in PK tests recorded in his absence".

This is completely wrong. In the PK tests on humans, according to the report in the *Journal of Parapsychology* (Vol. 34, 1970), the subjects always aimed at "willing" a light to move in a clockwise or counterclockwise direction among a circle of nine lights. We read there:

> . . . at the beginning of each run, the subject, having decided in which direction (clockwise or counterclockwise) he wanted to influence the light to go, set a switch on the panel accordingly. . . . From the experimenters point of view, the subject's goal was always to produce a high number of +1 counts. From the subject's viewpoint the equivalent goal was to influence the light in the direction desired and indicated by the position of the switch on the display panel. (p. 179).

Sargent continues: "Hansel seems to believe—and the casual reader will surely believe that subjects simply told Schmidt later which trials were run under which condition. In fact, separate recording systems were used for the two aim techniques so that subjects could not cheat here." But in the *Journal of Parapsychology* it is merely stated that the "sequence of generated numbers" was recorded "on the paper punch tape".

Assuming that Sargent confused the PK experiments with other experiments carried out by Schmidt his statement is still incorrect and misleading. In the case of precognition experiments where subjects could aim for a high or a low score, I wrote (p. 223):

> Whether to try for a high or a low score was decided at the beginning of each session, and the two modes of guessing were recorded on the tape in different codes (details of which are not given) so that the computer could separate the two types of test.

Schmidt himself wrote (Boeing Res. Lab. Report, p. 28):

The two modes of operation were recorded on tape in different codes such that the evaluating computer could separate the two types of test.

Further, contrary to Sargent's assumptions, I have at no time suggested that Schmidt's subjects cheated and consider it extremely unlikely that they could have done so. A further discussion of why this is so, and why Schmidt was a "careless experimenter" is being presented elsewhere.

Perhaps Sargent's biggest howler appears in his penultimate paragraph where he writes:

> . . . when discussing the Heymans' and others' experiment with the subject Van Dam, Hansel goes one better than this. He actually states that the subject scored better when the experimenters (who knew the targets and who could have given Van Dam sensory cues) were in the room with him rather than outside it when exactly the reverse is the case! Typical.

What I actually stated was (p. 36 para. 3):

> Some of the trials were made with the experimenters in the same room as the subject, but although he also succeeded under these conditions, his scores were not as high as when they were in the room above him.

In addition to these factual errors Sargent has inexcusably misrepresented what I said in my earlier book. He writes:

> After the publication of his ESP: a scientific evaluation in 1966 Hansel got a tremendous amount of stick for his assertion that one should assume that psi is impossible when examining the evidence. In this book he claims that such an assumption should be made provisionally and would have to be given up if for example Geller was repeatedly successful in ESP experiments run by skeptics.

What I wrote in 1966 was:

> Thus in analysing an experiment that purports to prove ESP, it is wise to adopt initially the assumption that ESP is impossible. If analysis shows that this assumption is untenable, then the possibility of ESP has to be accepted. (p. 21).

Exactly the same statement appears in the present book (p. 22), but also later in the book I went to considerable pains to remove any doubts about what I had said (pp. 301, 302) giving details of cases where my statement above had been misrepresented.

Other points raised by Sargent are covered in my book where I discuss the selection of experiments for review (pp. 24-28); and reasons for omitting experiments unless they afford a demonstration "which will rarely fail to give a statistically significant result" (pp. 211-212, 298-299).

As for what I wrote about mediums, I am no historian, but even the experts in this field disagree on what constitutes evidence and in their interpretation of events. My brief account of early investigations of Mediums was intended to provide an idea of what psychical researchers got up to in those early days.

In the case of "Edmund Gurney's suicide", I might have written that he died after administering to himself a fatal dose of chloroform and that evidence given at the inquest has since been disputed. (see Trevor H. Hall, *The Strange Case of Edmund Gurney,* given among my suggestions for further reading).

I would like to say, however, that among the early pioneers of Psychical Research, I have the greatest respect and admiration for Edmund Gurney. He always tried to get his facts straight.

ESP AND PARAPSYCHOLOGY
(A Review by Brian Inglis)*

Professor Hansel's *ESP: A Scientific Evaluation,* published 15 years ago, has remained the skeptic's *vade mecum* ever since; but so much has been happening in the interim that he has felt the need to update it. Much of the original material has been incorporated into the new book. He has also inserted replies to critics, and presented fresh material where it has become available on old controversies; and he has added a selection dealing with the post-1965 period.

Hansel is a disciple of David Hume. He does not claim that paranormal phenomena are a *priori* impossible; he maintains that they are so contrary to uniform experience that it is more reasonable to account for them by natural causes—coincidence, gullibility, delusion, sleight-of-hand, and so on. And his method of presentation is to take a succession of case histories of celebrated psychics, or of research projects, and to show how the phenomena can all be attributed to human frailty.

If Hansel were content to stick to this formula, he would be performing a useful service. But his premise, "an experiment must be judged on the weakest part of its design", only holds good for the experiment in question. If, as he clearly intends, his evidence is designed to cast doubt on the reality of paranormal phenomena in general, another aphorism requires attention: J. S. Mill's "an argument cannot be considered answered until it is answered at its best".

For Hansel to give a survey of the early psychical research of a century ago without even mentioning the work done with D. D. Home, is roughly comparable with offering the collected verse of the poets of the era without

New Scientist (February 7, 1980).

mentioning Tennyson. The cases selected as representative of the past 15 years' research are comically inadequate. His method of selection, too, is eccentric. He devotes a couple of pages to the tests which were rigged by American skeptics to discredit Eusapia Palladino—but only a brief paragraph to the remarkable range of scrupulously controlled experiments with her over a three year period at the Sorbonne by some of the most eminent scientists of the time—the Curies, Jacques D'Arsonval, Jean Perrin, Henri Bergson, Charles Richet. And to say they "detected many signs of trickery" is untrue.

Worse: Hansel cites as his sources works long since discredited. For example, he leaves the reader with no indication that the evidence for William Crookes' alleged collusion with the medium Florence Cook has since been shown to have been based on a misrepresentation of the source material.

REPLY TO *NEW SCIENTIST* REVIEW
(By C. E. M. Hansel)
The Editor:

I feel obliged to answer statements made by Brian Inglis in his review of my book "ESP and Parapsychology". These suggest (1) my failure to mention strong evidence that did not support my argument, (2) untruthful statements, (3) citing as sources "works long since discredited".

Almost the whole of Mr. Inglis' review of my book was concerned with a small section of fourteen pages in which I discussed four physical mediums, namely the Fox sisters, Eusapia Palladino, and Margery Crandon. These ladies who caused rapping noises, levitated tables and produced various "physical" phenomena, were selected for discussion as they had all been investigated by committees of scientists and because the methods by which they obtained their effects were revealed. D. D. Home was not investigated in this manner. His cabaret act performed at week-end parties in homes of the wealthy, included levitating himself and floating around in the horizontal position, feet foremost. Sir William Crookes, who investigated Home and believed in his ability to perform in this manner, discredited himself as an investigator through what he wrote about Kate Fox, a medium who later made a full public confession and revealed how she had deceived Crookes.

The most remarkable part of Mr. Inglis' review is where he compares "tests which were rigged by American skeptics to discredit Eusapia Palladino" with the "scrupulously controlled" experiments conducted "at the Sorbonne". The tests rigged by American skeptics were, presumably, those carried out at Columbia University. The investigators included R. W. Wood, Professor of Physics at John Hopkins, C. L. Dana, Professor of Psychology at Cornell, E. B. Wilson, Professor of Biology at Princeton and Dickinson Miller, Professor of Philosophy at Columbia. The findings were reported at length in *Science* (77, 1910). Mr. Inglis' "scrupulously controlled experiments" are, from the dates, those conducted at the Institut General Psychologique.

Mr. Inglis writes that my statement that "the committee detected many signs of trickery" is untrue. But in the report of the committee one large chapter is devoted to discussing tricks, and Mr. Inglis must agree that (1) Eusapia was detected "using what looked like a thread to move objects" (This quotation and those that follow are taken from Mr. Inglis' own account in his book *Natural and Supernatural*): (2) The committee noted that "A nail had been found where no nail should have been": (3) Eusapia's weight was monitored throughout the tests and "the balance registered figures which conformed with what would have been expected if she had been physically lifting the table which rose from the ground". It thus became apparent that Eusapia was raising the table in front of her rather than Spirit Guide, John King, whom she claimed to be responsible, was doing so: (4) We read "otherwise Eusapia had been detected in nothing more heinous than occasionally freeing her hands and feet". But since the whole idea of her act was to show that objects moved in her immediate vicinity when observers were holding her hands and feet she was presumably indulging in some form of trickery. In fact Mr. Inglis himself wrote: "The Sorbonne investigators declined formally to endorse Eusapia".

Mr. Inglis states that I cite as my sources "works long since discredited". He gives as a case in point the evidence for "William Crookes' alleged collusion based on a misrepresentation of the source material". I wrote "it was only in 1962, for example, that Trevor Hall made public his detailed study of one of the most prominent investigators of that time, Sir William Crookes, in which he revealed that Crookes and Florence Cook, a young medium whom he was investigating were both accomplices and lovers[2]". The reference given was: Trevor H. Hall "The Spiritualists: The Story of Florence Cook and William Crookes" (London: Duckworth, 1962). To anyone except a rabid psychical researcher Dr. Hall must be regarded as the most systematic, thorough and reliable contemporary investigator of the early history of Psychical Research.

Four years after "The Spiritualists" was published, Dr. E. J. Dingwall, at that time the foremost expert in the history of Psychical Research made a full survey of the evidence presented by Hall and the objections to it. In his *Critics Dilemma* (1966) he revealed that in 1922 he had himself met the man to whom Florence Cook had given details of her affair with Crookes, her trips to Paris, and the assistance that Crookes had provided in order to fake the spirit of Katie King. Dingwall supported Hall's conclusions and after considering attempts to explain away the evidence writes "If we are asked to think that Crookes really believed in all this, it appears that his modern defenders are reducing him almost to the level of an imbecile and denigrating him to a far greater degree than Mr. Hall has done".

Regarding the main part of my book, which he otherwise ignores, Brian Inglis writes "the cases selected as representative of the past 15 years research are comically inadequate". That is all he has to say. No instances are given of cases that should have been included. I gave full details of how I had made my selection (pp. 25-28). It was largely dependent on cases selected by Parapsychologists themselves in books they had written.

Cases arising in the past 14 years included:

(1) Helmut Schmidt's experiments on ESP and Psychokinesis using an electronic randomizer and scoring, one of which was published in the *New Scientist* (June 1971).
(2) Targ and Puthoff's research on Uri Geller, conducted at the Stanford Research Institute and reported in *Nature* (October, 1974).
(3) Experiments on Pavel Stepanek reported in *Nature* (October, 1968).
(4) "Remote Viewing" experiments carried out by Targ and Puthoff (*Nature*, October 1974 and in *Mind-Reach*, 1977).
(5) Experiments on avoidance of shock by mice conducted by W. L. Levy and others. (Reported in articles and in John Beloff's "New Directions in Parapsychology", 1974).
(6) Experiments of Sir Alister Hardy and J. V. Harvie. (Reported in "The Challenge of Chance", 1973 and discussed in *New Scientist* 1974).
(7) Experiments conducted at the Maimonides Dream Research Laboratory. (Reported in articles and in "Dream Telepathy" by M. Ullman, S. Krippner, and A. Vaughan, 1970).

If Mr. Inglis considers the evidence for ESP provided by these investigations to be "pitifully inadequate" I would agree, but what better experiments would he have had me include.

To send for review, a book that attempts to throw some light on the incredible claims made in parapsychology, to a confirmed believer in anything from levitation to spoon bending, is like sending a book on the shape of the earth to a member of the Flat-Earth Society.

BEYOND THE REACH OF SENSE: SOME COMMENTS ON
C. E. M. HANSEL'S *ESP AND PARAPSYCHOLOGY
A CRITICAL RE-EVALUATION*[1]
(By Charles Honorton)*

Introduction

This is an updated edition of Professor Hansel's 1966 book, *ESP: A Scientific Evaluation*. About 80 percent of the present edition consists of material retained without modification from the original. The author asserts that "no reason could be found to change what has already been written" (p. v). This is unfortunate because he fails to correct major factual errors or to address serious criticisms contained in various reviews of the original edition (e.g., Honorton, 1967; Medhurst, 1968; Stevenson, 1967). It is particularly unfortunate in that he repeats the same pattern of errors in his discussion of more recent psi

*The Journal of the American Society for Psychical Research 75 (April 1981): 155–166.

research. Despite his stated goal "to examine all the experiments and to make a further evaluation in the light of any new features that have emerged" (p. v.), Hansel's coverage of recent research is highly selective and grossly inadequate. Some of the major shortcomings will be discussed below.

Antecedent Commitments

"It is wise to adopt initially the assumption that ESP is impossible," Hansel says, since "there is a great weight of knowledge supporting this point of view" (p. 22). He provides no documentation whatsoever for this assumption. While other critics of parapsychology have assumed that psi phenomena are a priori improbable, few have been as bold as Hansel in proclaiming them to be impossible, and no critics, to the best of my knowledge, have ever shown where and how the existence of psi phenomena conflicts with "established" knowledge.

The philosopher C. D. Broad (1969, pp. 9-12) probably came closer to showing this than anyone else with his "Basic Limiting Principles." He identified four general classes of such principles which he said were "commonly accepted either as self-evident or as established by overwhelming and uniformly favorable empirical evidence" (p. 9). Briefly, these are (a) General Principles of Causation, (b) Limitations on the Action of Mind on Matter, (c) Dependence of Mind on Brain, and (d) Limitations of Ways of Acquiring Knowledge. Each of these principles has been challenged in the course of later scientific or philosophical investigation. In lieu of empirical confirmation, (b) and (c) require adherence to what Popper (1977) has called "Promissory Materialism." With respect to (a), consider the following comment by Columbia University physicist Gerald Feinberg (1975) concerning what is probably the most intuitively distressing parapsychological phenomenon—precognition:

> Instead of forbidding precognition from happening [accepted physical], theories typically have sufficient symmetry (between past and future) to suggest that phenomena akin to precognition should occur in a manner qualitatively, although not necessarily quantitatively, similar to the occurrence of retrocognition. Indeed, phenomena involving a reversed time order of cause and effect are generally excluded from consideration on the ground that they have not been observed, rather than because the theory forbids them. This exclusion itself introduces an element of asymmetry into the physical theories, which some physicists have felt was improper or required further explanation. . . . Thus, if such phenomena indeed occur, no change in the fundamental equations of physics would be needed to describe them (pp. 54-55).

This quotation reminds us that appeals to a priori knowledge are problematic, especially at a time when physics itself is engaged in controversy over whether its subject-matter exists independently of human consciousness (see, e.g., d'Espagnat, 1979, 1980; Weisskopf, 1980), and in which leading neuro-scientists such as Eccles (1977), Penfield (1975), and Pribram (1979) are abandoning speculative reductionism for a variety of equally speculative dualistic, emergent, or holographic "solutions" to the mind-brain problem.

The point here is not that "the millennium has arrived," as some sincere but naive enthusiasts would like to believe: the unresolved controversies of physics and neurophysiology are just that—unresolved. They constitute unfinished business for the practitioners of these fields. It would be fool-hardy and opportunistic for parapsychologists not trained in these disci-plines to advocate a particular position merely because it seems more supportive of the existence of psi than its competitors. At the same time, the existence of legitimate controversy in these areas is a clear indication that the state of "established knowledge"—circa 1980—is still sufficiently incomplete, as it pertains to such basic problems as the foundations of physics and the nature of consciousness, to make any final assignment of antecedent probabilities—for or against the reality of psi phenomena—totally unintelligible.

On Examining the Evidence

In order to examine the empirical evidence, Hansel is forced to admit the possibility, however remote, that there is something real to examine. How he makes the qualitative leap from an initial assumption that psi is impossible to one that asserts psi to be possible, albeit extremely unlikely, is—like justification for the a priori argument itself—left to the reader's imagination. Somehow Hansel manages to make the leap, and having done so, he describes his guidelines for evaluating the evidence. The most important of these may be summarized briefly.

Because psi phenomena are assumed on (unspecified) a priori grounds to be extremely unlikely, "proof for the existence of ESP obviously must depend on conclusive experiments . . ." (p. 25). *"An experiment that has any defect such that its result may be due to a cause other than ESP cannot provide proof of ESP"* (p. 20, Hansel's italics).

"A possible explanation other than extrasensory perception, provided it involves only well-established processes, should not be rejected on the grounds of its complexity" (p. 21). *"If the result could have arisen through a trick,* the experiment must be considered unsatisfactory proof of ESP, *whether or not it is finally decided that such a trick was, in fact, used"* (p. 21, my italics).

Despite his own admission that "no single experiment can be conclusive," and the statements that "repetition after repetition of an ESP experiment by independent investigators could render the possibility of deception or error ex-tremely unlikely . . . if the original result is repeatedly confirmed, the probabil-ity of ESP becomes increasingly likely" (p. 21), Hansel is undisturbed by these contradictions and continues to be preoccupied by individual experiments.

"Conclusive" Experiments and Evaluation of Experimental Flaws

I believe that most experienced researchers would agree that there can be no single conclusive experiment in any area of the social sciences. There are good and bad experiments, but there are no perfect experiments. Real or suspected flaws can be found in any study.

Consider Hansel's enthusiastic endorsement of the U.S. Air Force VERITAC experiment (Smith, Dagle, Hill, and Smith, 1963), which in his earlier book he described as "an acceptable model for future research" (Hansel, 1966, p. 241). Had VERITAC produced significant ESP results, Hansel could have found a number of legitimate reasons for questioning the experiment. VERITAC was a good effort in its time, but its methodology was inferior to many of the Schmidt-type random generator experiments that followed. For instance, unlike Schmidt (1970), who provided schematic-level descriptions of his test equipment, the VERITAC investigators gave no technical documentation whatsoever on theirs. We are told only that it was developed by an electronics engineer "adept at designing such systems" (Smith et al., 1963, p. 2). The investigators' claim that VERITAC produced sufficiently random targets (numbers between 0-9) might be questioned since it is predicated on control data apparently taken only in unreported pilot studies of unspecified length and using unspecified criteria of randomness (p. 11). Considering that subjects received immediate feedback on each trial and could conceivably learn (over 1500 trials) to recognize subtle patterns if they occurred in the target sequence, this experiment is hardly a model for future research! Since Hansel criticizes Schmidt on the same grounds (p. 228), we might also expect him to be dissatisfied that the VERITAC investigators did not specify the number of subjects and trials in advance of the experiment, but merely set a minimal limit of 30 subjects (Smith et al., 1963, p. 12).

I could go on, but I think most readers will agree that potential flaws can be found in any experiment, given sufficient determination to find them. The identification of potential flaws is a useful classroom exercise, but it is hardly a sufficient basis for rejecting experiments out of hand. Clearly a more sophisticated approach is called for. There are several common approaches to evaluating real or suspected flaws in experiments. Here are two examples.

When real weaknesses in design are discovered, their effects upon the experimental conclusions can often be weighed by looking at blocks of similar studies and comparing the results from "flawed" and "unflawed" samples. If there is a difference in results between the two samples, our suspicion that the first result was artifactual will be confirmed and our rejection of the experiment will be empirically justified. If, on the other hand, we find little or no difference in the "flawed" and "unflawed" samples, we would not be justified in rejecting the experiment. For instance, in a recent discussion of free-response methodology, Kennedy (1979) raised the possibility that significant ESP results might be due to subtle handling cues in experiments where subjects used picture judging packs that had been previously handled by the senders. This hypothesis was empirically tested by comparing the results of studies in which the suspected flaw was present with others in which it was not (Honorton, 1979). Since there was no difference in the results of the two groups of studies, the handling cue hypothesis was rejected. As John Stuart Mill put it, "A difference, in order to be a difference, must make a difference."

Another approach is to repeat the experiment, systematically varying the presence or absence of the suspected flaw. An excellent illustration is a study by Palmer and Lieberman (1975) exploring the relationship between ESP performance and a measure of mental imagery. In an earlier study, Palmer (Palmer and Vassar, 1974) had found a significant relationship between ESP performance and the same imagery measure. However, since the subjects in that study received feedback on their ESP scores prior to completing the imagery scale, Palmer was concerned that knowledge of their ESP scores may have biased their responses to the imagery scale. Therefore, in the replication study Palmer and Lieberman compared the earlier procedure with one in which the subjects did not receive ESP feedback until after completing the imagery scale. Palmer's suspicions were confirmed: the significant relationship between ESP and imagery was only present in the suspect condition. The original finding was therefore discarded.

The moral here is simply this: Disputes over empirical claims can only be resolved through empirical methods. This is the hallmark of science and what differentiates it from other approaches to knowledge such as religion. Both science and religion seek understanding, but only the latter promises the attainment of Perfection. When a critic calls for "proof" of ESP—or, for that matter, of any empirical claim—that is "beyond all doubt," as Hansel does in this book (pp. 314-315), he is appealing to something other than science, which must always stop short of dogmatic claims to absolute certainty.

The Ubiquitous Fraud Hypothesis and the Blunting of Occam's Razor

Hansel's suggestion that counterhypotheses should not be rejected because of their complexity also conflicts with accepted scientific thinking. Most scientists adhere to the principle of parsimony, which states that simpler explanations are preferred to more complex ones.

Hansel, however, repeatedly engages in complex scenarios based on speculations of fraud. This is perhaps most graphically illustrated in the earlier book (Hansel, 1966) by his "Road Runner" scenario of the Pearce-Pratt distance ESP experiments conducted at Duke University in 1933-34. It is repeated in the present edition, complete with the famous "not to scale" diagram of the rooms in the former physics building at Duke where Pratt was stationed with the targets in three of the four experimental series. Pratt's desk was near the window in room 314 and he could see Pearce cross the quadrangle and enter the library about a 100 yards away at the beginning of each session. Hansel speculates that Pearce or an accomplice could have secretly returned to the physics building and looked through the window of Pratt's office as he recorded the target order at the end of the session. According to Hansel, this could have been accomplished by standing in the hallway outside Pratt's office or by standing on a chair and looking down through the transom from a room across the hall, which Hansel says was room 311.

During the second series, Pratt was stationed on the third floor of the Duke medical building. The "scenario" for this series is described by Hansel as follows:

> There was a transom above the door and a window, but both of these were of ripple glass, and it is doubtful whether the cards could have been identified through them. In this room there was, however, a trap door in the ceiling, measuring about 4 feet by 1½ feet and situated immediately over the position occupied by the table at which Pratt sat during the experiment. Its cover had a large hole that looked as if it had been made recently. There was also a small metal plate on the trap door that could have covered another hole, and this plate looked as if it had been there a long time.
>
> The room was on the top classroom floor of the building, and the main staircase went up another flight to a large attic, which extended over the floor beneath it. At the time of my visit (1960), the attic was used for storage purposes, but I was told that most of the contents had been put there well after 1934. It would thus have been possible for an intruder to have positioned himself above the trap door to see the cards on Pratt's table (pp. 115-116).

Hansel's account of the Pearce-Pratt experiments was challenged by Ian Stevenson (1967) in a review of the original edition of the present book. Stevenson also visited the scene of the supposed crime and, in addition, obtained copies of the plans of the layout of the rooms. While admitting that deception by Pearce or an accomplice cannot be ruled out, Stevenson showed Hansel's "not to scale" plan of the rooms in the physics building to be grossly inaccurate; for example, Room 311 is not opposite the office used by Pratt, as shown in Hansel's diagram, but down the hall and "could under no circumstances have served as the sighting point for the inspecting of the cards" (Stevenson, 1967, p. 256). Stevenson also dismisses the possibility that anyone could have seen the cards by looking into the window of Pratt's office, since the bottom of the glass is six feet above the floor.

Incidentally, Hansel identifies Stevenson, who is Professor and former Chairman of the Department of Psychiatry at the University of Virginia, only as "a leading expert on reincarnation" (p. 122), and the complete reference he gives for Stevenson's review is "Ian Stevenson, *Journal of the American Society for Psychical Research*" (p. 123).

At the end of his discussion of the Pearce-Pratt experiment, Hansel says that "a further unsatisfactory feature lies in the fact that a statement has not been made by the central figure, Hubert Pearce. . . . what would Pearce have said?" (p. 123). While it is difficult to see what possible value a statement by Pearce could have, those who are interested will find it on p. 258 of Stevenson's 1967 review.

This approach is scientifically sterile since it is unfalsifiable and cannot lead to a resolution of the empirical issues. It is ethically irresponsible since it casually questions the personal integrity or competence of individuals without just cause.

Accusations of fraud or incompetence are serious and should not be made unless there is strong supporting evidence. The Levy affair, tragic as it was, provides a model that is probably unique in the history of science. When Levy's associates in the Institute for Parapsychology at the Foundation for Research on the Nature of Man became suspicious of his behavior, they quietly set up recording devices and caught him in the act of manipulating the data. Even here, Hansel finds it necessary to twist the facts to suit his own purposes, saying that "thanks must go to the laboratory technicians, who displayed a critical attitude singularly lacking in the parapsychologists involved in the research" (p. 297). These "laboratory technicians" were J. W. Davis, J. E. Kennedy, and J. Levin, all members of the research staff at the Institute. Davis was co-author with Levy of a number of published experimental reports, and Kennedy was co-experimenter in the animal series during which their suspicions were aroused. Those making accusations of fraud or incompetence should be especially careful not to engage in deceptive practices themselves.

The Importance of Replicability

Replicability is a progressive development in any new problem area, and signals achievement of sufficient understanding of the problem to enable specification of the important determinant conditions. In parapsychology, as in most other areas of behavioral science involving complex human interactions, replicability is partial, but not, as Hansel implies, nonexistent. Replicability serves as a check on the validity, or at least the generalizability, of a claim and—if the claim is valid—allows productive work to be done on it.

The "key" experiments of the Duke era were useful and important because they stimulated further productive research, not because they "proved beyond all doubt" the existence of psi. But their value is clearly limited. I cannot replicate the Pearce-Pratt experiments without Hubert Pearce. I can, however, replicate investigator A's claim that procedure P, device D, personality trait T, or state of consciousness C shows statistical evidence of psi in X proportion of experiments. If A's claim is spurious or he fails to specify the necessary antecedents, my replication effort will fail and A's claim will soon be forgotten. If A's claim is valid and I include all the necessary ingredients, my replication should succeed—in roughly X proportion of experiments—and A's claim may be remembered.

Given Hansel's own statement on the importance of replicability that I cited above (p. 157), he deals with it in a very peculiar way. In fact, his tactics are so extreme in this regard that it is tempting to describe them in clinical terms as repression and denial.

Regarding Schmeidler's sheep-goat experiments, for example, Hansel repeats the claim he made in his earlier book that "repetition of the test by other investigators did not confirm the original result" (p. 200). Some replications of the sheep-goat work have, of course, failed to confirm the effect. But what about the successful confirmations, some of which were cited by Hansel's earlier reviewers? Why does he completely ignore these?

Hansel also ignores Palmer's (1971) detailed analysis of the sheep-goat research. Assuming the sheep-goat effect to be a small but real effect whose magnitude is on the order of Schmeidler's own group experiments, Palmer computed a theoretical sampling distribution of mean differences between sheep and goats. This led to three predictions that are in reasonably close agreement with the pattern of experimental findings: (a) sheep should score higher than goats in approximately 84 percent of the experiments, (b) significant differences between sheep and goats should be expected in only about 16 percent of the experiments, and (c) less than one percent of the experiments will show significant reversals (i.e., goats scoring significantly higher than sheep). Surveying the goats scoring significantly higher than sheep). Surveying the sheep-goat literature, Palmer reported that six out of 17 experiments showed significant sheep-goat effects, 13 of 17 studies were in the predicted direction, and there were no significant reversals.

Those familiar with psi research during the past decade will be shocked by Hansel's totally erroneous claim (pp. 228-231) that there have been no significant independent replications of Helmut Schmidt's work with electronic psi testing machines. Surveying the random generator PK work published between 1969 (Schmidt's initial report) and 1977, I found a total of 54 such experiments, 35 of which were independently significant (Honorton, 1978a). Thirty-five of these experiments were conducted by investigators other than Schmidt and 19 were significant. Significant independent confirmations were reported in five out of seven laboratories as of the time of my survey. Since Hansel was present at the 1972 Parapsychological Association Convention in Edinburgh where several of these confirmations were reported (Honorton, Ramsey, and Cabibbo, 1973: Kelly and Kanthamani, 1973); he cannot claim total ignorance of successful replications of this work.

It is important to critically examine these reports, to raise questions concerning their methodology, interpretation, methods of assessing unpublished studies, etc., but it is dishonest to pretend, as Hansel does, that they do not exist, and it is irresponsible of him to attribute Schmidt's results to carelessness or incompetence.

Hansel provides no discussion whatever of psi research with sensory isolation techniques, which has been successfully confirmed in at least eight different laboratories (see Honorton, 1978b), or related lines of research with other internal state procedures such as progressive relaxation (Braud, 1978) and hyponosis or meditation (Honorton, 1977). Nor is there any mention of conceptually consistent patterns of psi-personality correlates (see Palmer, 1977).

Hansel's failure to address consistent and meaningful patterns of findings in systematic lines of research is a direct consequence of his monolithic focus on individual experiments and constitutes one of the most serious weaknesses of his approach.

Some Concluding Thoughts

A much longer review would be required to document all of the factual errors committed by Hansel. I have given a small but representative sample of some of these errors here, and many more can be found in the reviews, cited above, of the first edition of his book.

Science is a highly pragmatic enterprise and valid scientific criticism must lead to empirical resolution of the contested issues. I believe that a careful analysis of Hansel's assumptions and attitudes toward the evaluation of evidence reveals his approach to be fatally flawed precisely because it is incapable of leading to such resolution. His all-purpose fraud theory can, as he again demonstrates in this edition of his book, be extended to cover any new experimental data, and is therefore unfalsifiable. Even those readers who are highly skeptical of the existence of psi phenomena will, I think, agree that it is inconsistent to propose such a theory and then to call for new and better experiments!

Parapsychology will stand or fall on its ability to demonstrate replicable and conceptually meaningful findings. Future critics who are interested in the resolution rather than the perpetuation of the psi controversy are advised to focus their attention on systematic lines of research which are capable of producing such findings.

NOTE

1. I wish to thank Nancy Sondow and Mario Varvoglis and especially Donald McCarthey for their helpful comments and suggestions on earlier drafts of this review.

REFERENCES

Braud, W. G. "Psi Conductive Conditions: Explorations and Interpretations." In B. Shapin and L. Coly (Eds.), *Psi and States of Awareness*. New York: Parapsychology Foundation, 1978.

Broad, C. D. *Religion, Philosophy and Psychical Research*. New York: Humanities Press, 1969.

d'Espagnat, B. "The Quantum Theory and Reality." *Scientific American*, 241 (1979): 158-174.

d'Espagnat, B.. Correspondence. *Scientific American,* 242 (1980): 8-9.

Eccles, J. C. "The Self-conscious Mind and the Brain." In K. R. Popper and J. C. Eccles, *The Self and its Brain.* New York: Springer-Verlag, 1977.

Feinberg, G. "Precognition: A Memory of Things Future." In L. Oteri (Ed.), *Quantum Physics and Parapsychology.* New York: Parapsychology Foundation, 1975.

Hansel, C. E. M. *ESP: A Scientific Evaluation.* New York: Scribner's, 1966.

Honorton, C. Review of *ESP: A Scientific Evaluaion,* by C. E. M. Hansel. *Journal of Parapsychology,* 1967, 31, 76-82.

————. "Psi and Internal Attention States." In B. B. Wolman (Ed.), *Handbook of Parapsychology.* New York: Van Nostrand Reinhold, 1977.

————. "Replicability, Experimenter Influence, and Parapsychology: An Empirical Context for the Study of Mind." Paper presented at the National Meeting of the American Association for the Advancement of Science, Washington, D.C., February 17, 1978. (a)

————. "Psi and Internal Attention States: Information Retrieval in the Ganzfeld." In B. Shapin and L. Coly (Eds.), *Psi and States of Awareness.* New York: Parapsychology Foundation, 1978. (b)

————. "Methodological Issues in Free-Response Psi Experiments." *Journal of the American Society for Psychical Research,* 73 (1979): 381-394.

Honorton, C., Ramsey, M., and Cabibbo, C. "Experimenter Effects in ESP Research." In W. G. Roll, R. L. Morris, and J. D. Morris (Eds.), *Research in Parapsychology 1972.* Metuchen. N.J.: Scarecrow Press, 1973.

Kelly, E. F., and Kanthamani, B. K. "A Note on a High-Scoring Subject." In W. G. Roll, R. L. Morris, and J. D. Morris (Eds.), *Research in Parapsychology 1972.* Metuchen, N.J.: Scarecrow Press, 1973.

Kennedy, J. E. "Methodological Problems in Free-Response ESP Experiments." *Journal of the American Society for Psychical Research,* 73 (1979): 1-15.

Medhurst, R. G. "The Fraudulent Experimenter: Professor Hansel's Case against Psychical Research." *Journal of the Society for Psychical Research,* 44 (1968): 217-232.

Palmer, J. "Scoring in ESP Tests as a Function of Belief in ESP. Part I. The Sheep-goat Effect." *Journal of the American Society for Psychical Research,* 65 (1971): 373-408.

————. "Attitudes and Personality Traits in Experimental ESP Research." In B. B. Wolman (Ed.), *Handbook of Parapsychology.* New York: Van Nostrand Reinhold, 1977.

Palmer, J., and Lieberman, R. "The Influence of Psychological Set on ESP and Out-of-body Experiences." *Journal of the American Society for Psychical Research,* 69 (1975): 193-213.

Palmer, J., and Vassar, C. "ESP and Out-of-the-body Experiences: An Exploratory Study." *Journal of the American Society for Psychical Research,* 68 (1974): 257-280.

Penfield, W. *The Mystery of the Mind.* Princeton, N.J.: Princeton University Press, 1975.

Popper, K. R. Materialism criticized. In K. R. Popper and J. C. Eccles, *The Self and its Brain.* New York: Springer-Verlag, 1977.

Pribram, K. "A Progress Report on the Scientific Understanding of Paranormal

Phenomena." In B. Shapin and L. Coly (Eds.), *Brain/Mind and Parapsychology.* New York: Parapsychology Foundation, 1979.

Schmidt, H. "Quantum-Mechanical Random-Number Generator." *Journal of Applied Physics,* 41 (1970): 462-468.

Smith, W. R., Dagle, E. F., Hill, M. D., and Smith, J. M. "Testing for Extrasensory Perception with a Machine." Hanscom Field, Mass.: Air Force Cambridge Research Laboratories, Office of Aerospace Research, United States Air Force, 1963.

Stevenson, I. "An Antagonist's View of Parapsychology. A Review of Professor Hansel's *ESP: A Scientific Evaluation." Journal of the American Society for Psychical Research,* 61 (1967): 254-267.

Weisskopf, V. F. Correspondence. *Scientific American* 242 (1980): 8.

RESPONSE BY HANSEL*

(Replies to the various points raised by Honorton are given using the subheadings he used in his review:)

(1) Antecedent Commitments

The conflict of "psi" phenomena with existing knowledge was certainly acknowledged by J. B. Rhine who considered ESP to be radically at variance with contemporary scientific ideas. If current ideas in Psychology can be considered as representing established knowledge, ESP is at variance with what is known about Perception and about the relationship between psychological phenomena, the nervous system and the brain.

I explained what I meant when using the term "impossible". I could have used the expression "speculative, not in accordance with existing knowledge and unsupported by experimental evidence after a century of efforts to establish such support."

(2) On Examining the Evidence

Honorton writes: "In order to examine the empirical evidence, Hansel is forced to admit the possibility, however remote, that there is something real to examine". It is difficult to see what this is meant to signify. I thought that my approach was made clear on the first page of my book when I wrote "the public has become aware of reports that abilities such as clairvoyance and telepathy have been demonstrated in the laboratory by means of rigorously controlled experiments. These claims are puzzling to many persons who are interested in natural processes and scientific experimentation, for the investigators appear to have established, by means of carefully planned experi-

---

*First published here

ments and conventional statistical analyses, the reality of phenomena that conflict with well-established principles."

If we assume that the earth is not flat. It is still possible to examine claims made by those who believe that it is. This is particularly so if such claims are being given wide publicity in the media where they are discussed as part of accepted scientific theory. The "something" that is real in an ESP experiment is the result in the form of a score that is unlikely to have arisen by chance. We may be interested in ascertaining the cause of this high score without invoking new hypothetical, processes to account for it.

I would agree that in my account there was some preoccupation with individual experiments. This was necessary if those experiments were to be examined that were considered by parapsychologists to be "conclusive" and the remainder rejected. Ideally it should not be necessary to hunt through the literature of parapsychology research in order to extract experiments called "conclusive". If a single repeatable demonstration were available, this would be enough, but such a demonstration has not been made available for any of the processes postulated by parapsychologists after a century of effort to obtain it.

Anything is possible in the sense used by Honorton. It is possible that we are mistaken in our present ideas about the shape of the earth or that Queen Victoria never existed.

Honorton writes "When a critic calls for 'proof' of ESP—or for that matter, of any empirical claim—that is 'beyond all doubt', as Hansel does in this book (pp. 314-315), he is appealing to something other than science, which must always stop short of dogmatic claims to absolute certainty."

What I wrote on pp 314-315 was:

"After 100 years of research, not a single individual has been found who can demonstrate ESP to the satisfaction of independent investigators. For this reason alone it is unlikely that ESP exists. But this empirical finding confirms the theoretical viewpoint that sensory information is required to provide the causal link between objects and events in the environment and events in the brain that determine perception.

In this research a number of properties of ESP are assumed to have been discovered. Since if ESP is nonexistent these properties are also nonexistent, only utter confusion can exist if the findings from the experiments are retained. The aim of parapsychology should be to produce one individual who can give a reliable and repeatable demonstration of ESP.

In the event such an individual is found, confirmation by independent investigators could easily be arranged. If parapsychologists were to undertake systematic forms of investigation and eliminate all that is not confirmed beyond all doubt, they would have a better chance of revealing any new human abilities that may exist."

(3) The Ubiquitous Fraud Hypothesis and the Blunting of Occam's Razor

The parsimony principle relates to scientific theory that seeks to account for empirical observations. It does not relate to the observed facts of nature. That the cod-fish lays a large number of eggs in order to produce a limited number of offspring may appear to lack parsimony but it is a fact not an explanation or theory. Theories to account for this lack of parsimony in the cod-fish may be subject to Occam's razor but not the observed facts. Similarly the activities of human beings that they undertake in order to deceive those who are investigating them may lack parsimony but be necessary in order to escape detection by parapsychologists such as Honorton.

The case of Hubert Pearce is surely of little further interest. The fact that my diagram was not to scale or that room 311 was not directly opposite Pratt's office but further up the corridor is in no way at variance with what I wrote in my original report. This matter of the room across the corridor has been a main point for criticism by a number of parapsychologists.

In my original report after stating that sight of the records could have been obtained by anyone in the corridor I wrote:

"There is, however, a clear pane of glass above the door in a room *on the opposite side further down the corridor* through which sight *might have been got* of the cards by anyone standing on a chair inside the room with the door shut. This possibility was difficult to test owing to the structural alterations which had been made." (italics mine)

Honorton writes: "According to Hansel this could have been done by standing on a chair and looking down through the transom from a room across the hall, which Hansel says was room 311."

(4) The Importance of Replicability

It is clear that Honorton used the work "replicable" to denote that an experimenter can—if he is lucky—carry out a similar experiment and obtain the same result as some other investigator. Any ESP experiment in which the result is assessed in terms of the odds against chance of the result will be replicable in this sense. Experiments giving results at low levels of significance as commonly reported in the literature cannot form the basis for a repeatable demonstration.

It is a simple matter to increase the number of observations required in an experiment that is to provide the repeatable demonstration.

Most of what Honorton has written requires merely a more careful reading of exactly what I wrote. His last paragraph raises a fundamental point.

Critics would no doubt welcome the opportunity of focussing their interest on systematic lines of research. There would be little point in continuing to discuss Rhine's research or many of the experiments producing very high antichance odds that figured in the past. It is the continued reluctance on the part of parapsychologists to forget anything in its history other than admissions of fraud or revelations of gross experimental ineptitude that makes it necessary to discuss such experiments. If they are omitted the critic will be accused of ignoring the best evidence. It would be of interest to know what constitutes the "systematic lines of research" on which critics should focus their attention and which experiments are to be rejected as failing to comply with the standards required.

Suggested Reading

CRITICAL ASESSMENTS

Alcock, James E. *Parapsychology: Science or Magic?* Elmsford, N.Y.: and Oxford: Permagon Press, 1981.

Gardner, Martin. *Fads and Fallacies in the Name of Science.* New York: Dover Publications, Inc., 1957.

———. *Science: Good, Bad and Bogus.* Buffalo, N.Y.: Prometheus Books, 1981.

Kurtz, Paul (Ed.). *A Skeptic's Handbook of Parapsychology,* Buffalo, N.Y.: Prometheus Books, 1985.

Marks, David and Kammann, Richard. *The Psychology of the Psychic.* Buffalo, N.Y.: Prometheus Books, 1980.

GENERAL REVIEWS (Mainly Uncritical)

Edge, Hoyt L.; Morris, Robert L.; Rush, Joseph H.; Palmer, John. *Foundations of Parapsychology.* Boston, London, and Henley: Routledge and Kegan Paul, 1986.

Wolman, Benjamin B. (Ed.). *Handbook of Parapsychology.* New York: Van Nostrand, 1977.

EARLY HISTORY OF PSYCHICAL RESEARCH

Hall, Trevor H. *The Strange Case of Edmund Gurney.* London: Gerald Duckworth, 1974.

SPIRITUALISM

Hall, Trevor H. *The Spiritualists:: The Story of William Crookes and Florence Cooke.* London: Gerald Duckworth, 1962.

Rinn, J. F. *Searchlight on Psychical Research.* London: Rider & Co., 1954.

GHOSTS

Dingwall, E. J.; Goldney, K. M.; and Hall, Trevor H. *The Haunting of Borley Rectory: A Critical Survey of the Evidence.* London: Society for Psychical Research, 1956.

Hall, Trevor H. *Search for Harry Price.* London: Gerald Duckworth, 1978.

Index